101 Reasons To Be A Mentor

★ ★ ★

Andrew M. Mecca, Dr. P.H.

California Mentor Foundation

This book is dedicated to my wife Kate, whose tireless dedication to children inspires me everyday and has done so for twenty-seven joyous years!

I wish to acknowledge my deepest appreciation to:

Mary Piasta (senior editor) for her enormous talent and tenacious assistance in making this book possible,

Jenny Svanfeldt and *Pete Anderson* for enthusiastically assisting in bringing this book to fruition, and

Jim Kooler and *Alison Elsner* who have been by my side from the beginning.

While crisscrossing California inviting groups to become part of the mentoring initiative, I collected stories. This book represents not 101 but millions of mentoring success stories that are changing the face of America one child at a time. Read on, be inspired and become a mentor.

International Standard Book Number: 0-9713680-1-5
Library of Congress Control Number: 2001118602
Printed in the United States of America

For more information on all mentoring efforts visit our website **http://www.calmentor.com.**

Foreword

When you hear the word "mentor" different images of friend, guide, listener, coach, teacher, resource and helper may come to mind. But likely we do not think about ourselves. Dr. Andy Mecca, of the California Mentor Foundation, is helping to shift our perspective to see that each of us can make a difference in the life of a child. He has the vision and commitment to see mentoring as a cornerstone for the positive development of young people.

This book, *101 Reasons To Be a Mentor*, shows how we as ordinary individuals can have extraordinary impacts. This book helps us see our potential in bringing out the best in our young people. I am certain that you will find this book a great resource as you embark upon your journey with a young person.

California is very fortunate to have Dr. Mecca as a friend, guide, coach, teacher, resource and helper, in short a mentor, to our growing mentoring movement.

Jim Kooler, Dr.P.H., Director
Governor's Mentoring Partnership
State of California

Introduction

First and Foremost, this book is an imperfect attempt to share scores of stories I collected between 1995 and 2001 while crisscrossing California in my work with the California Mentor Initiative.

Most of this work coincided with my tour of duty as Drug Czar for California. Thus, a great number of these mentor stories are provided by people in recovery or involved in drug abuse prevention work.

Many of these stories were written as free standing OPEDs for local papers or short articles for Journals and Magazines.

As you will quickly discern, I am in awe of the dedicated adults and young people committed to growing this "mentoring movement." In my opinion, mentoring is the most potent youth development strategy we have to break the back of the social epidemics kids face and insure their healthy future!

While honored that I was invited to compile this first volume, I invite you to grow volume two and three.

If you have an inspiring "mentor story" you wish to have considered for Volumes 2 or 3, please submit it in no more than 500 words to <info@calmentor.com>.

Finally, this volume is probably best enjoyed a few stories at a time. The people and dedication reflected in these vignettes encourages me daily in this work to grow mentoring opportunities for every child who needs and wants a mentor.

I hope you enjoy this as much as I have in hearing them and sharing them with you.

Story 1

Mentoring is spreading like wildfire because it takes very small doses of it to work, and because those same small doses come back to reward the giver.

Almost 40 years ago, a vigorous young President, John Fitzgerald Kennedy, seized the reigns of power and exhorted a nation toward greatness. He enkindled in me, a member of the notorious "boomer" generation, a burning desire to serve this country I love so much.

Lulled to passivity in the wake of post-World War II prosperity and seemingly doomed to a life of sameness and striving for the status quo in the soporific 50's, Kennedy's admonition to "Ask not what your country can do for you; ask what you can do for your country" was a clarion call to a new level of consciousness.

The shift was essential, and it began in earnest. Faded photographs of a broadly smiling Kennedy mirror the nation's burgeoning sense of reinvigorated youth. Citizens answered his call to take 50-mile hikes, they enlisted in droves in his newly created Peace Corps.

The dust had been blown off the long-dormant ideas of participatory democracy, and Americans were literally chomping at the bit to make this country hum with efficiency and happiness.

Something happened along the way, of course. Vietnam and domestic strife fueled by racial tension bubbled up from the once-placid underbelly of the American machine. On the one hand, Kennedy's youthful enthusiasm was the perfect elixir for a country grown bored with the monotonous 50's; on the other hand, it was his naivete that could not foresee long-festering wounds that now oozed from the veins of the nation into the streets of its beleaguered cities.

As pockmarked with controversy as it was, as scarred by dissent it came to be, Vietnam nevertheless served as the backdrop for my own sense of patriotism—I served my country in its darkest hour, feeling the pain of human tragedy in my stint running two hospitals in Vietnam where I came to grips with the gaping stares of hopelessness and despair.

Giddy with a sense of new freedom and unlimited possibilities on every horizon, America was now an awakened giant, but we were out of control. Race riots and anti-Vietnam demonstrations polarized and paralyzed families and institutions. At the precise moment we were supposed to rekindle a sense of democracy as a standard-bearer of freedom throughout the world, we were coming apart at the seams with the cancer of confrontation and dissent.

The strength and beauty of America, the very genius of this idea called a republic, however, is that we survived even our own best efforts to self-destruct. We took it to the brink, to the breaking point in some cases, but even a cursory survey of the damages shows that democracy is still intact, albeit battered and bruised, while communism, once our greatest threat and fear, is dead.

Many Americans in the 80's and early 90's got slammed and severely criticized for being overly greedy and materialistic, but one way to look at their hunger for wealth would be to see it through the gauze of the healing process. They wanted America to be better, and they wanted it to happen fast. In that light, their excesses might be forgiven.

At any rate, the healing process had begun, however imperfect. In many ways, we were a nation under the influence of drugs and alcohol and material greed. We may even smile with sadness now at the naive notion flower children had about marijuana. They vehemently condemned their martini-wielding parents while, at the same time, inhaling themselves into toxicity, self-righteously asserting that cannabis sativa was much more organic and healthy than demon alcohol. As we would soon discover, AA meetings do not differentiate between drunks and stoners.

So now where are we?

Outside enemies like Vietnam no longer pose serious threats to our new-found democracy. Internal discord is a long way from being resolved, but we have at least discovered the tools with which to handle our conflicts. We are learning how to conquer our demons without killing ourselves.

However, the reality is that we are still a country in recovery.

Twelve-step programs for every conceivable malady under the sun dot the landscape like fuel stations for the soul. Talk-show programming continues to reveal an America with serious internal dysfunction. And, every once in a while, just to demonstrate that we are a long way away from stable mental health, demonic eruptions occur as sobering reminders that insanity stirs just beneath the thin ice of a seemingly tranquil nature scene—domestic terrorism like Oklahoma City and Waco, harrowing madness disguised as religious zealotry in the case of the Heaven's Gate cult, and the widening, horrific litany of child abuse, spousal violence and urban street crimes that pepper our collective soul with so many shards of shrapnel.

Someday when historians attempt to chart the moment when America took stock of itself and moved toward recovery, the focal point will not be Kennedy's New Frontier or Johnson's Great Society, but rather a less specific tidal wave of phenomena and events that created what appears to be the single most effective weapon in the struggle for sanity and the restoration of health. What we are talking about here is mentoring.

How fitting that mentoring has some of its roots in the ancient Greek civilization, the original and most radical breeding ground for democracy and participatory government in the history of mankind. Other roots for this ethic of mentoring come from indigenous village life all over the world.

In modern-day America, the landscape is dotted with the wreckage of excess and addiction. Dreams have been dashed, hopes trashed, marriages splintered, families disintegrated, and children made lonely. Perhaps the greatest, most grievous wrong absorbed by our young people is the lack of a significant adult role model in their daily, formative lives.

The feeling of alienation and loneliness experienced by a child of divorce or family dysfunction is a gaping hole of despair that's a dangerous launch pad into the same kind of downward spiral of hopelessness and addiction that afflicted the parents.

What this child needs more than anything is to be embraced and accepted into the life of a stable adult role model.

This is the definition of mentoring—an ongoing, sustaining commitment of an adult to a young person lacking basic tools that will guide the youth toward a realistic, productive life choice. The mentor respects his mentee and recognizes the innate goodness and worth of his charge. Sheathed with this sudden infusion of light and love, the mentee is finally able to come to grips with the challenges of life in the real world, drawing upon the mentor's example and his own newfound inner strength to travel the path of righteousness and productivity.

We are witnessing today an explosion of mentor/mentee awareness. The human quilt of caring is a colorfully woven healing blanket that stitches together people of all races and backgrounds, matching individual involvement with corporate engagement. Mentoring is a healthy virus of vital human energy surging through the veins of a nation desperately thirsting for a transfusion of new blood.

It's a miracle of human recovery, actually, that the many-headed demon afflicting our youth can be so brilliantly remedied by so simple and so painless a task as mentoring.

Legions of our young—torn apart and alienated by the scourges of drugs, alcohol, gangs, teenage pregnancy and school dropout rates—are being repaired, resuscitated and rehabilitated by one caring hand placed on the shoulders of one needy life. We are rebuilding America one child at a time.

And we are doing it in a way that works, one of the only proven ways that works, just like AA is the only known antidote to alcoholism.

As any recovering person will attest, there are no shortcuts to full recovery, but once the first taste of health and sanity is experienced, the hunger for wellness is every bit as strong and as compelling as was the wayward striving for addiction.

And the brilliance of the mentoring movement is that it recognizes diversity while hailing individuality. Just as drugs and alcohol don't discriminate along the lines of age, race or social status, mentoring, too, is not exclusive, narrow or prejudiced. If we want to stop killing each other, if we want Americans to learn to walk together hand in hand, producing once more a nation for the ages, then we must teach each other the true meaning of respect, love and dignity.

This is what mentoring accomplishes, the ability to unleash in each individual that special essence of independence and personhood that has been stagnating, dormant, undernourished, unfed.

How mentoring is saving lives from the clutches of substance abuse, gang entanglement, teen pregnancy and educational failure is the most critical American story of the new millennium.

The California Mentor Initiative is ambitious and explosive. Having accomplished raising the public investment of $76 million, we achieved the initial goal of 250,000 matches by 1999. General Collin Powell, Governor and Mrs. Davis then challenged this when they set an ambitious goal of 1 million matches by the year 2005.

An emerging patchwork stitched together by individual citizens and corporate donorship alike, the Initiative is a tidal wave of human evolution that shall produce a sea change of dynamic social and economic growth, vaulting California into a leadership position as a mentor to the rest of the world.

The genius of mentoring is that it abandons tired old language, meaningless clichés like: "We care about our children because they are our future."

Kids today hear empty rhetoric like that, and they run away shrieking. Besides, within that weary and ancient politicians' anthem is the very problem itself—lack of esteem. Think about it: We care about our children because they are our future? Isn't that a bit selfish? Doesn't that reek of the same empty-headed sugar talk that made our kids rebel in the first place?

Instead, how about more hard-nosed, straight-talking language like: I am going to spend a lot of time with you because you are worth it, and, with a little bit of guidance and practical tip, you can become the person you've always wanted to be, and you can walk into adulthood capable of providing for yourself and your family. In a word, I am going to help you become whoever you want to be.

And yes, by the way, our future *will* be better, because they, in fact, will have one.

Mentoring is spreading like wildfire because it takes very small doses of it to work, and because those same small doses come back to reward the giver, as well. Mentors are discovering that their work with young adults is creating a life force of joy and satisfaction they never expected, and they begin to wonder why it took them so long to discover this absolutely worthwhile venture.

Mentors' own families are reporting high rates of happiness and increased amounts of impending serenity, which is quickly replacing turmoil and restlessness. So not only is the mentee being given concrete steps to adulthood, so, too, is the mentor discovering deeper wells of maturity.

And none of this even mentions all the delicious side benefits, like the collapse of stereotypes, the creation of communication between generations, the disintegration of prejudice and hostility, and the regeneration of goodwill among men and women of all races.

Mentoring is the vehicle whereby we can put an end to ignorance and despair, open conflict resulting in mortal wounds, and the insanely insatiable appetite evil needs to stifle good. Mentoring keeps hope alive, and, in an America that's driven by the hunger for recovery, that's slowly being re-crafted and re-designed child by beautiful child, this hope springs eternal.

In May of 1997, the Presidents' Summit for America's Future was the culminating focal point for a cresting new phenomenon promising to paint America in bold fresh strokes of renewal and resurrection. The Summit is every bit as important as Kennedy's New Frontier and Johnson's Great Society.

Thanks to the tireless efforts of organizers Ray Chambers and General Colin Powell, the Summit will forever stand as the blueprint for hope among the nation's youth.

Hear it from General Powell as he addressed the throngs gathered in Philadelphia for the Summit:

"Despite more than two centuries of moral and material progress, despite all our efforts to achieve a more perfect union, there are still Americans who are not sharing in the American dream. There are still Americans who wonder, is the journey there for them, is the dream there for them, or whether it is at best a dream deferred.

The great American poet Langston Hughes talked about the dream deferred, and he said, 'What happens to a dream deferred? Does it dry up like a raisin in the sun, or fester like a sore and then run? Does it stink like rotten meat, or crust and sugar over like a syrupy sweet? Maybe it just sags like a heavy load. Or does it explode?'

"For too many young Americans, that dream deferred does sag like a heavy load that's pushing them down into the ground, and they wonder if they can rise up with that load. And as we see too often in our daily life, it does explode in violence, in youngsters falling dead, shot by other youngsters. It does explode, and it has the potential to explode our society.

"So today we gather here to pledge that the dream must no longer be deferred and it will never, as long as we can do anything about it, become a dream denied."

Your chance to join in the campaign to change society one child at a time is at your fingertips.

Story 2

Over the past three decades, I have witnessed firsthand and the steady rise of the four social epidemics of drug abuse, educational failure, teen pregnancy and kids joining gangs.

There was an ebb of these social epidemics in the early 80's, but then the steady rise returned—for example, a virtual doubling of drug abuse among 12-year-olds the past four years.

During this time, I have been involved professionally in the drug abuse treatment and prevention arena. This experience included administering the drug treatment programs in Vietnam, building and directing treatment and prevention services in Marin County for 12 years, and representing the United States in assisting a dozen foreign countries develop treatment and prevention programs.

My interest in prevention efforts grew enormously, through, by recognizing the obvious—we would never have enough resources to keep pulling people out downstream, when more and more kept jumping into the chaos upstream.

This interest was buttressed by Governor George Deukmejian's invitation for me to chair the California Task Force on Self-Esteem. Initially parodied by cartoonist Garry Trudeau's "Doonesbury" strip for two weeks, this three-year project soon became a scholarly investigation.

The final report stated unequivocally that low self-esteem is central to these four social epidemics. The hundreds of research studies on self-esteem also documented the core ingredients of an environment that promotes self-esteem.

- you feel you belong
- you are made to feel significant
- you are acknowledged for your efforts
- you are recognized for your competence

This work challenged traditional thinking and policy that relied on talking to kids about these programs, for example, classroom curricula, publishing brochures and responding to the crisis once it occurred.

In 1991 former Governor Pete Wilson appointed me to the post of "California's Drug Czar." In this capacity, I was responsible for a department of 300 with a budget of $350 million. In addition, the Governor asked me to chair his Drug Policy Council to ensure coherence to California's Drug Policy execution.

One of the first things I accomplished in this capacity was to design a research protocol capable of documenting the effectiveness of the $300 million a year being spent on treatment.

Ironically, the self-esteem research was corroborated by this, the largest drug treatment outcome study ever conducted. The California Drug and Alcohol Treatment Assessment (CALDATA) was designed and implemented in California and in 1982, results were published in 1994.

This study documented that drug treatment works. For example, 50% reductions in crime and hospital admission one year after treatment. A closer look at the most successful programs shone a light once again on those four "esteeming ingredients"—belonging, feeling significant, acknowledgement for effort and recognized for competence.

During this same time, my long-time friend and colleague, Terry Pearce, was sharing his insights on successful businesses and ethical communities. They promoted these very same qualities. Terry pointed me toward the vast literature on "Excellence in Business"—for example, Tom Peters—and safe, nurturing and ethical communities—for example, John Gardner.

It was at this time in 1994 that Governor Wilson, being aware of my deep interest in prevention, asked me to co-chair with his wife Gayle, the California Commission on Improving Life Through Service. This additional duty was a blessing. The challenge of working with a team to design, build and implement a new program is always exciting. This particular opportunity to launch AmeriCorps, though was very special.

At this time, I was also serving as a member of a teen pregnancy prevention task force, a juvenile justice review panel, a school drop-out prevention discussion and the ever-ongoing debate concerning action to prevent drug abuse. In all these areas, the bulk of prevention policy and resources were being directed at classroom-based curricula and strategies reliant on talking to not involving kids.

This experience was juxtaposed against the efforts being mobilized within and around the AmeriCorps Initiative. Mentoring, Service Learning and School to Careers were all elements that clearly required human engagement and led to the mentor and mentee feeling a sense of belonging.

Gayle Wilson and I had the opportunity to convene public hearings around the state on the Service Initiative. We heard hundreds of testimonials from former gang members, drug abusers, teen moms and school dropouts.

All now were on a positive path towards finishing school and securing employment. They expressed feelings of pride and dignity obtained by participating in community service.

But the universal statement by everyone was that someone had taken the time and interest to become their mentor. Hardly rocket science to recognize the opportunity for a coherent Prevention Initiative. But there was a little more homework. Review of the scientific literature on mentoring offered a floodlight on the enormous opportunity mentoring had on breaking the back of these four social epidemics.

The literature highlighted that young people in high-risk environments who did not get in trouble had one thing in common. They had someone who cared, was there with consistency, held aspirations for the young person, and coached them to success.

No one would suggest that mentoring replace loving and effective parenting. But when you consider the Los Angeles Times' December 1996 headline that "only Twenty-Five Percent of California Homes Have Two Parents"—you realize it is a healthy and safe human investment that science says is essential to promote well being.

These social epidemics have a core cause of isolation. Therefore, a core solution must be human engagement. We cannot buy the solutions, although we have certainly tried. We cannot talk our way home or legislate these problems away.

Our failures to date have been opportunities to learn, our successes a clarion to future direction and investment.

Nothing short of building a cultural army for mentoring every child who needs one will secure the positive change we eagerly seek. Absent this, the rising trend of these social epidemics will drain our sprits and resources, leaving us in the carnage of unrealized human potential.

How do we get there? We have already started. We have mentoring programs that have built tools to successfully recruit, train, match and support mentor-mentee relationships. In California alone we estimate that there are currently 340,000 matches. However there are 80,000 kids on waiting lists for mentors and an estimated one million who need one.

The California Mentor Initiative (CMI) sets forth a goal of recruiting one million new mentors by the Year 2005. This initiative recognizes the opportunity for mentoring to offer, for the first time, a coherent prevention strategy.

The CMI acknowledges the wisdom and courage of current efforts—Big Brothers/Big Sisters, School to Careers, Communities in Schools, and others. It also invites all of the other prevention programs and businesses to reinvest themselves into mentoring organizations and support systems.

A good example is the statewide Friday Night Live program. Approximately 200,000 young people in California have received this leadership training with a primary focus on drug abuse prevention.

Now this organization in conjunction with the California National Guard is reinventing their mission to focus on mentor training and matching with younger kids. This strategy alone should realize 50,000 new mentors a year.

Add to this the agreement that when a grade school or middle school student gets a mentor, they agree to be trained and become a mentor when they get to high school. How simple, yet in 10 short years this strategy alone will establish a deep-rooted mentoring ethic.

Another opportunity that exists in the coherence of this movement is the potential of the sum of the parts. Usually called synergism, I think there will be a new word realized out of this real-life experience of multiple organizations coming together to execute a shared strategic plan that supports comprehensive mentoring.

Programs usually focus on one more piece of mentoring—for instance, character building, tutoring, service or careers. Why not have all of these elements work coherently and harmoniously to ensure a mentee can matriculate through all the phases, uninterrupted.

There are community coalition support systems that some people focus on—school system pieces, (K-12, and higher education), business support (School to Careers for example), technical assistance and government support that can collaborate to realize this more coherent approach.

Rigorous documentation of outcomes is also an essential piece to support the growing mentoring ethic and how the child, mentor society, and democracy all benefit.

I cannot restrain the urge to offer an editorial comment here.

Coming from an immigrant family, I have a profound love and appreciation for democracy. I have worked in countries where people were still giving their lives to realize a democratic form of government.

Yet, I have observed a growing sense of entitlement in this country of what deTocqueville called an "experiment" in democracy. That young French philosopher observed that Jefferson's (et. al.) experiment would work if people participated.

If Frank Marshall and Kathy Kennedy are right and mentoring does become a movement, then the human participation will mean we are maturing as a Nation. Perhaps we are recognizing our personal and social responsibilities to our children and communities, Nation and most important of all to this vital experiment in democracy.

In our affluence, we no longer share in the labor of a barn raising, but invest in government agencies and experts to fix it. This approach has not secured the desired outcomes, and our dissonance rose ultimately to confront us with our cultural values of personal and social responsibility.

What if two million persons in the United States become mentors by the year 2008? What if we succeed in actually turning the tide of these four social epidemics representing an annual cost to the GNP of half trillion dollars?

Perhaps, then, we really could envision the devolution of a centralized government with enormous wealth and authority, returning to the communities of America Everyone could add scores of other wonderful implications to the "What ifs," but at the heart of them will be—"We earned it!" We came of age as Nation—no longer blaming and scapegoating, but rather as mature and engaged citizens, which each did a little and together had an extraordinary effect.

Story 3

Mentoring is the easiest, simplest way to fulfill a vital part of being an American, which to paraphrase President John F. Kennedy, surrounds the notion that "to whom much is given much is expected."

In her book, *The Healing of America*, author Marianne Williamson writes:

"Mentoring is the only known antidote to juvenile delinquency. One hour spent with a responsible adult each week can turn a young person's life completely around, even if that adult is not a family member and even if the young person is already in his or her late teens.

"Millions of Americans would respond to an intelligent call to join a citizen crusade to mentor our young and otherwise repair the broken places in American society. They would do it if they actually knew where to go, who to call, and how their work might make a difference."

Precisely.

Today, with the ongoing installation of the California Mentor Initiative, these people do know where to go, who to call, and how their work might make a difference.

Mentoring is the easiest, simplest way to fulfill a vital part of being an American, which, to paraphrase President John F. Kennedy, surrounds the notion that "to whom much is given, much is expected."

Participatory democracy calls for active reinvestment in the nation. We cannot survive as a free country if all we are about is self-aggrandizement and materialistic accumulation. Social conscience and progressive awareness are cornerstones of liberty, the nesting ground for a truly free republic.

No longer does active personal engagement in the democratic dream have to be a complicated commitment draining career dreams and personal aspirations. No more does civic duty have to be performed in dramatic strokes like Peace Corps membership, military enlistment or political volunteerism.

Asking not what your country can do for you but asking, rather, what you can do for your country is now literally under your nose—the next wayward, sad, confused, isolated, alienated young person you come across on the street just might be your first introduction into the phenomenon of mentoring.

Instead of being on the street, perhaps this kid needs a conversation from someone like you who can happily point him toward a library, an arts and crafts college, a summer theater group or a Christian fellowship.

Active engagement in democracy means to connect people less fortunate and aware than you to movements, ideals, organizations and lifestyles that can trigger personal involvement in something greater than themselves.

So…if mentoring is the only known antidote to juvenile delinquency, what are we waiting for?

Well, it may surprise you to discover we're not waiting at all. The movement has been engaged. For nearly four years, responsible, caring adults have been signing up in droves to bolster, support and elicit strength from legions of young people who are only momentarily adrift and cut off from the flow of dynamic, self-sustaining life work.

If we're waiting for anything, it's for you. Mentoring affords you the opportunity to complete the cycle of your citizenship.

Again, from *The Healing of America:*

"There is a new prophetic voice in America, saying, as do all prophets, that we must repent—which means literally to 'rethink.' This new prophetic voice is not a soloist but a choir.

"This time it will not be possible to silence one prophet, or even a few, and thereby stymie a broad-based social impulse for decades. This time, a prophetic calling is seizing the hearts of a critical mass. It is a voice of group conscience and a redefinition of citizen activism in American democracy.

"It is time once more for the average American citizen to turn to the dominant power structure of our time and say, as did our Founders over 200 years ago, 'We have a better idea.'"

That better idea, my friends, is mentoring. Won't you join?

Story 4

America 2001 is, in fact, primed to look inward and refine the moral fiber of its soul so that we can be, for the ages, a truly great civilization in every sense of the word.

In the first decade of the 21st century, we are blessed to live in an America that is bursting with prosperity, a declining unemployment rate, and a budget deficit that has vanished.

Wouldn't this be a dream country if we could erase crime, character flaws, social unrest and moral turpitude with the same kind of results as those cited above?

Actually, now that we are in a state of a flourishing economy that comes about, for a change, without the injection of a mobilized military-industrial complex fully engaged in war, we are in a perfect position to challenge the domestic decay that threatens to undermine the aforementioned successes.

This is the best time ever to reflect on our inner selves, our national spiritual profile that will help maintain and sustain all the outward signs of soaring national pride and accomplishment.

It doesn't take a wizard historian to point out that the classic downfall for the great empires of old was for them to rest on their laurels of physical achievement and allow themselves to be corroded with the infestation of cancerous growths brought on by complacency, greed and self-indulgence.

America 2001 is, in fact, primed to look inward and refine the moral fiber of its soul so that we can be, for the ages, a truly great civilization in every sense of the word.

In California, we are getting ready for the turn of the century by creating a massive re-tooling job for our younger citizens.

For an entire host of sociological, cultural, economic and spiritual reasons, the state found itself in the mid-90's mired in an epidemic of maladies afflicting our teenage residents.

Drug and alcohol usage spiraled toward record numbers among minors. Teenaged mothers found themselves looking in bewilderment for their own lost childhoods. School dropout rates reached tidal wave figures of failure. And headlines blared, guns blazed, as statewide youth gangs multiplied in numbers.

It is not news to report that even the most sage of observers looked at this holocaust-like horizon, peered into the future of our offspring, and shook their heads sadly. We may not have been seized with panic—that has never been the proper American spirit—but we were certainly closer to despair than we were to positive confidence that things could be reversed.

Traditional avenues of social programming were folding their tents. Church groups knew they had been licked by demons they had never before witnessed—crack cocaine, wanton violence, utter disrespect for authority, an absolutely terrifying absence of fear, and an equally horrific hole where once stood proudly something called a respect for life.

For kids without parents, there was no hope. Gangs became the last refuge for lives ultimately cut short. Educational failure was inevitable. Mothers too young to smoke were getting pregnant. And booze and nasty drugs raced through the veins of our kids like acid in the streams.

An epidemic is not an understatement. We needed to do something fast, effective, radical and healing.

Nearly six years ago, we implemented the California Mentor Initiative, a miracle, really, that has become the model program for problems like this around the nation and, more recently, around the globe.

Mentoring has proven to be the only viable, lasting, effective and authentic remedy to alter the downward spiraling war of attrition the young wage against themselves through self-destructive behavior.

To introduce a capable, caring, mature, experienced role model into the life of a dispirited, hopeless young person has the same effect as the miraculous transformation that occurs when a drunk finally crawls into his first AA meeting. Once this first step is taken, the miracle of life begins to heal the suffering person immediately.

From reports we've gathered from around the state, there is such a quenching of thirst achieved by the mentor/mentee relationship, there is such an intoxicating hunger for more and more infusions of health, that we are richly blessed by the wondrous ripple effects this phenomenon has charged into the social strata.

Families are reunited, lives are elevated to new levels of accomplishment, wrongs are amended, peers spread the news to companions still adrift in hopelessness, and the underpinnings of what we call the California Experience are solidly re-rooted in a foundation of recovery.

Story 5

What we are discovering from mentors around the state is that young people are beginning to realize there is actually a place for them in what is too often merely the rhetoric of America.

As an enthusiastic champion of the California Mentor Initiative, I am frequently asked about the seemingly futile war we are waging on behalf of our kids. Far from caving into futility, however, my spirit is constantly buoyed by the many-faceted preventive measures we currently have in place to turn our youth away from drugs and alcohol and toward active, healthy, citizen participation in the greatest liberating high anyone could ever experience—America.

Personally, I cannot help but reflect on the philosopher and historian Alex de Tocqueville's comments in the mid-19th century about the American experiment in democracy. To paraphrase, he said: "Thomas Jefferson is right about this democratic experiment in democracy—it will work if people remain involved at the local level, and will fail if left to experts and central control."

The epidemic of drug and alcohol abuse—specifically among our young citizens—is eroding the foundation of our participatory form of government, but it is far from a lost cause. Those of us who have battled for the implementation of self-esteem in the lifestyles of the young know in our hearts that it is this very return to the core of dignity that will resuscitate America like the mythic bird of hope; the Phoenix rising from the ashes of despair.

Leaders, poets, scholars and historians from the earliest of times believed what we now know today. They saw a correlation too strong to be ignored—that personal and social responsibilities are the manifestation of an individual's high level of self-esteem.

We have only to look to Aristotle's ethical philosophy in which he plumbs the depth of the meanings of "good" and of "happiness" for a deeper understanding of self-esteem and its co-parts, personal and social responsibility. It is no surprise really to see that Aristotle sees both good and happiness inextricably interwoven with participation in civic matters. *The highest good is right action and the person so directed has the greatest chance at happiness.*

Does all this sound a bit too esoteric for those of us living in the modern morass of big-city violence, youth alienation and rampaging drug criminality? Not at all. Happiness and living righteously are the flip side of drug and alcohol abuse. Our job is to find the right key to unlock the disturbed soul from the grip of addiction, and set him free into the land of illumination.

Further proof of the philosophical foundation for the work being done in the realm of self-esteem is seen in the "unreal city," the nightmare landscape of T.S. Eliot's poetry. The landscape he creates is filled with the clutter of despair. His work is peopled with sallow unbelievers and ruined dreams. But ultimately, Eliot's poetry establishes a paradigm of hope. He reminds us that from death comes resurrection; from ruin comes repair; and only after the dead of winter can there be hope for spring.

That a person experiences an increase in his self-esteem when he acts effectively toward others and toward his community is not surprising. We recognize this as true and as vital. And so the extension goes that a healthy quotient of self-esteem in a person can be what initiates the cycle of good works and of a high level of personal and social responsibility.

As in any endeavor worth striving for, there are steps toward the goal. Required is self-esteem and personal and social responsibility, the best ingredients for the effective prevention of drug and alcohol abuse.
Six specific steps show the way—A return to dignity, self-knowledge, self-acceptance, integrity, realization and permission.

These steps form the foundation for one of the most exciting social revolutions yet developed in the late 20th century—the California Mentoring Initiative, which is a proven and solidly effective weapon in the arsenal of drug and alcohol prevention among the state's young.

When a parent, teacher or other role model alerts a child to the possibility of his entering into a vitalizing cycle of self-esteem and social and personal responsibility, the adult enters the cycle, too. With a high level of self-esteem, personal and social responsibility will follow. This is the engine room of the mentor/mentee relationship that is currently the genius behind the California

Mentor Initiative, a social phenomenon that is returning America to itself. What we're discovering from mentors around the state is that young people are beginning to realize that there is actually a place for them in what is too often merely the rhetoric of America.

Almost universally, mentors point happily to the fact that their job is sometimes as easy as pointing the young person toward the front door of a university or into the foyer of jobs fair or onto the front step of a workplace that employs their skills.

The truth is that none of these young people has ever had an adult believe in them. It's not that they are unskilled, unintelligent or incapable. It is quite the contrary. Empowerment is about knowledge and belief. Knowledge unlocks the door of opportunity, and belief in the person makes it possible for him to flourish as a responsible citizen.

Just as 12-Step programs like to say they are based on attraction, not promotion, so it is with the American Dream—once a person breathes the fresh air of full engagement in the process of freedom and the pursuit of happiness, the intoxication toward health is an all-powerful elixir.

The sense of fun and joy that occurs when a young person has a chance to blossom as an active participant in democracy is something that can't be adequately bottled or described.

Story 6

For mentoring to work authentically, people have to step up responsibly. This isn't an exercise in mere altruism or an outgrowth of one's feeling good about himself on any particular day

Directing the alcohol and drug programs for the State of California has given me a renewed sense of participatory democracy in its most radically effective form—restoring sanity and hope for upcoming generations of young Californians.

Participating in service oriented programs is what American democracy is all about. Bringing disenfranchised youth into the watershed of full engagement of their lives heals the wounds brought on by alcohol and drug abuse.

We should not underestimate the epidemic of social alienation currently surging like cancer through the veins of our younger citizens' lives. Our work on the grassroots level in cities and communities around the entire state has boiled this epidemic of estrangement down to four raging symptoms—teenage drug and alcohol abuse, educational failure, gang involvement, and teen pregnancy.

Kids gripped in the vise of emotionally wrenching primal screams are mortgaging their precious futures by acting out devastating and life-threatening behaviors that are nothing more than dramatic cries for help. They live in fear and isolation, bereft of any significant adult role models. Abandoned emotionally and physically, they are unleashed into the world without a map, without a clue. The pitfalls have pitfalls, and kids without direction are, quite literally, lost souls.

What terrible thing happens to adults making them forget what it's like to be young, restless, without roots? What horrible indifference to life's very pulse seeps into an adult's arteries to make him turn away and reject that very young life which is his responsibility? What makes people turn away so perversely from the bouncing bundle of joy they once so warmly embraced at life's onset?

We can't bemoan tired old adult behavior because that would be tired old adult behavior. We don't have time for that kind of sanctimonious whining. We are living in a crisis situation. We need to change urgently and fundamentally the way we think and act.

One of our successes in this regard is the California Mentor Initiative, which is in place throughout the state and flourishing as an essentially healing and guiding principle in the lives of our younger citizens. Isolation is the disease of the young and the disenfranchised, and mentoring is the tool whereby we reintroduce these people to themselves. We have come to realize that the best way to heal the scars of absentee and non-existent parenthood is the return of community. Mentoring is the beginning of community, and the ripple effects from its dynamism are re-sodding the once barren emotional and psychological fields of California's adolescents.

For mentoring to work authentically, people have to step up responsibly. This isn't an exercise in mere altruism or an outgrowth of one's feeling good about himself on any particular day. With its roots firmly planted in ancient time, the birthplace of an actively free citizenship yearning for democracy, mentoring is quite literally a function of society. It is a good citizen's duty, every bit as vital as jury summons, taxpaying or watchful neighborhood vigilance.

It does not take much thought to fully understand that mentoring crushes isolation, which is the disease eroding the underpinnings of a healthy society. Mentoring is not designed as a full-service package equipped with all of life's answers, but it is offered as a creative way to trigger self-reflection and realization. It is a catalyst that helps inspire and motivate a scarred and scared youth toward adulthood. It is a spark that ignites the engine, which will propel youth from the perils of adolescence to the opportunities of maturity.

I would like to present the concept of mentoring in its most simple terms because it is a giant phenomenon built with tiny steps. It takes minimal effort for an adult role model to nudge himself toward activism, and the fruits of his labor yield maximum results. It is a joyful decision of citizenship that induces one good person to come to the assistance of another good, albeit troubled person.

And mentoring really is as simple, as straightforward, as refreshing, and as wise as saying to a young person: "The goodness in me salutes the goodness in you." That, my friends, is a power-packed salutation that will re-stitch the fabric of California currently at stress and strain under the oppressive weight of the four-headed epidemic hounding our kids. It's time to reclaim what is rightfully ours, and that is our future. It is far better to light a candle than to curse the darkness, and mentoring is the candle and the path to personal maturity and civic responsibility.

There is a chance, already proven, that life can be bright and fun again for once-beleaguered, overly tortured souls. There is a chance, already in action, that young people mired in negativity and unhealthy life choices, can still opt for positive, growth-enhancing, and satisfying lifestyles.

Story 7

HOSTS is a cornerstone to growing mentoring in America

As a fond admirer and participant in the classroom setting you are able to see many students on a daily basis, each group that you see is unique but holds some similarities. Every class includes superstars, class clown, as well as among the group will be the athletes who spend what seems to be all of their outside time competing, and even a few that spend their breaks writing stories. One day I noticed a student was struggling in school. Struggle is not by any means an unusual occurrence, but it seemed that over the years more and more students struggle with academia and this student faced a different battle.

My mind became consumed with thoughts of the academic system and how I could help this student to succeed. This child in particular needed something more than motivational speeches. The following day upon a visit to a southern California school in the San Diego area, I became aware of a program that could aid this child and other students in our school. The school decided to implement the program. From that day Helping One Student to Succeed was a great idea for this school that enabled students to not only attain personal TLC but also personalized academic tutoring.

I learned that with HOSTS, mentoring matches mean academic success. HOSTS has a brilliant formula for successful academic performance in that they formulate an academic plan based on the student's instructional and developmental level, learning style, and learning objectives. Students were able to realize their potential through tutoring sessions and regular progress reports. Tutors were matched to the students, and these tutors met with them on a regular basis. The tutors were given an agenda for that day's meeting with the student to attain success. Meetings between the student and tutor led to friendship, faith in their own abilities and renewed sense of academic achievement. The tutors became mentors in the truest sense of the term. They reacted to the immediate needs of the particular students and were able to chart their academic progress, which led to further academic achievement.

This was my first exposure to HOSTS and the results were seen weeks later as the student gained confidence in their abilities and was able to tackle the academic monster. Many other students in this school benefited from the specialized attention of the newly implemented HOSTS program. As a result the students participating in HOSTS rose from the bottom ten to the top percentiles of their academic world.

To see students excel and tackle their own academic challenges renews my own belief in the wonders of the human mind and spirit.

Story 8

The mentor/mentee relationship will work only if it is based on attraction, not something forced through promotional means. You can become a mentor today by simply being yourself.

Americans don't like to be told what to do.

We are, after all, revolutionaries, born in a spirit of rebellion against authority figures. We like to think we have a thick red stream of rugged individualism surging through our veins.

Chiseled of jaw, eagle of eye, our self-image is one of every man for himself. Patriotic, of course, but long live narcissism.

This is one reason it's so difficult for those of us in the public policy sector to mount a grassroots campaign on behalf of anything. People erect boundaries taller than their frailties; a welcome mat for new ideas is not a common sight on the doorsteps the Silent Majority.

Just ask any political campaign consultant worth his salt. Long ago was abandoned any notion that new ideas from politicians should be floated forth above the electorate. The winning strategy for seizing votes has for a long time been the simplistic tactic of imposing a grid of agreement upon the public, then fashioning a candidate to reflect that image.

Political leaders, if you'll forgive the oxymoron, are spokespersons that mirror the results taken from focus groups and market surveys. The underlying rule of thumb is check your brain at the gate. Little wonder, then, why many baby boomers feel that the last original political thought was uttered in Bobby Kennedy's last speech.

Sadly, we are a nation with no major heroes. Traumatized, we echo each other's packaged thoughts and bounce truisms off each other's damaged radar.

In many ways, the land of the free and the home of the brave has become a vacuum sealed tight through fear, pursuit of comfort and an unwillingness to have our fragile fortresses poked or probed by unwanted gadflies.

So then … after this somewhat dreary forecast of the country's social consciousness, how do we motivate citizens to come out of their castles to perform basic civic tasks like helping out young people.

Those who have the resources and luxury of time to assist youth in crisis are too often overly consumed with acquiring more resources and time. You cannot pry the unwilling to venture forth into a world of service.

That's exactly why we have designed the California Mentor Initiative to be a public policy program of attraction, not promotion. These, in fact, are words taken directly from the founding traditions of Alcoholics Anonymous, perhaps the most famous and most effective self-help organization in the United States.

Shunning self-promotion, AA relies on word-of-mouth and the spiritual power that comes from its success to create an atmosphere of attraction to something that really works. Recovering alcoholics flock to this program with the same urgency and thirst for improvement that used to propel them towards alcohol.

People whom we need to be mentors in this state are asked to be nothing more than themselves. In fact, it is the very gift of self in its most unpolished form that gives mentoring its greatest thrust.

For one hour a week—who really can't afford to give 60 minutes four times a month?—we ask settled, mature, professional adults to share their experiences, their lives with young people who are struggling mightily to find their way in the world.

The mentor/mentee relationship will work only if it is based on attraction, not something forced through promotional means. Thousands can attest to the satisfaction attained by both mentors and mentees in what is really the simplest, most effective measure yet created to nudge troubled teens out of isolation into the challenges and opportunities of the real world.

Take it a gospel from our nearly six years of experience working in the mentoring field—we are reaping a harvest of youth rehabilitation far beyond our wildest dreams, and we have the young lives to give testimony to the fact that mentoring works better than anything else yet imagined.

You can become a mentor today simply by being yourself.

Story 9

With the young, any point is a starting point, and the healing process begins with the slightest application of hope.

Once people find out how easy it is to become a mentor to a needy, deserving young protege, our fondest hope is that the floodgates of commitment and service will open.

We are trying to dissolve the misconception that to be a mentor is a complicated process. The opposite is true.

For young people who have been victimized so early in life by the multi-headed epidemic of drug and alcohol abuse, educational failure, teen pregnancy and gang attachment, what they so desperately need is someone who will simply listen to their dearest aspirations.

With the young, any point is a starting point, and the healing process begins with the slightest application of hope.

You may want to take an inner city kid to a baseball game, for example. Chances are, a kid with no father has never experienced this most basic of all-American treats. No profound conversation or complex interchange of grandiose ideas is necessary. Exposure to a new phenomenon is all that matters. Choices abound.

Perhaps during the game, the kid will volunteer how he has secretly yearned to be a part of a sports team, but that he has never had anyone to play catch with. The simplest act of father-son bonding, playing catch, has not been available in this kid's life.

You tell him next time you meet, you'll bring a baseball and a pair of gloves. His eyes shine with expectation. During the game of catch, back and forth, back and forth, you exchange tidbits of information about each other. He now feels comfortable enough about you to share some private doubts, fears, hopes.

You suggest ways to get him hooked into a youth athletic league. You accompany him to the sign-up, you introduce him to his teammates, and before you know it, you've enjoined him to a life-sustaining force infinitely more satisfying and enhancing than, God forbid, an association with a gang.

The mere act of taking a kid to a ballgame has opened for him an entirely new world of options heretofore foreign to him.

★ ★ ★

Years ago, there used to be a private Catholic institution in San Francisco's Richmond District. It was called St. Elizabeth's Home for Unwed Mothers, housed in a red-brick mansion surrounded and secured by wrought iron fences and gates.

A stately home, it looked like a fortress of doom. Indeed, it was.

There was such a death-knell connotation about the place, a burial ground for youthful dreams. Not only was a young woman's mistake being paid for, it was being institutionalized, and she'd be stigmatized for life.

The rock-solid building stood as a sober reminder that, in life, you play, you pay. Passers-by would walk past the edifice and peer inside. Staring back at them with hollow stares would be teenage girls whose eyes no longer sparkled with joy or promise. It was one of the saddest walks in San Francisco.

In today's world, such a scene is unimaginable. Far from being locked up and pilloried as outlaws, teenaged mothers now appear on talk shows. But their angst is the same.

Teen motherhood is one of the most damaging symptoms of personal alienation, a malady that could've been stemmed with the simplest introduction of a mentor into the young girl's life.

Without a significant adult in her natural family to steer her away from such reckless mistakes, the child has made a brutal error in becoming a mother before her own childhood has advanced.

What we've discovered with mentoring is that a secure role model, with just the slightest of influence, can alter a young woman's life away from fatal mistakes like this and toward self-fulfillment and maturity.

With the gentlest of nudging, we've witnessed mentors urging young girls to focus on their God-given skills long before they even begin to think of bringing new life into the world.

The girls soon realize that babies aren't meant to fill the emptiness in their wombs; infants need to be nourished by stable, caring, genuinely loving mothers. Once the mentors can educate unhappy young girls about these urgent facts of life, there can then be a return to sanity and balance in their young lives.

Story 10

As we walk that bridge to the next millennium, we can either accept the complexities of a modern society and embrace wonderful concepts like mentoring, or we can pretend that difficult problems do not exist, and move in fear backwards to a warmly nostalgic but ultimately hollow past.

★ ★ ★

In the latter part of the '90's, there is a rosy outlook on the horizon of American prosperity.

Strictly in materialistic terms, life is abundant. The economy is often booming, places like Silicon Valley become fabulous oases of wealth, and people are bursting at the seams with accessible cash, ready credit and dreams of gold.

Like anything in life, there is a flip side to this nirvana. It has to do with examples we set for our children, who must be instructed that all of this came about through hard work, unwavering faith during the tougher times, and an unswerving devotion and commitment to character, integrity and dignity.

And, with newspaper stories bristling every day about the booming bonanza of new wealth and material accumulation, we must always be mindful of the parallel phenomenon that exists for those who have yet to find their niche.

Thousands of California kids still go to bed every night without a responsible parent affirming their aspirations, without a solid role model of any kind telling them they love them. That kind of emptiness cannot be sated by the most fantastic news about a booming economy.

Each child must still find his or her own way through this perilous world, and the key to unlocking their success resides deep within their own hearts. This is where will, integrity and self-respect dwell. This is where integrity of the person is guarded, and this is the wellspring whereby young kids will learn to be self-sufficient, contributing members of society.

We want our children to know, without firsthand experience, that drugs and alcohol mute these aspirations, muzzle these hopes. Addiction to anything is a quick-fix feel-good remedy to alter what they perceive is wrong in their lives, but the ultimate knowledge is that caving into addictive substances and influences only create more problems and crises in their lives.

This is not the time to abandon disenfranchised youth by uttering pious cliches about rugged individualism in the land of plenty. You don't command someone to pull himself up by his own bootstraps when there's nowhere for him to walk.

The best and finest minds in today's recovery movements—the tireless, committed people who work with drug and alcohol-afflicted youth—swear that mentoring is what kids need today, not angry rhetoric.

Hear it from Martin Jacks, one of California's leading proponents of mentoring as a social motivating force:

"As responsible adults in an ever-changing, complex society, we need to 'walk through' our kids step-by-step. We need to expose them to new, daring situations that will enable them to grow as people. And, even as adults, we are not above the maturation process, either.

"We encourage training. We need to take a look at the man or the woman in the mirror before we interface with the child.

"After all, we have our own bad habits—we cuss, smoke, drink, whatever, so we must take a look at ourselves before we can begin to understand and serve the kids.

"And one of the first things we must learn as adults is to understand the attitudes of youth—kids are just being who they are culturally, so often times their behavior is wrongly assessed as negative.

"Multi-culturalism is designed to show that there are other considerations in personal behavior, and it is up to us to understand these. It's not that the European culture is bad, *per se*, but that there is a myriad of other influences to consider."

His thoughts are echoed by Tandy Isles, who works with Indian youth in San Francisco's Mission District:

"I see a lot of fighting about whether someone is whole blooded or mixed-blood. This is oral history passed down from families. But what we teach is that each person is respected for who he or she is. We use readings and a lot of traditional stories. We personalize history for the kids, and it gives them a certain amount of pride and respect.

"When you come right down to it, each of us *is* history, and we must instill both a sense of respect and a sense of history and pride in those whose skin bears that heritage."

To refine the point: As we walk this bridge to the next millennium, we can either accept the complexities of a modern society and embrace wonderful concepts like mentoring, or we can pretend that difficult problems don't exist, and move in fear backwards to a warmly nostalgic but ultimately hollow past.

Story 11

In our efforts to reinvigorate California one child at a time, there is no greater blessing for us than to see the cycle of mentoring solidified and completed through a functional and fully reciprocal mentor/mentee relationship.

★ ★ ★

As an enthusiastic advocate for the California Mentor Initiative, it frequently occurs to me that we have one of the easiest recruitment programs in the history of progressive social reforms.

While we have witnessed mentoring become the most effective device to help kids gain confidence and self-esteem in their return to sane and healthy lifestyles, we have also witnessed a phenomenon we could never have anticipated accurately.

Time after time, case after case, the mentors who are assisting their young mentees come to us and report how much they themselves have gained from the experience. While it's impossible to construct a consistent prototype of the "average" mentor, it's fair to say that most are well-educated, at least moderately successful, and possess a social consciousness that nudges them into the public fray to contribute to the community's greater good.

Because they are good citizens acting on their own awareness to give back to society, this being their driving motivation, it really doesn't occur to them at the beginning of their mentor relationship that they will also gain from the experience.

For all of us trying to orchestrate this great symphony of rippling effects and healing currents, it provides a wonderful sense of gratification to witness the testimony of mentors who emerge from the experience eager for further involvement.

In our efforts to reinvigorate California one child at a time, there is no greater blessing for us than to see the cycle of mentoring solidified and completed through a functional and fully reciprocal mentor/mentee relationship.

The ease with which this dynamic is created can be attributed to the fact that this is not a dramatic rescue mission. It is, rather, a calm process whereby the mentor introduces the protege to his own vast potential.

Take the case of Ben, a Mill Valley financial consultant who has been working as a mentor to a young man named Carlos, a former Mission District gang member who's been long alienated from his alcohol-wracked family, discarded and disenfranchised since early childhood.

When Ben took on the assignment of shepherding Carlos into a life that would have more meaning, it struck him that Carlos already possessed most of the smarts and savvy that Ben's colleagues in the Financial District had long displayed as successful professionals. Ben knew that, save for a few twists of fate and ill fortune, there was a very thin line between the world of Carlos and the world of thriving prosperity.

Ben also recognized early on that Carlos was a gift—a quiet, reflective young man who drew from a deep well of brilliant creativity. Driven downward and inward from neglect and parental abuse, he found strength from the quiet recesses of his inner soul. Once Ben was able to tap into this powerful reservoir of personhood, he was able to set Carlos free from his demons.

In dealing with Carlos, Ben remembered a talk he once had with a minister when he and his wife were pregnant with their first child. The minister had told them that while parenthood was a great challenge, remembering one thing would make the job extremely easy. That one thing was the acceptance and recognition that every child is a gift.

Says Ben today: "I have lived by that simple rule every day of my parenting life, and I am extending the same spirit to Carlos. It covers everything, from showering the individual with affection to learning to communicate honestly on all levels; from never trying to control the person to always being mindful of his needs; from accepting the person for who he is, to learning how to share tough-love pearls of wisdom."

Ben says his influence upon Carlos has given the young man the kind of confidence he's needed to make it on his own, away from the lawlessness of gang involvement. He's enrolled in art classes, and he's even sold some oil paintings depicting Mission District family life at street fairs. On weekends, Carlos helps coach children's soccer teams.

This is why Ben signed on as a mentor, to make a difference in a young man's life, but he's still in awe over how much he has gained from the experience himself. Not only does he enjoy the ongoing friendship with Carlos, but he also feels enriched by the success of their partnership, a richness he can bring to his own family and one that wraps him in a very happy and warm aura of well-being.

Story 12

We are actively engaged in the struggle to make democracy work most effectively once again. This is an inclusive battle that honors the diversity of each individual participant, and there is a place for everyone.

★ ★ ★

In our work rebuilding California one child at a time, those of us driving the machinery of mentoring must constantly caution ourselves against the illusion of cliche and misguided motivation.

Our work is about repairing the soul of youth that's been abused and shattered by the swirling vortex of drug and alcohol involvement, educational failure, teen pregnancy and gang violence. By addressing these problems with the proven technique of solid mentoring programs, we must always be aware of false prophets mouthing empty promises.

Caught up in the vigor and enthusiasm of the work that is reshaping our glorious state, their stumbling might be forgiven, but it must be checked. Language expands reality, and where it is wrong, it should be repaired.

I speak specifically about a misconception that's too often the prop of rhetoric. Frequently, you will hear a legislator or social commentator talk about the importance of mentoring because, to paraphrase roughly, "The youth of today represent our future." This is buzzword chitchat that needs to be deleted into oblivion.

Kids today are hip, savvy, street-smart and informative. They can cut through such propaganda like scissors through onionskin. They know intuitively that they are worth more than seedling exhibits for "our future." They are worthy and esteemed for who they are in the moment.

Take the case of Lamar, an 18-year-old Marin City man who has matured as a person after three years of active mentoring; he is now almost ready to complete the cycle and become a mentor himself. He minces no words when it comes to lancing cliches and thoughtless phrases.

"If anyone had said to me in my angrier, younger days that they were helping me because I was their future, I would've laughed in their face, man," he says. "I was desperate to find myself for me, not for anyone else. Kids can see right through patronizing people, folks who condescend. They may mean well, but they're actually turning us off with empty promises like that."

This may seem trivial or hair-splitting, but the discussion cuts right to the heart of what we are trying to accomplish with the California Mentor Initiative. We are actively engaged in the struggle to make democracy work most effectively once again. This is an inclusive battle that honors the diversity of each individual participant, and there is a place for everyone.

Spinning forth from this is other avenues of awareness that we must constantly heed. Genuine mentoring, for example, is not about false edification. Heaped-on praise where none is deserved serves only as a sham. Hollow and empty acceptance, a desire for a feel-good-now payoff, rather than an earned and true level of high self-esteem does nothing more than to fan the flames of hypocrisy.

Mentoring is about being a confident, secure, solid role model. There should be less emphasis on rescue missions and more attention given to how life should be lived in a healthy, functional fashion.

Even a small child (*especially* a small child) instinctively knows that acknowledgment and appreciation where none is called for is gratuitous and cheap. This is because of the reality of the system we live in. Before we came along, the system was working. And long after we are gone, its wheels will continue to turn.

The system is not a perfect one. There are homeless people. Illnesses hit the unexpected ones. Life is hard and bullies exist. Within the system are built-in values, limits and equations that give merit to some actions and scorn to others. The level of a person's self-esteem can only grow and flourish when the rewards of right actions or of true intent are in a valid and proper framework.

Like villainous tentacles, crime, unemployment, drug and alcohol abuse, teen pregnancies, welfare dependency and violence have reached into our homes and lives and dragged us to the floor. What Alexis de Tocqueville saw as the almost charming experiment, democracy, with all its responsibilities would seem now terribly anachronistic. The infant called democracy has grown up. The grand experiment is working, but some of the hinges squeak, some are non-functioning, and others have fallen off and have left the door gaping open.

In Walden, Henry David Thoreau acknowledged: "The mass of men lead lives of quiet desperation." The insidious nature of passivity can rot the roof and warp of society. Like the crew on Odysseus' ship who got waylaid on the land of the Lotus Eaters, we sit in front of television sets letting ennui smother us in her warm fog. To do nothing is an evil action. To sit and be passive gives energy to all that can bring us down.

Again Thoreau, who was only a boy when de Tocqueville was visiting young America, remarked, "That which a man thinks of himself will determine his fate." Exponentially, this works for a man, a family, a town and a country.

When John F. Kennedy asked us what we could do for our country, our democratic heritage was being fleshed out. This is a country founded upon participation, right action and accountability. And our nation's journey, not unlike the hero's own path, has just begun.

Begin right action. Participate in the system. Watch the benefits accrue. The California Mentor Initiative might just be for you.

Story 13

13

A child cannot be wise, but he can have the strength, the integrity and the resolve of the most profound thinkers and doers of the world. Those very qualities will serve our society well. We must be proud of nurturing that.

★ ★ ★

I am proud to say that one of my boyhood heroes, John Fitzgerald Kennedy, is largely responsible for the choice I have made to devote the bulk of my adult life to public service.

The Kennedy family, maligned as they are in the modern media, was always fond of saying: "To whom much is given, much is expected." They did not wear their wealth gaudily, but accepted it in a spirit of gratitude, always mindful of returning something of worth and benefit to the greater community.

I am constantly aware of the Kennedy admonition, and I see heroes every day. When Joseph Campbell wrote *The Hero With A Thousand Faces*, he drew our attention to a link we have both to the past and to the future.

We are not new to this earth. We are ancient in our habits, propensities, and yearnings. Perhaps we Fax and e-mail our scribbling across the Pacific in a wink of time, sending ideas and information, but the idea we transmit is grounded in the bedrock of time, and the information received is only a puny little strata, a ribbon line in the rock. We forget that we are the rock, as formidable and as lasting.

In the journey man makes toward the self, which is the path to true heroism, this perilous adventure can involve many permutations. Each of us, as a hero, must answer his own particular call. As Campbell points out: "A hero ventures forth from the world of common day into a region of supernatural wonder: fabulous forces are there encountered and a decisive victory is won. The hero comes back from this mysterious adventure with the power to bestow boons on his fellow man." This pattern of outward travel and adventure, of course, forms a comprehensive metaphor for the inner journey of the hero.

When the adolescent child seeks his own way to truth, perhaps causing a family uproar in these tumultuous '90's, he is encountering the dragons in the dark wood. He must slay the dragon; he must endure and fight so that his return will be replete with the capacity to give. His newfound wisdom of the world and his outward maturity are his gifts.

But his journey might take him to places his parents and teachers don't understand or approve. Must the journey be along the path the parents like? Here is the juncture at which the hero's trail becomes rocky and difficult to traverse. The Roman philosopher Seneca remarked that the road to happiness is a rough one. Yes, I should say it is.

The amazing strength of purpose required to pursue a goal is the most visible sign of a person's high self-esteem. That sense of personal integrity and honesty of purpose arms the hero for his journey. He is "following his bliss," his sense of purpose. When a child is encouraged to be self-reliant, he may want to strike out on his own, sail across an ocean, start a backyard business, play cacophonous music in the garage, and wear tattered clothes. When a child is taught to question and to challenge, he may question you and challenge his very environment.

A child cannot be wise, but he can have the strength, the integrity and the resolve of the most profound thinkers and doers of the world. Those very qualities will serve our society well. We must be proud of nurturing that.

The man who leaves behind his low regard for himself casts off the rags of isolation. His nurturing substance now becomes: feeling likeable, significant, as if he belongs, and sensing an acknowledgment of his hard work. With efforts to involve ourselves in the affairs of the community, we are rescued.

The daily acts of heroism wounded people perform need not be melodramatic or documented by media frenzy. They can be as quiet as a reflective moment on one's knees or as kind as a hand extended to a person in need or as silent as an unspoken prayer uttered to God Almighty on behalf of a suffering friend.

Mentors can certainly help in these never ending journies.

Story 14

The beginning of mentoring, the acceptance of another person into a young person's life to serve as a role model, is the end of isolation which is the antithesis of what America is all about..

★ ★ ★

Fax machines weren't around in American writer William James' day, but if they were, his frequent repartee with Henry David Thoreau could have been communicated with much more alacrity.

When James wrote, "Let everything I do be done as if it makes a difference," it took many days for the thought to be delivered with dispatch to Thoreau, who took even a few more days to respond: "There is no beginning too small."

These magnificent men of historical American letters may have been limited by the means of their comunicados, but their essential message is just as relevant in today's madcap, information-ready age of instant communication.

We are a society of many individuals, and there can be no solution to the problems we face except the individual motivation to take action. Any effort to alleviate the darkness of our cities, schools and families must be a common effort. The process by which a person is made to realize his worth and the efficacy of his bolstered high self-esteem will feed back onto the alienating world he stepped from.

It's truly wonderful how the word "mentor" has crept back into popular usage. The word's origins date back to the classical cultures of Graeco-Roman days when it took an entire city-state to raise a child. And it's doubly refreshing that a word with genuinely timeless roots finds itself once again in the lexicon of the aware and the newly enlightened.

In a community like Marin, for instance, it is not at all uncommon to hear young people in coffee shops and on bike trails refer to someone as "my mentor," a warmly endearing term that conveys the sense of community, democracy and purpose once imagined by James and Thoreau. Its very utterance is reassurance that our way of life in a free democracy is working in its most radical form.

The word "mentor" was heard on a recent episode of "Seinfeld," for example, that wacky comedy which prides itself on being about "nothing." One of the zany female characters introduced her lady friend to someone as "my mentor." It wasn't used as a throwaway phrase or as a dig at a culture of old—it was mouthed casually and sincerely.

And, laced throughout the seemingly endless menu of daytime talk shows, the word has taken on bold new significance. Psychological experts and counselors for the dysfunctional are frequently paraded onstage toward the end of a show to prescribe therapy, medicine or a guiding hand to the emotionally wracked panelists who have been chosen as guests.

Many times, these experts emphasize that what this child needs in life is a mentor, or what that recovering alcoholic/dope addict/sex fiend should seek out is a mentoring center.

This is a marvelous experience to behold—it's just the genesis, a sneak peek, if you will, at what America would look like if mentoring became as commonplace as, say, TV watching.

The beginning of mentoring—the acceptance of another person into a young person's life to serve as a role model—is the end of isolation, which is the antithesis of what America is all about. Through mentoring, it does not have to be a lonely way to full self-esteem. We know that it blossoms forth from within, but we also know that those around us are extremely important to its nourishment. Our teachers, our parents and our communities give us constant feedback as to how we are doing. Very much like a radar tracking system, we bounce our decisions and actions off a sounding screen.

The validity and integrity of a radar screen is paramount. When a child comes in a distant fourth in a swimming race, he looks at the screen and reads the results. He looks to see how his parents treat that event. Did they acknowledge his valiant effort and his crushing disappointment with kindness and respect? Did they patronize him with trite and empty responses?

The student looks at the teacher in the same way. How are his victories as well as his failings showing up on the screen? So self-esteem is engendered via these mentors. So self-esteem takes hold in a person, and he becomes a hero to himself who can one day bring to his community and his family the fruits of his accomplishments.

The key is self-discovery, not bold imposition from a hovering authority figure. The key is living well, the most potent form of being a good example for those still in the throes of discovery.

So, with so many young people wanting a positive, caring person in their life, coaching them to success, would you consider being a mentor?

Story 15

15

She says mentoring is especially important to her because she is the single mother of a 10 year old girl, and she would really like to have her daughter benefit from a strong role model.

★ ★ ★

Angie is a 29-year-old African American woman who grew up in O.J. Simpson's San Francisco boyhood neighborhood of Potrero Hill. In fact, she recalls meeting Simpson when he was in grammar school. Angie's family was moving into the Simpson house when O.J. and his brood needed larger quarters.

"I'm not sure how these things happen," she explains, sitting on a grassy knoll in downtown San Francisco, the sun splashing her raven hair with rays of gold, "but it was shortly after the verdict setting Simpson free when I had this moment of clarity."

"It was like I was looking into the very absurdity of life. I mean, this guy was my hero. I knew him. He was my one link with fame. But I was also absolutely convinced that he was guilty."

"So, I had this roller coaster emotional upheaval, first of all trying to reconcile the shock I felt when I was convinced he was the murderer, then trying to get through the betrayal of the system. Now, I know it's not popular for a black person to take this position, but I really wanted to see the system work. When it didn't, I had this very clear, very sudden awareness that we are only responsible for ourselves in this world. I never felt so alone, yet so strong, in all my life."

Angie decided, literally on the spot, to look into becoming a mentor for a needy young person from her old San Francisco neighborhood.

"I really needed to reach out immediately to help someone in worse trouble than me," she recalls. "I had this burning rage and restlessness within me, and it was devouring me. I desperately wanted to turn this negative energy into something positive and wonderful."

Angie's own road has not been that easy. Although she's been clean and sober for eight years, she had her "dance with the devil" in high school, drinking away her innocence and nearly losing her life smoking crack cocaine.

"My cousin jumped off the Golden Gate Bridge when I was nine," she says, "and many times I've walked across the span contemplating the same thing. But I've always felt that I had something 'special' to offer, and that always kept me from leaping. Growing up like I did in the projects, I was no stranger to pain and fear. There is so much suffering going on there, it's incredibly difficult to rise above it. But something deep inside me continues to burn, and I refuse to quit."

"I'm not proud of it, but when I needed money I danced at one of those sleazy Market Street joints where men pay you to dance in their laps. I can't believe how may lonely people there are out there who'd shell out money for a few moments of mindless chatter and giggling. All the time I'm performing, I'm thinking, 'If all these well-dressed, successful men are paying me for company, then there's hope for me after all.'"

Angie squirreled away her money from dancing, and enrolled in a drama class at San Francisco State. She's a glib, quick-witted personality with a flair for humor, and she has a dream of appearing in a TV sitcom one day. She says mentoring is especially important to her because she's the single mother of a 10-year-old girl, and she'd really like to have her daughter benefit from a strong role model.

"If mentoring were available to me when I was my little girl's age," she says somewhat ruefully, "maybe I would've saved myself a lot of agony and trouble. I do have faint memories from my childhood of all these other adults having authority over me. A lady from the neighborhood would come in to do the ironing, and another woman would do my mother's books. Both were like extended parents for me, but there's nothing like that in today's world."

"That's why I embrace mentoring so wholeheartedly. It gives the young person a solid way to view the world, to survive in the world. It provides structure, meaning and love, and it offers a path to success."

Angie squints a smile in the noonday sun, then says: "You know, it's really true God works in mysterious ways. There's so much disillusionment and rage and pain around the O.J verdict, but it's also opened up a whole new world of awareness."

"I decided not to get swallowed up in the cynicism, and I chose instead to take positive, definite steps to help turn someone else's life around."

Story 16

To experience the power of turning a young person's life around toward righteous, self-fulfilling behavior is an intoxicant more exhilarating than any assortment of fake highs induced by drugs, alcohol, or material aggrandizement.

Would you consider being a mentor?

Maybe if you knew just a little bit more about this phenomenon that is sweeping the state, you just might be moved to sign on with the California Mentoring Initiative.

The first thing I should tell you is that it is not complicated. All you have to do is be yourself, and you will be an excellent mentor.

The second thing I should tell you is that there are thousands of kids right here in Marin County who would love to have you as a mentor. Marin has one of the highest divorce rates in the nation, and kids have a gnawing hunger for more stability in their adult relationships.

You wouldn't be replacing either one of their parents as an important role model. You would, however, be augmenting the kid's need for a significant, stable, adult influence, thereby filling a terrible gap that something like divorce creates.

Too often, the adults going through marital strife are so utterly consumed and too frequently destroyed by the experience that they have little left of emotional strength to offer their kids. One harsh reality of life is that, while the adults are working through their various issues, the kids' needs remain unchanged and unfilled.

It is not a negative reflection, necessarily, upon the divorcing parents. No man should ever judge unfairly the kind of anguish that dissolution creates, but neither parents should live in denial about the ongoing needs and wants of the children, who in truth are no doubt yearning for the kind of free, refreshing, no-strings involvement a neutral third-party is able to offer.

The third thing I should tell you about mentoring is that you stand to gain even more than will your mentee. This is a truly phenomenal fact of life that we see time and time again in our studies of cases up and down the state.

As previous Director of Alcohol and Drug Programs for California and as Governor Wilson's point man for the California Mentoring Initiative, I heard feedback all the time from Californians who have given up a slice of their lives to be mentors, and it as unanimous as it is gratifying—mentors are overwhelmed by how much they themselves are rewarded for their services.

So then, as for my first point, it really is simple.

If you are reading this, it already tells me you are an engaged, caring citizen of the world. In the profession of your choice, you have applied your God-given talents on a daily basis to the task at hand. You are worldly, in that you've steered your life through the various pitfalls and icebergs of reality. You've learned how to negotiate yourself in what is an ever-increasingly cold, unconditional world.

You have succeeded in family life, the business world as well as sustaining these triumphs with an active, ongoing spiritual commitment. Yes, you are as vulnerable as the next ever-changing organism, but you have the tools, the will and the know-how to deal with whatever situation life dishes up.

You've done it for yourself making you the perfect candidate to do it for someone who has yet to learn the tools.

My second point is where you place your talent—directly into the life of someone who suffers for the lack of a person like you. Maybe the kid simply needs someone to really listen to him. You can do that. Perhaps it's a case of the kid needing to vent to someone the stress caused by his parents' problems. You can do that, too. Or maybe he needs some recreational release—a walk on the beach, a trip to a Giants' game, a ferry ride to Angel's Island. You're qualified to do these things.

Or maybe the kid has never been to a museum. Perhaps he's never seen Golden Gate Park or an aquarium. Maybe he doesn't know about SAT scores as preparation to college, or perhaps he doesn't know the first thing about dating someone from the opposite sex. These are all things you take for granted that are still wrapped in mystery for a novice child. Take him there, and enjoy it for yourself once again.

And this leads directly again to my third point. "To give is to receive," and nowhere in life is this aphorism more deeply experienced than by a mentor in a nurturing relationship with a mentee. To experience the power of turning a young person's life around toward righteous, self-fulfilling behavior is an intoxicant wildly more exhilarating than any assortment of fake highs induced by drugs, alcohol or material aggrandizement.

If you become a mentor, you are enlarging not one life, but two.

Story 17

Sometimes it takes only a fraction of adjustment to induce a young person toward the light away from the darkness. One of those precious fractions is the concept of mentoring.

If you knew you had the opportunity to prevent a teenager from taking his first drink of booze, would you?

Well, you do.

If you knew you had the chance, today, to talk a girl through an emotional crisis that would lead to her pregnancy while still a mere child herself, would you?

Well, you do.

If you could snuff out a beautiful young child's first careless toke of a joint, first awful puncture of virgin skin by a hideous needle bearing crack cocaine, or first thoughtless flirtation with the initiation rites of a dangerous gang, would you?

Well, you could.

You could be a mentor. In fact, you probably already are one, and you don't even know it.

There is today in California a tremendous movement of hope sweeping the state. It's called mentoring, and you can be a part of the revolution by the time you finish reading this column.

Preventing our children from harm's way and leading them toward a life of self-fulfillment is what mentoring is all about.

The bewildering teen years have claimed far too many victims, and it is time for us to step up to the challenge—teenagers should be poised on the brink of maturity, hopeful and eager for the future and not making disastrous choices that end their young lives before they've even had the chance to enter adulthood.

Sometimes it takes only a fraction of adjustment to induce a young person toward the light away from the darkness. One of those precious fractions is the concept of mentoring.

Prevention from addiction, prevention from teen pregnancy, prevention from educational failure, prevention from gang involvement—these are wishes we bestow upon our children, yet so many of them falter. Why?

Why, indeed, would a teenager cave into peer pressure and start drinking alcohol? Many times it's simply ignorance of the consequences that leads to such a mistake. If an adult with even a modicum of experience and knowledge about alcohol could speak evenly, frankly and soberly about the immediate dangers of alcoholism, that adult would be saving a life.

And, if a teenager came to realize that the satisfaction of talking things out with a solid role model is infinitely more life-enhancing than stuffing things in by way of substance abuse, that teen can be spared a lifetime cycle of affliction, recovery and relapse.

Same is true of teen pregnancy. A mere child desperately craving a child of her own is wildly trying to fill a gaping void within herself, a crazy, futile notion that will rob her of her own childhood and set her on a course of emotional and financial ruin.

Hear it directly from Tawny, a recent graduate of Drake High School, who shivers with fear over how her life would be without the influence of her mentor:

"My parents just weren't available to me, and I had so many questions. I had, in fact, this insatiable need to fill myself with anything—that's how large my emptiness felt.

"After a week of binge drinking and sleeping around, one of my friends introduced me to her support group, and I got hooked up with a woman who would become my mentor. It was this simple—she looked into my eyes, she opened her ears, and she let me talk forever about anything I wanted to dump on her.

"I know in my heart that without her being there, I would've gotten addicted to booze and drugs, and I definitely would've been a child mother. And all she did was listen. We worked problems out together, she made herself available to me at all hours of the day, and she guided me through my last year of high school."

Tawny is currently enrolled at a college in Los Angeles where she studies dance and music, and she is pursuing a career in entertainment. She is discovering the power within herself to become an independent person without dulling her senses. And she is happy. And she owes her life to her mentor.

This is a wondrous, magnificent phenomenon, and it is here to stay. You can become a part of this exciting revolution, and the gains you will experience far outweigh any investment of time. Indeed, it is the giving of time and attention, not an impersonal check that will generate the most profound changes of all.

Story 18

18

Mentors are vital to these young people because mentoring provides the texture, flavor and appeal to change young people's environment and future

In his clumsy, yet heartfelt stabs at rhetoric, former President George Bush was fond of talking about "a thousand points of light" that illuminated America's path for struggling citizens.

The illusion was a poetic attempt to cast praise upon the nation's unsung heroes, toilers in the trenches who steadfastly maintain in their hearts and chosen vocations a determined vision for all that this nation promises.

In California, the most diverse and troublesome of the country's 50 states, there are thousands of points of light in each major urban sprawl.

One of those is Gregory Hodge, an eloquently upbeat African-American historian/activist/minister who helps shepherd California youth through the perils of adolescence.

To hear Hodge speak is to embrace hope—he is that dynamic.

When he speaks on his favorite subject, mentoring, the passion of his convictions is palpable, the power of his message profound.

"I like to talk about both the challenges and assets of the mentoring movement," Hodge told a recent gathering of mentors in California.

"There are immense challenges facing African-American kids today, but I always quickly follow this up by asserting that they are *children*, not an endangered species—not an owl or a whale that we need to save from extinction."

"In California, roughly 47% of African-Americans live in poverty, yet nearly 84 % of school suspensions are handed out to black students, even though we comprise only less than half the student population."

"Mentors are vital to these young people, because mentoring provides the texture and flavor and appeal to change young people's environment and future. It's going to take mentors to create the rich fabric. Social isolation among black kids is a huge challenge, and mentors will fill in the gap to show the opportunities."

As the California Mentor Initiative takes root in this vastly diverse state, Hodge emphasizes that it is absolutely vital to be consistent—there should be nothing casual or half-hearted about a mentor's approach to a child, who needs structure and continuity.

He also points out that programs and ideas must be culturally based. Culture is to people what water is to fish. There will be hope and an opportunity to do better, but it must be based on a cultural value system, one that accepts the young person for who he or she is today.

Culture is a way of looking at life—it's not just about music and books. First, you learn history, and then there is hope. And mentoring is all about a sense of history—the effective mentor shares, for example, that your African-American ancestors are a great people because they survived slavery.

What's particularly unique about the mentoring movement as it exists in California today is that, perhaps for the first time in the history of government, this is not a program that induces people to swivel their heads toward the establishment for help. It is, rather, an inspiring tidal wave of hope and promise that empowers citizens to cultivate themselves as talented and worthwhile human beings.

Most importantly, we have to be honest with children, because they're good, sharp thinkers, and they've shut down to most role models. Very simply, mentors provide the surrogate example of what should have been in place quite naturally from parents and the extended family members.

There's an ancient African-American adage that best sums up the whole concept of mentoring—"It takes a whole village to raise a single child."

That is the essence, the beauty and the simplicity of mentoring as it prospers today.

Story 19

Scapegoating youth as a way to smokescreen adult misbehavior is no longer acceptable, politically correct or morally justified, and statistics back the argument.

Just when you thought that youth violence and teenage gangs were out of control, now comes a headline from a recent edition of the *Sacramento Bee's* "Forum" page:

Adults now more violent than youth

What follows is a lengthy article by Michael A. Males, a social ecology doctoral student at UC Irvine and author of *The Scapegoat Generation: America's War on Adolescents.*

The article is a huge relief to thousands of people toiling in the fields of teenage problems, because part of the burden constantly saddling them is the misconception dramatized by the media that America's young are on an unbridled spree of crime and lawlessness.

The mere perception of hopelessness and disdain perpetrated downward from adult to youth often times generates a vexing phantom problem that feeds the fear and widens the generation gap.

Not that anyone should exult over the fact that adult crime patterns are on the rise, but Males' findings do give some solace to countless numbers of adult mentors who strive tirelessly to bolster adolescent hopes toward full inclusion in worthwhile lifestyles.

Scapegoating youth as a way to smokescreen adult misbehavior is no longer acceptable, politically correct or morally justified, and statistics back the argument.

Males nails the thesis with strong language:

He writes, "A nation whose top political leaders are engaged in a relentless campaign to scapegoat its own young for a complex array of social problems is suffering a fundamental crisis of accountability."

This is rich stuff for people in the mentoring movement, people who have committed a healthy slice of their lives to facilitating self-esteem and independence among the young.

What this de-mythologizing suggests is precisely this—problems of youth violence are extremely complex, and, much like racism, they refuse to be cured by simplistic methodology.

Like with racism, there are a lot of misguided do-gooders who think they can impose their somewhat strict and rigid belief systems upon an oppressed people.

But it doesn't work that way, just like white liberals who long ago discovered that you can't legislate integration. The key ingredient is empowerment. Black people don't need "permission" from white people to attain their rights; they need to be left alone to assert the rights they already have.

This is similar to the problems of youth. The last thing a troubled teen wants or needs is input and advice from an adult whose own life is totally out of the loop of what transpires in the world of the young.

Author Males' parting shot is a resounding volley:

"If California and the nation face a violent future, it is not due to some mythical teenage menace, but the personal misbehavior, economic abuses and official indifference inflicted by older generations that seem not to care what happens to the young."

The genius of mentoring as a vital social force in the world today is that its dynamics provide for the emerging citizen his or her own blueprint for becoming exactly the kind of person they've always yearned to be. Mentoring is a lightning rod for hope, not a mandated governmental control.

In life, if not always in government, all things have a way of working themselves out. Sometimes the most vital step in the process of healing is letting go, which provides fresh air and new life.

Story 20

20

A mentoring relationship means meeting on a regular basis, over an extended period of time, with the goal of establishing a special bond of mutual commitment based on the development of respect, loyalty and self-esteem. The essence of mentoring is the sharing of one person with another.

It's funny how American life in the 90's invents new buzzwords, isn't it?

With TV, the fireplace of our instantly intimate global village, catchy new phrases and twists of grammar spill forth like fashion fads.

Have you noticed the phrase "24-7" being used more and more by people of all ages?

This was actually a code word for the so-called "Generation X" kids, who, instead of saying something like, "I work and study around the clock," shortened it to "24 (hours)-7" (days a week).

Then there's that black culture-inspired replacement for "Hello, how are you?" It's now, "Wassup?" or its less refined offspring, "Waddup?"

Some of these slangy, trendy detours through the much-embattled English language actually become legitimate after years of use, and others receive the sublime honor of being invited into the dictionary.

Tracking words through the paths of our lives is not an idle, frivolous exercise. Words and how we express them actually expand the reality in which we live. This is why we must choose our words carefully.

How they are uttered and the accents with which we stab at them are important, too. To quote the late sage Marshall McLuhan, "the medium is often the message."

But, while words come and phrases go, there is an exciting new word, bursting with hope and meaning, that is creeping solidly into daily use and understanding—mentoring.

The word is not an invention, and it actually has roots as far back as the ancient Greek Empire, but its impact on American people today is giving the word an entirely new sense of importance.

There is a bold new public policy program in California, in fact, being built around this word. It's the California Mentor Initiative, a public commitment of nearly $30 million to instill a grid of care and grassroots re-birth among the state's young and (temporarily) stray citizens.

Addressing the epidemic of educational failure, pregnant teenage girls, alcohol-and-drug-inflicted minors and misdirected members of youth gangs prone to violence, the California Mentor Initiative is a classically grounded, courageous effort to offer solid support, guidance and, most importantly, empowerment to a state whose youth problems have crested in plague-scale waves of discontent.

In essence, mentoring is the active presence of a caring individual, one who provides one-on-one support and attention, one who is a friend and a role model, and one who can boost another's self-esteem. A mentor is someone who can instill values, guide curiosity, develop innate self-worth, and encourage the effective pursuit of a purposeful life.

A mentoring relationship means meeting on a regular basis, over an extended period of time, with the goal of establishing a special bond of mutual commitment based on the development of respect, loyalty and self-esteem. The essence of mentoring is the sharing of one person with another.

Yet, for a great number of today's youth, the mentoring experience has been the exact opposite. Too often, their mentors have been negative role models, coming as they have from the criminal elements within our neighborhoods, gangs, drug culture and disrupted marriages.

Mentoring experiences of this kind have led to crime, violence, teen pregnancy, school dropout, and general misery for which society pays a tremendous price in lost lives and wasted human productivity.

The results we've reaped to date show we're exactly on the right track when it comes to a successful mentor/protege relationship. That is, the mentor acts as the nourishing water source for a long thirsty potted plant that suddenly springs to life when it drinks freely.

The California Mentor Initiative (CMI) has the specific mission to provide at-risk youth with the support and guidance they require to become productive members of society.

Story 21

Mentoring is evolving. It introduces a service ethic, it instills in kids a sense of community, and it sows the seeds in young people the desire for service outside themselves

Taxpayers hear the term "public policy program," and they usually wince. They see dollar signs and volumes of boring paperwork, which they'll never read or appreciate.

In a way, the taxpayers are right. Most public policy programs, built into the infrastructure of government like housing insulation in an attic, are out of sight, out of mind, expensive and seemingly unnecessary.

When a public policy program arises from a state's dire needs, however, and presents itself as an investment rather than a liability, and starts reaping invaluable rewards immediately, it is time to rejoice.

One such public policy program is the California Mentor Initiative, signed as an executive order by Governor Pete Wilson in April of 1995.

The epidemic problems have been staring us in the face for some time—teenage drug and alcohol abuse, gang violence, school dropout rates, teenage pregnancy, and the overall sense of malaise and alienation that spirals downward from these societal ailments.

The California Mentor Initiative stares down these hard facts of life and address the needs of young people desperately looking for meaning, fulfillment and survival.

The California Mentor Initiative's initial goal was to recruit and train 250,000 mentors. We accomplished this and are now well on the way toward the new goal of one million new matches by 2005.

Governor Wilson's and new Governor' Davis' budget commitment of $30 million per year marks the first time in the country's history that such a significant public policy step has been taken on behalf of mentoring activities.

The money streamed toward community-based groups like Big Brothers/Big Sisters, at an estimated cost of approximately $300 per child per year.

The underlying theme of this radical approach to re-seeding our state's investment in youth is that prevention programs for youth will only work if whole communities become involved and adults take their share of responsibility by providing kids with healthy role models.

The rest of the nation will be looking at California very closely, as this state attacks the problems of drug abuse, teen pregnancy, educational failure and gangs.

It is estimated that these problems cost Californians $100 billion a year in hard costs, lost productivity and missed opportunities—catastrophic economic hits that are every bit as debilitating as earthquakes, fires and floods.

The program for mentoring is like no other, because we know that it works before we even implement it.

There are volumes of research already in print that show mentoring succeeds in relationships between high-risk kids and their mentors. Mentoring creates a 50% reduction in school dropouts, and a 55% reduction in drug abuse.

We also see more kids going on to college.

We emphasize that this is not a Great Society-style social program of mammoth proportions. This is not a huge rescue mission with frantic legions of soldiers armed with desperate battle plans. This is a brilliant option for troubled teens to embrace in order for them to move their lives in more healthy directions.

Mentoring is evolving. It introduces a service ethic, it instills in the kids a sense of community, and it sows the seeds in young people the desire for service outside themselves.

Keeping hope alive for kids is as tangible as life itself—it guides kids in going from nowhere to somewhere.

For taxpayers weary of opening their pocketbooks for programs that are pathless, this is a journey that is already making returns on the public's monetary investment.

Story 22

Leading someone to hope and a new life is what mentoring is all about. Mentoring is the courage of someone in a stable position of life extending promise and opportunity to someone less fortunate.

One of the mysteries of the human animal is that we show more compassion and mercy toward pets than we do toward each other. Take a walk around the streets of San Francisco.

Natives are used to the sight, but tourists and visitors look shocked when they encounter homeless forms of humanity sprawled out in various postures of despair. Pedestrians literally stumble over lifeless bodies sleeping inside cardboard packing boxes on downtown pavement, cold from the fog and stinking of human waste.

The few feeble hands that have the strength to stretch outward in a begging position are left with nothing as passers-by rush past, trying very hard not to notice the disasters sprawled beneath them. It's a grim picture, this battlefield of human wreckage splayed against the backdrop of what should be the most healthy, giving, and upbeat city in the universe.

Imagine the outcry that would be heard if these were small animals, household pets, wounded and scarred, moaning for food, shelter, hope. First of all, it wouldn't happen. Not in America. Think of the words—Society for the Prevention of Cruelty to Animals—so soothing and compassionate, so kind and protective.

Is there any agency or organization that promotes such gentleness and empathy toward humans? Not really. Fittingly enough, the few homeless people in the streets fortunate enough to receive a helping hand do so because they usually hang a sign around the neck of a scrawny kitten or puppy. Only then will someone feel a tug at their heart strong enough to cough up a few coins…ostensibly for pet food.

This is one of the truly vexing problems facing modern-day America—the individualistic sense of "Me First" and self-aggrandizement that, actually and ironically, flies in the face of the spirit of the Statue of Liberty. Give me your tired and hungry, your poor and oppressed, indeed.

But, even if it were fictional, what would San Francisco look like if people transferred their pet-loving ways to other people? You'd have a bustling town of active intervention, concerned citizens assertively stepping in to arrest and alter the disease of others.

You'd have aggressive folks loudly expressing outrage and indignation about the carnage in the streets. You'd have people physically guiding these lost souls to food lines at churches, shelters at community organizations. You'd have the true spirit of America rekindling hope where there was desperation.

How could this begin to happen? How do you break through the thick wall of denial and hopelessness that surrounds seemingly unsolvable issues like homelessness and poverty? You do it by humanizing—in the finest, highest sense of the word—the problems at hand. You do it by viewing each separate case of despair and destruction as someone special, as a person who was once an infant cradled with care in his mother's arms. And you do it by reaching out a hand of hope where before there was only a path to death.

People simply must know the help that is available to them before they can learn to ask for it. Restoration of human dignity begins with a hot meal and a clean place to live, yes, but it also begins with the proper information. Leading someone to hope and a new life is what mentoring is all about. Mentoring is the courage of someone in a stable position in life, extending promise and opportunity to someone less fortunate.

In AA, it's called one drunk helping another drunk not to drink. In real life, it's called social responsibility. And, in the nuts and bolts of personal recovery, it's called mentoring —fostering a caring, ongoing and stabilizing influence in another person's life.

We don't blink or flinch when a precious little animal bats its eyes for a free meal. In our country, neglect of animals is simply not tolerated. The really tough challenge is to summon the same kind of spontaneity of feeling when a fellow human being pleads with us for a new life.

The brilliance of mentoring is that it offers a positive choice for a troubled citizen to finally tap into himself to find out exactly how to turn his life around toward hope and health.

Story 23

23

Telementoring could visually display true heroes of history, genuine role models whose lives would lead the viewer from despair to hope, modern-day mentors that could easily trigger points of greatness currently dormant and passive in the viewer's mind, body and spirit.

As a real believer in the value of mentoring, it is very gratifying for me to see how the word "mentor" has crept back into popular usage.

Laced throughout the seemingly endless menu of daytime talk shows, the word has taken on bold regularity.

Psychological experts and counselors for the dysfunctional are frequently paraded onstage towards the end of a show to prescribe therapy, medicine or a guiding hand to the emotionally wracked panelists who have been invited as guests.

Many times, these experts emphasize that what this child needs in life is a mentor, or what that recovering alcoholic/dope addict/sex fiend should seek out is a mentoring center.

This is a marvelous experience to behold—it's just the genesis of what America would look like if mentoring became as commonplace as, say, TV watching.

Baby boomers who were born roughly at the same time as the TV was conceived are the same people who used television as a babysitter/mentor while raising their own kids.

Just think about *Sesame Street.* Here was a show that offered education, advice, values, entertainment, knowledge and opportunity—all components of a model-mentoring program.

Sesame Street could not provide the ongoing, tactile, tangible, sustaining sense of continuation that is carefully built into the most effective mentoring programs.

Perhaps what is needed for an entire generation of videophiles is something we can refer to as telementoring.

Where have the kids gone now for information, play and knowledge, those same kids that used to sprawl on the living room floor, hands cupped under chin, gazing slack-jawed at Bert, Ernie and the Cookie Monster?

They've gone to two places, actually—the TV room and computer screen.

Thus enters the concept of telementoring. View it as a cleansing solution surging through the satellite beams of television and the micro-thin channels of energy that fuel the Internet.

Think of the garbage currently spewed by both TV and the Internet. One of the great arguments of the 90's has been about censorship, whether or not to install a so-called "V" chip that would monitor and delete offensive material.

But where are our great thinkers? Instead of controls bordering on censorship that will ultimately fail, how about coming up with better, loftier, classier options?

Telementoring could be simple and basic—it could teach young people how to balance a checkbook, where to search for work, how to get involved in church groups and social occasions.

And it could be more complex and profound—it could visually display true heroes of history, genuine role models whose lives would lead the viewer from despair to hope, modern-day mentors that could easily trigger points of greatness currently dormant and passive in the viewer's mind and body and spirit.

The essence of telementoring is the message to the young people of America today—you can control your life and you can become exactly whom you choose to be.

We could have telementoring as accessible as the nearest electrical outlet.

Story 24

Already in our six years of existence we have amassed a legacy of testament to how young lives have been saved, turned around and sparked toward success by volunteer mentors who merely talk to these kids about choices they never knew existed.

This is a gentle appeal to men and women who might be suffering what is commonly called an "identity crisis."

There is a tremendously bulky new population of early-retired "baby boomers" who, now in their early 50's, enjoy deep-rooted financial security and robust good health.

Many of you have raised children of your own who are now away at college, independently situated, and certainly not draining your time and resources.

Many of you are also single, and, for the first time in your busy lives, staring down a long path of multiple options.

Some of the tired old choices have no appeal, given the stability of your health and the acumen of your mind and spirit.

Inactivity has never become you. Inertia is most assuredly not how you achieved career satisfaction and personal comfort. Golf and hunting, both to excess, do not define you as a person.

You are poised on the precipice of happiness. You've done a marvelous job raising your offspring, you've carved a niche of independence and maturity for yourself, and you still have a solid mind and spirit definitely capable of contributing something of substantial worth to society.

You are exactly what we are looking for to help us continue to build the most exciting, dynamic movement in America today.

It's the California Mentor Initiative, and if you fit the profile above, it's designed precisely for you.

Do you have any idea the impact you can have on a disenfranchised young kid if you spend as little as one hour a week with him or her?

Already in our almost six years of existence we have amassed a legacy of testament to how young lives have been saved, turned around and sparked toward success by volunteer mentors who merely talk to these kids about choices they never knew existed.

California is an amazing state. You've probably spent your entire adult life in a career that's prospered while, in the same neighborhood, a little kid goes to bed every night not having someone to say "I care, I love you, I hold aspirations for you!"

He has no clue about who loves him, he has less of an idea about what to do in this drama called life.

Embittered by the neglect that surrounds him, enraged that he's been ignored by a stable, caring adult in a childhood starved for nourishment, his choices are narrow and dangerous—school means nothing, drugs are readily available both as a commodity to sell and an escape to ingest, gangs provide instant albeit twisted sense of identity, and sexual license leads to teenage, unwanted pregnancy.

But within this kid's heart—in that same space of will and hope that propelled you to a successful career—there lives and breathes an untapped well of potential. It's just that nobody has ever taken the time to say something as simple as, "You know, you're a worthwhile, capable, very talented young person. What would you like to do with your life? Did you know there are ways I can help you get there?"

The apparatus for this kind of reaching out exists today in the California Mentor Initiative, and it has proven to work better than anything yet attempted, precisely because it waters the seeds of self-esteem and self confidence and self hope that have so long been neglected.

The California Mentor Initiative is offering kids the chance to get to know and love themselves, which is really the only road to true success in America today. If you don't have that self love and understanding of survival, nobody in life is going to take care of you all the way to the grave.

All we ask from you is a simple phone call. You will be amazed how even more enhanced your life will become.

Story 25

25

What beats in the heart of the California mentor initiative is the pulsating drive to seed the kids' will to thrive, to use their own god given talents to overcome their man-inherited obstacles

At conferences, conventions, workshops and seminars, many people have asked me why the California Mentor Initiative works so well.

It seems that I have a different answer each time the question is asked. I say this happily, because there are as many reasons as there are participants in our program. That is the strength of our success.

The key, you see, is based on the power—the hidden awesome power—of the individual.

Our original intent when forming the California Mentor Initiative was to find the right way for kids to discover themselves.

This is not a rescue mission as much as it is a sparkplug for kids to finally trigger the impulses that will make them happy, successful and safe in a life that didn't start in their favor.

The power that drives the California Mentor Initiative is a simple force. It's the same power that surrounds our freedom as Americans.

"Make something of yourself, you have the ability to do it." This is the anthem, the daily affirmation of anyone fortunate to wear the mantel of American citizenship.

Youth gangs and other maladies associated with juvenile delinquency—educational failure, drug and alcohol abuse, teenage pregnancy—are sorry manifestations that this anthem was never sung to these wayward kids.

Cheap thrills and shortcuts to fake highs do not a complete American make. Ask any 18-year-old staring at a blank future from behind steel prison bars.

Among many of my own personal affirmations that help me in my career and my spiritual life, one of my favorites has to do with what I call the engine of America. It has to do with "awakening," which is the juice inside the mentor philosophy:

"Whereby we find our own wisdom and reassert our personal power, reeducate ourselves concerning things we've ignored or forgotten, seek to be free thinkers, rethink love, reclaim the political process, create a citizen-based politics, move beyond war and find the field of peace."

Don't the tones of that declaration send a surge of genuine Americanism through your veins? Doesn't it resonate with hope, courage, renewal and faith?

Nowhere in those words are there any allusions to free handouts, patronizing charity or condescension from some higher source.

What beats in the heart of the California Mentor Initiative is the pulsating drive to seed the kids' will to thrive, to use their own God-given talents to overcome their man-inherited obstacles.

What a horrible thing it is to neglect the aspirations of a young heart. The audacity of anyone who brings a child into the world without the parallel duty to nourish his mind and heart is downright appalling.

But, on the flip side, what a tremendously gratifying experience it is to offer this second chance, one that works as well as the most functional, mutually gratifying relationship in healthy family structures that don't cry out for mentoring.

When something works as well as our program does, it is not important to dissect the miracle, to define the mystery. That would be putting a severe limitation on the phenomenon.

The importance is to celebrate life, and the best way to do that is to make sure that the ripple effect continues to widen by inviting more participants into its dynamism.

Won't you enhance your Americanism today? Even if you're just curious to see what all this wonderful healing is all about, give us a call. You'll learn for yourself why it works so well. Thank you.

Story 26

26

It takes a happy, productive person who has found or her own bliss to positively influence a kid who is still foundering in the abyss of adolescent confusion and uncertainty.

Sterling examples of mentors are everywhere in America today.

One of my constant worries as an enthused advocate of the California Mentor Initiative is that people think they are not qualified to be a mentor.

But, again, I tell you—mentors are everywhere.

I've been thinking a lot these past few days, for example, about Frank Sinatra. It may surprise you that I think of him as a mentor given his mercurial, famously explosive temperament.

But I think Sinatra is an excellent mentor for one simple reason—he was nothing more than himself at all times. Friends and associates say he was literally incapable of being anything but himself.

Unlike so many of us who gauge our behavior according to how we think it will be received, Sinatra was missing this particular chromosome that dictates civility over genuineness. And I think this is a good thing.

Witness the kids who appeared on TV mourning his death the same way aging bobbysoxers grieved for their fallen idol. His entire life exuded this one constant quality—he did it his way.

But he didn't like people who fawned all over him, and he expected nobody to be like him. He even told his daughter Nancy, who aspired to be a singer also, not to attempt to be like him. He encouraged her to sing, of course, but to find her own way.

I don't know of a better definition of what mentoring does. It takes a happy, productive person who has found his or her own bliss to positively influence a kid who is still foundering in the abyss of adolescent confusion and uncertainty.

We don't want mentors who expect kids to be just like them. We want mentors who want their proteges to unlock the secrets to empower themselves to find their own way in the world. Nothing short of this basic mentoring tenet works.

Sinatra—an incredibly gifted, complex individual with as many glaring flaws as there were shimmering assets of character. His talent didn't come unworked; nobody toiled harder. But he was fortunate enough to know what it was, then to utilize it almost to the day he died.

I don't need to extend the Sinatra metaphor any further than to assert that we ask nothing more of our mentors than to be themselves, purely themselves, when they meet their proteges. We need stable, mature individuals who can look into the eyes and hearts of our young ones and learn how to care for the potential that resides within.

In one of my favorite books, *To Kill A Mockingbird* by Harper Lee, the character Atticus Finch (played so brilliantly in the movie by Gregory Peck) says to his daughter: "You never really understand a person until you consider things from his point of view—until you climb into his skin and walk around in it."

Call it compassion, empathy or genuine concern. In this case, Finch was trying to instill in his daughter a sense of social awareness, specifically about the events surrounding a wrongly accused black man in the South.

But the message is universal, and its application springs from a solid, mature, evolved heart, someone secure enough in his own self knowledge to be able to impart the wisdom to someone still learning life's major lessons.

So then, if you follow this seeming contradiction, it follows that the most effective mentors are those who don't make loud, assertive suggestions or commands about how to live. Instead, they live hard and well themselves, and, by their example, release a potent desire in the protege to say to himself: "I want what he has, and I'll do anything to find that ingredient in me."

Only one person can ever be Frank Sinatra, but—think of it this way—he'll never enjoy what it's like to be you.

Story 27

27

All she brought was her gift of self, and it was enough. Mutual respect was born, and the two embarked on a working mentoring relationship that enhanced both lives

People often ask me if the concept of mentoring can be summed up in a short descriptive sentence.

As one of the California Mentor Initiative's enthusiastic champions, I like to think that mentoring involves this simple process: The goodness in me salutes the goodness in you.

This is really all we ask of prospective mentors who come to us saying they have the time, the energy and the interest to join the ranks of volunteers stepping forward to assist troubled young California teens.

I first heard this—"The goodness in me salutes the goodness in you"—at one of the original mentoring conferences held in the state. It was at Mills College in the Fall of 1996, and hundreds of us were split up into classrooms where we would hear from mentors and mentees alike, all sharing their experiences in this pioneering venture.

I was struck by the account told by a white woman in her late thirties.

She told us she was terrified when she first met her protege, a 16-year-old black girl from Oakland. The mentor was a traditionally raised college graduate from the suburbs currently on leave from the phone company. She was coming out of a soured relationship, she had a lot of time on her hands, and she feared becoming lazy, indolent or lapsing into bad habits like drinking too much with all her spare time at home.

And then, when she met this young girl, she remembers feeling greatly intimidated by the kid's street-smart savvy and worldliness.

In a word, she was in a world of hurt and fear, and she was wondering whether or not she made the right decision to become a mentor.

The two sparred for awhile when they first met, both kind of circling each other, asserting their turf, as it were. The mentor told us she had never been exposed to a different culture like this at all, and there were all sorts of barriers—language, eating habits, friendships, musical tastes, attitudes toward authority, the whole ball of wax.

She told us she was staring at her young protege during this meeting, and she felt her fingers strangling the cup of coffee wedged into her hand. She doesn't know how it happened, but she recounts a breakthrough moment when something just snapped.

"I looked up from my coffee and looked directly into this girl's eyes. She was still checking me out, fiercely, and all I saw was fear and mistrust. I felt more like a probation officer than a prospective mentor.

"I knew this was a defining moment. I knew right then I could either stand up and say goodbye or make something of what looked like an impossible situation.

"So, I took a deep breath, smiled as best I could, and said, 'You know, we're both coming here from totally different directions and for probably vastly different reasons, but you know what—so what? The goodness in me salutes the goodness in you.

"'I'm not here to be intimidated by all your hostility and bad experiences. I've had my share, too. Let's get beyond all this. I've got a lot to learn from you, yes, but I also have a lot I can share with you. Step by step, starting right now, we can talk about life and your place in it. If it works, great. If it doesn't, we walk away. But I'm not going to dwell on any negatives. From this moment on, we can be friends. You can trust me. And together we can both get on with our lives and make something of ourselves.'"

The woman told us it was like a scene out of a movie. Ever so slowly, yet ever so perceptibly, fear and mistrust drained from the eyes of her new friend, and something resembling a very thin smile replaced all the anxiety and attitude.

The young girl extended her hand across the table, and said, 'Thank you for your honesty. I think we can do this.'"

The mentor told us this was the beginning of a great working relationship. She told us, at that moment, she realized she didn't have to bring anything profound or weighty to the table. How could she compete, anyway, with a street survivor who had been living by her wits all of her life?

All she brought was her gift of self, and it was enough. Mutual respect was born, and the two embarked on a working mentoring relationship that has enhanced both their lives.

Story 28

Mentoring is such an important part of reviving America as we begin the millennium. Won't you join in the adventure?

Becoming a mentor is the best, most effective way to combat racism in America today.

Racism is the cancer that corrodes the fabric of diversity in this great melting pot we call America.

Racism is the ignorant beast that corrupts the pillars of our Constitution like millions of termites gnawing away at a once-mighty structure.

Racism—institutional or personal—is what will bring America down. Not a foreign enemy but rather a domestic malady is our country's greatest threat to freedom today.

Sometimes the feeling of hopelessness is a bit overwhelming.

Those of us who worked in the battlefronts during the emotionally charged Civil Rights era—marching with Dr. King, organizing with Cesar Chavez, doing precinct work for Jack and Bobby Kennedy, visionaries of social justice all—sometimes wonder where we are headed in today's glossed-over, quick-fix era of computer sameness and multi-media intoxication.

Those of us with battle scars don't trust life without pain, and we worry that giant strides can't be made without the price that needs to be paid.

What makes me so excited about the California Mentor Initiative, among other reasons for enthusiasm, is that it helps eliminate the effects of racism, one child at a time.

Working as a mentor is a great way to make reparations for social injustice. This is where the real work of America is today—in the gaping maw of disenfranchisement, in the jaws of racial inequity, in the clanging isolation of poverty, hunger and alienation from the great American dream, which means full inclusion in the equal pursuit of life, liberty and happiness.

I know a mentor who keeps a prayer pasted to his headboard. He says this prayer every night, because it heightens his awareness of what he is about when he leads his young protege out of the clutches of racial injustice and into healthy participation in the American experience:

> *Dear God, please forgive our grievous errors. We atone and ask forgiveness for our early treatment of the indigenous people, the natives of the North American continent who suffered devastation at the hands of our forefathers.*

We atone and ask forgiveness for the racist streak in American history, the slavery in both body and spirit of African-American men, women and children, who have lived among us and suffered among us the sting of our unfair dominion.

We atone and ask forgiveness for the mistaken places in us, wherein we have sought to suppress and harm the children of the Lord. We atone and ask forgiveness for the places where we do this still, where we hate, dear Lord, and do harm, dear Lord, and lay unfair judgment on our brothers and sisters.

Help us, Lord, to mend our thoughts that we no longer rebel against Your Spirit, which is Love. Forgive us now. Turn our darkness into light, dear God, through Your power which does these things, that we might awaken to a new America. May hatred be replaced by love and true justice prevail.

May we meet each other in newborn brotherhood now and forever. Take from us the burdens of our history, our transgressions toward others. To people of color whom we have offended, please forgive us.

We acknowledge the evils of past behavior and the suffering, which it caused. We ask that God in His glory compensate for the evil done unto your people. We apologize for the past, and ask that you open your hearts to us now.

We bless your children, and acknowledge their brilliance. Please bless ours. Wash us clean, dear God, and heal us. Amen.

(The preceding prayer can also be seen in Marianne Williamson's book, "The Healing of America.")

Mentoring is such an important part of reviving America as we head toward the millennium. Won't you join in the adventure?

Story 29

The brilliance of this story is that it captures for me the whole idea behind the California Mentor Initiative. Adults doing something of specific value for troubled youth.

Horsetail Falls is a majestic waterfall that careens down a mighty Sierra mountainside on the North Slope of Highway 50 adjacent to the American River.

It's as breathtaking a sight as anything inside Yosemite, which is a more remote and inaccessible visual landmark many miles to the south.

Horsetail is gorgeous, splitting as it does a moonscape-type mass of granite, spires of pine and gently landscaped grottos of shady ferns adorning the roaring banks of the foamy-white falls.

The falls originate inside Desolation Valley high atop these mountains, which are adorned at the summit by Pyramid Peak, a shimmering diamond of snow-capped perfection.

With El Nino's ravaging downpour bringing abundant water and nourishment to the Sierra highlands, Horsetail has never looked mightier or more robust than it did in the spring of 1998.

Lost and absorbed in this incredible beauty as I hike down along the deafening whirlpools of raging whitewater, I almost hike right past an endearing sight along the way.

It is a small pack of eight young black kids from Vallejo, eating lunch on sun-parched river rocks which jut into Horsetail Falls. The looks on their faces is a vision of the word "awe." It is truly a sight to behold.

They are all 12-years-old and it is their first time ever in the glories of Mother Nature.

Sitting and eating silently, they munch on bologna sandwiches and stare happily at the unfolding scene just past their eyeballs.

I approach one of them, a pretty young girl named Janeece, and ask her about this adventure. She says it was the idea of one of the kid's uncles, who serves as the group's mentor.

He had been asked by his nephew to help him purchase a new pair of Nike shoes for a little over $100. The uncle laughed, then said to him, "You know, for that price, I can do something much better for you, and it'll be something you can have for the rest of your life."

Thus originated the idea for this trip. The uncle offered to take the kid's friends by van for a day into the incredible wilderness near Horsetail Falls. For the price of bologna sandwiches and a full tank of gas, these kids were exposed to something far beyond the pinched environs of their daily lives.

The brilliance of this story is that it captures for me the whole idea behind the California Mentor Initiative—adults doing something of specific value for troubled California youth.

Now, Vallejo is not without its own merits. A bayside community comprised mostly of hard-working blue-collar types, the city is a working-class enclave with a rich history of maritime involvement in World War II.

But its lower classes are certainly not able to afford regular visits to the Tahoe Wilderness.

But, for the cost of a pair of sneakers, one man was able to organize a field trip that would have lasting lifetime impact upon the young hikers.

There is a certain stress that builds up in young people who have never been given the opportunity to explore beyond their limited neighborhoods. Maybe it's not always visible, but the imprint of ennui leading to depression can be indelible, and there is nothing more refreshing than a clean, radical departure from the norm as a way to cleanse the soul and spirit of young ones.

And who knows? Maybe someone in that little troupe will be so moved by this experience that a career in forestry or environmentalism may have been seeded. Or perhaps the trip will inspire another young soul to write poetry or prose in an attempt to describe the splendor. And, most certainly, nature's panoply of beauty will always reside in their hearts long after they return to Vallejo.

Mentoring sometimes is just as simple as this. Won't you help?

Story 30

Always keep your dignity and integrity intact. Believe in your opinions, trust your feelings, and honor both by being consistent in your actions. Don't let anyone ever sway you from what beats in your heart.

One of the people involved in the infrastructure of the California Mentor Initiative has two sons. His younger son is a graduating senior from a private Sacramento high school.

Toward the end of the school year, the senior class went on a traditional retreat called Kairos, which is Greek for "The Lord's time." His son wanted some reading material to contemplate during the four-day session, so he called Dad for what turned out to be the most flattering request he could ever make.

"Dad," said the young man, "you may not know this, but you're my hero and my mentor. I've gained so much from you already, but would you mind jotting down some of the guidelines you've used in raising me and my brother, who feels the same way about you?"

Flabbergasted and overwhelmed with an enormous sense of gratitude, Dad responded quickly. His list is printed here because it closely reflects the types of things we like our mentors to impart to California kids enlisted in our program:

1. Know that you are loved. God loves you. I love you. Your Mom loves you. In this, you already have the most important ingredient for success in life.
2. Surround yourself with positive people and positive influences. Feed yourself good, healthy experiences and habits. Listen to your innermost calling and find ways to honor your best wishes.
3. Don't ever give up, no matter what you are doing or how you feel. You will discover that the very act of not giving up will in itself yield tremendous rewards you don't yet see.
4. Carry the courage of your convictions. Speak out against injustice and wrong-headedness and be quick to come to the aid and defense of those who are attacked or belittled.
5. Do not look for comfort in outside influences like alcohol or drugs. These are way too much trouble than they're worth, and you'll be interfering with the God-given molecular structure that keeps your body in sync with your soul.
6. Don't shout your way through life. You'll be amazed how much you can learn in the world of silence. There will be such a sense of serenity and

peace rushing to you in these moments that you will want to make them a daily ritual. Consider meditation as a way to trigger these precious moments in the day.

7. Love yourself first and foremost. It really is true that you won't be able to love another until you learn to love yourself, and, believe me, it is a learning process with no short cuts. You came into this world alone, and no matter how intimate you may become with a lifelong mate, you truly must be your own best friend, because, in the end, you will be leaving this world alone, too.
8. Always keep your dignity and integrity intact. Believe in your opinions, trust your feelings, and honor both by being consistent in your actions. Don't let anyone ever sway you from what beats your heart.
9. Think about your impact on the world. Do little things every day that help someone else, even if it's anonymously. Of small actions are moral fiber and personal character built.
10. Be not afraid of pain, emotional or physical. Really listen to what lesson the pain is giving you, live through it and gain from having the courage to withstand the test. You will see the next time it happens that you are a better person for having faced it the first time.
11. Manhood doesn't come easily. Treat others with dignity and respect, lavish good things upon yourself, work hard on studies and personal responsibility, and you will find that the yearning for manhood will be a hunger re-triggered every day's new dawning.
12. Know that the unexamined life is not worth living. Avoid cesspools brought on by stale thinking and lower companions. Keep your mind razor-sharp, your body in tip-top shape, and your soul whole.
13. Learn to laugh away your troubles. Nobody has yet to get through life undamaged, and you'll find that laughing at yourself is as good a medicine as there exists for any malady under the sun.
14. Pray so hard and so often that you find yourself yearning to utter the next affirmation. It works. And so will you. Be grateful you're alive and thank God frequently.

Story 31

One's deepest pain, integrated, becomes one's greatest strength. Mentoring is the vehicle whereby the realm of pain evolves into the kingdom of strength

★ ★ ★

A young single father of two teenage daughters tells a national TV audience he has founded a support group whose chief focus is to address the special problems of teen girls.

He is a mentor.

A burly, middle-aged black male corners three young black youths spraying graffiti on the walls of an Oakland grocery store, cajoling them with dark charisma into diverting their "brilliant, artistic talents into something useful down at the youth center." They actually listen to him.

He is a mentor.

A San Francisco Muni bus driver stands up from her seat. She is a very athletic-looking Chicano woman. Sternly walking down the aisle, she stops in front of two teenaged girls, demanding they apologize to an elderly woman they insulted, and refuses to let them off the bus until they do so. The teenagers apologize, and then sit humbly and quietly, mulling their actions, gazing silently out the window.

She is a mentor.

The handsome, 19-year-old white male stands proudly in front of his young team's baseball dugout. He exhorts this team, largely a minority group of kids in a lower class section of Marin County, not to take the game too seriously, but to have a truly good time and to play their absolute best. Their faces shine back to him with the kind of confidence that comes when someone has really made an impact.

He is a mentor.

The beautiful folksinger with waist-length, golden hair charms a small group of school children beneath the canyons of high-rises in San Francisco's Justin Herman Plaza. Her guitar case slowly fills with dollar bills and silver coins. Her lyrics about hope and love, peace and joy crease the grins of the kids with laugh lines of promise and opportunity.

She is a mentor.

The self-deprecating juggler at Pier 39 in Fisherman's Wharf admonishes his young crowd of gawking admirers not to watch so much TV, but rather to focus instead on their God-given talents. He says, "with any luck, you'll learn to use your hands like me, except maybe you'll grow up to be a surgeon, not a circus fool."

He is a mentor.

The bubbly lady clerk at a Safeway grocery store in Novato has something pleasant and genuinely caring to say to each and every customer in her cashier line. She blushes only slightly when a female shopper tells her that she, the clerk, is the reason why she comes to this store, to receive the charming banter and feel better as a person.

She is a mentor.

The middle-aged father of two teenaged boys sits with his sons in the upper deck of 3Com Park, where they are watching a Giants-Cardinals game. Sitting a few rows away from them are three boys dressed in gang-attire, sharing tokes from a marijuana joint. The young father approaches them, and says, "I don't care that you are oblivious to breaking the law and facing its consequences, but I refuse to witness this and do nothing in front of my sons. Either put that thing out, or I will call security." They put it out, and the father returns to his seat amid a chorus of applause from the surrounding fans.

He is a mentor.

A single mother from Sausalito became suspicious about her 17-year-old son's whereabouts when, for two nights a week and without a word about his activities, he'd leave the dinner table and wander into the fog-shrouded evening. When she finally followed him one night, she felt overcome with emotion when she saw him parking his car outside a Mill Valley convalescent home where, she later discovered, he had been volunteering long hours reading to several of the patients who had vision problems.

He is a mentor.

A lady on the San Francisco radio talk show line was choking back tears as she told the host she had a new heroine in her life, a little 10-year-old girl who, anonymously, wandered into a community center in South San Francisco and gave away half of her birthday gifts to less fortunate children, saying only, "I have enough video games and stuff."

She is a mentor.

Two boys and a girl, clearly present against their will, giggled and scuffled in the back pew of a Sacramento Episcopal church, rudely disrupting the attention of those around them. A small girl, five years younger than the roughnecks, turned around and said, "You're not honoring me and my need to pray, and you're certainly not honoring God." The youths sat still in stunned silence for the rest of the ceremony.

She is a mentor.

You read these anecdotes and decide to muster at least one small act of courage a day, to join society's ripple effect.

You are a mentor.

Story 32

The essence of mentoring establishes in young people the fundamental seeds inherent in becoming a motivated, evolving, emancipated young adult.

The mentoring programs and concepts endorsed by the State of California are far more than Band-Aid, babysitting-type remedies to the complex problems youth face today.

To the uninformed, the idea of mentoring may sound too passive, soft, and perhaps excessively permissive.

The cynics might say that hot-button issues like gang violence, drug rampages, teenage pregnancy, early alcoholism and educational failure need something far more radical than an idea whose roots harken to the ancient days.

In actuality, mentoring is a very radical and effective concept, one that we wholeheartedly embrace today as the most effective tool working for the betterment of California's youth.

The essence of mentoring establishes in young people the fundamental seeds inherent in becoming a motivated and emancipated young adult. As we begin this century, the choices become starkly limited: Grow up or never catch up, get with the program or perish.

It's important for taxpayers to know that this is not a rescue mission funded by massive public funds. It is a message of attraction with amazing results that have ripple effects.

Hear it from Lilly Manning, a Detroit native in her late 30's currently working as a mentor in Oakland:

"It's basically the old concept of either giving a kid a fish, or teaching him how to fish. It's easy to see which one is better.

"The key is finding out what makes someone want to change and to become a better, happier person. This is what mentoring helps unlock, that desire to be a productive citizen."

Manning says that being a mentor can still be a challenge. She's the Operations Manager at the Oakland Mentoring Center, so she sees kids of all ages with all sizes of problems. A business major studying for her Master's at Golden Gate University, Manning is absolutely sold on the concept of mentoring as a tool for a better society.

"Young people today don't want to sacrifice. With so many broken homes and marriages ending in divorce, their threshold of pain is limited. But once you overcome that barrier, it's so sweet to witness the growth, the hunger for independence and happiness."

"We hear so much about the turmoil and violence in young people's lives today, the temptation is to feel overwhelmed by all of it. But the solution can be simple. Just reach out and embrace one kid at a time. Mentoring gives you that tool."

The brilliance and genius of mentoring is also reflected in the reality that mentors gain at least as much as their protégés. What we are witnessing in California today is the social phenomenon of one fairly evolved adult reaching out to bolster the hopes and dreams of one struggling younger citizen.

In a mysterious formula of goodwill we have yet to completely fathom, we are finding that the giver is reaching high levels of happiness and fulfillment while the recipient is finally enjoying essential adult direction and respect in his or her young life.

It's an experience of mutual emancipation—a caring adult sharing accumulated wisdom with a young citizen starving for attention and know-how.

Story 33

The key to transforming a troubled youth into a self respecting, productive young person rests in how to replace the tools of negativity into positive instruments of growth and maturity.

Every day in San Francisco, there are 600 meetings for Alcoholics Anonymous. From church meeting rooms to hospital conference centers, from cozy storefronts to converted saloons, thousands of recovering alcoholics and drug addicts walk into these rooms on a daily basis seeking spiritual recovery from a debilitating illness.

The power of AA is magical, mysterious and absolutely effective. It is the only known authentic antidote to what is medically perceived as a progressive, incurable disease. What if we in California took a model city like San Francisco, and applied the principles and structure of AA to the special concerns of our youth? What if we built an organization exactly like AA, and addressed problems like teen pregnancy, gangs and guns, high school dropouts, alcohol and drugs?

And what if we made meeting places available on a 24-hour basis, to insure that kids in crisis, wandering the streets could find a safe haven for their needs and aspirations? Actually, we already have part of the apparatus in place, as young and burgeoning it may be.

It is called mentoring, which like AA, has already proven itself to be an effective and ongoing remedy to the sins of low self-esteem and crippling family dysfunction. Kids desperately want to acquire a sense of belonging and a feeling of self worth. If you examine the dynamics of a gang, you will see that they are a mirror of more traditional and lawful organizations that exist in America today, albeit a little more edgy and raggedy.

Gangs have strict rules and disciplines. They have well-defined initiation rites. They have promotions based on performance and commitment. They have uniforms and regimented codes of behavior. Unfortunately, they also have guns and knives, drugs and booze. The key to transforming a troubled youth into a self-respecting, productive young person rests in how to replace the tools of negativity into positive instruments of growth and maturity.

Most disenchanted, disenfranchised young people have sprung, and bolted from dysfunctional families sadly lacking in strong role models. Simply put, there was no one visible at an early age to say to these kids—"You are a fine, worthwhile, loving and lovable human being. You deserve respect and a happy life."

Mentoring is the agent of change from dysfunction to function and fruition. All it takes is the courage of an adult or a peer to say to a troubled kid: "I trust you and your ability to change. I understand your anger, and I do not blame you alone for any of your troubles. I want to help you turn your life around, and I will not desert you in what will be a difficult but very satisfying journey to health and self-esteem."

Like AA, mentoring is a phenomenon based on attraction, not promotion. The profound nature of recovery is such that miracles and the grace that flows from honest personal growth work, seed it.

Of all its many-faceted virtues, perhaps the most appealing of San Francisco's images is that the city has long been a cauldron of progressive social change. It is a city of tolerance and compassion, a town of joy and understanding, and, in the brilliant words of author George Sterling, "The cool grey city of love." Love will save our young people. Love is what mentoring is all about.

Imagine what it would be like to have an entire city poised on the threshold of recovery. Imagine what it would look like to have throngs of young people entering and exiting mentoring centers, thirsty for enlightenment, starved for a sense of community. Imagine how it would be not to have to live in fear. Imagine roving gangs of youths all of a sudden converted into thriving, prosperous citizens. Imagine former graffiti artists now etching true art on the canvas of their lives.

This is not a pipe dream. All around California, mentors and mentees alike are dotting the landscape of the state like so many spring poppies, full of vigorous freshness and colored in the many taints of recovery. For all its breathtaking physical beauty, San Francisco's finest asset is its human resource treasure—professionals and struggling amateurs striving toward progress and maturity. If there are any doubters casting shadows on a concept like mentoring being capable of saving human lives, they should look no farther than Alcoholics Anonymous.

It is a program of acceptance, courage, spirituality, conversion and healing. It is a program of hope, prayer, understanding, love and compassion. It is a program of profound personal change and effective social restoration. And ... it works.

Story 34

Mentoring does not have to be a tedious, highly developed, rigorous and sequentially stepped routine mentoring—mentoring is best revealed in subtle, truthful, momentous shards of mirroring other people's behavior.

The 19-year-old African American male sat defiantly on the hot seat of Jerry Springer's nationally syndicated TV talk show. The young man's face was a cauldron of rage, his body language a coiled power pack of human abuse.

Shocking for his sense of cool, he admitted to Springer and America that he had killed 15 people in his short life. Most of his victims were rival gang members and drive-by shooting targets. Even more spine tingling was his cocky assertion he had served only 20 months in jail for this monstrous behavior. Never mind that the talk show host ignored the issue of his non-imprisonment. What was most chilling was the youth's savage vow that he would, indeed, butcher again ... in a New York minute.

"So," countered Springer, "say for instance I meet you in the streets for the first time, and tell you I don't like the pants you're wearing. What would you do?"

"I'd kill you," responded the murderer, not batting an eye.

The audience was made up mostly of pre-teen inner city youth. The astonished looks on their faces were frozen in fear upon the scrawny killer. The scene captured the perfect microcosm of America today—one bad apple instilling fear, panic and chaos in a generation whose dreams had barely begun to take shape.

But, about a quarter of a way into the program, something of a positive note began to arise from the young people gathered in the audience. They started to hurl insults and epithets toward the boastful young killer. Yes, the onlookers were initially transfixed and horrified by his early bravado, but their reactions as a group began to coalesce in open hostility once the "ice was broken" by a nine-year-old black girl.

"I could be just like you," she chirped, "but I chose Jesus into my life instead."

The crowd went bananas at the innocent brilliance of her statement. The lonely murderer, suddenly realizing his status as a heroic gunslinger had abruptly dwindled, stared at the little girl with a blank look of death. There's no describing the elation that swept the studio audience of young minds and hearts. Caught up in the little girl's act of verbal courage, the crowd began to attack the culprit with well-aimed words.

They might not have been aware of it, but what the group of youngsters experienced was mentoring in its purest, most fundamental form—the example of one spilling forth into the enhancement of all. This is how the world works, with small acts of bravery creating a ripple effect of profound proportions.

Mentoring doesn't have to be a tedious, highly developed, rigorous and sequentially stepped routine—mentoring is best revealed in subtle, truthful, momentous shards of mirroring other people's behavior. It's simply part of what it means to be human—we naturally want to emulate in others what feels good in ourselves. Madison Avenue knows all about mentoring and peer pressure. In fact, the world of advertising is built upon the premise that we seek happiness and abundance based on how we perceive other people.

The cool guy with the red convertible. The gorgeous blonde in the skimpy bikini. The tanned stud sipping a beer. It is all mentoring with a distorted, skewed angle of commercial acquisition. But when you strip away the outward, consumer-oriented drive toward external possessions and focus instead upon what makes someone an integrated, happy and wholesome person within, you can then grasp the power of real mentoring. Then you can see the power of that little nine-year-old girl's statement about Jesus.

The power of a good life well lived cannot be underestimated. No torrent of words or cavalcade of sermons can ever be as effective or as intoxicating as the clout of an exemplary life.

None of us lives in a vacuum. We have mentors whether or not we are even consciously aware of the phenomenon. Part of our makeup constantly pushes us toward self-improvement, and implicit in that is the way we look to other people as examples. But to over-analyze this is to strip life of its mystery, diluting genius moments like the magic of Jerry Springer's little girl in the audience.

As the talk show's camera pans back from the lonely figure of the pathetic murderer, revealing instead a wildly waving, cheering crowd embracing the little girl in their midst, the once-cocky killer suddenly looks like the loneliest man on the planet.

Story 35

Once we understand as adults that there are options for survival—nay for actual thriving *as individuals- then we can finally unleash the enslaving claws of addiction and reach instead for the liberating embrace of freedom.*

What would the City of San Francisco look like if mentoring centers became as commonplace a sight as, say, flower kiosks? Dare to think about it—it might not be as strange a notion as you imagine.

San Francisco sits perched on the edge of the continent as the last great hope for hundreds of thousands of Americans. The Golden Gate Bridge, which ideally should be a glorious symbol of promise, has tragically become a tool of self-destruction. Estimates put the number of suicide leaps from the span at well over 1,000 victims.

San Francisco is proud of its reputation as a free-swinging, bawdy, tolerant, irreverent town, sometimes shocking for its leniency toward outrageous human lifestyles. For a city of its cosmopolitan sophistication, however, it also reveals a dark, sleazy side. Witness the number of Tenderloin peep shows, street corner drug dealings and rat-infested dwellings that reflect the diseases working their havoc within the human mind, soul and body.

There simply aren't enough havens providing help for a city that holds out so much promise. It can no longer afford to let its young people down. Not to be frivolous, but if crisis centers were as omnipresent as drive-through fast-food joints, San Francisco could well be a model for self-help availability throughout the world. Think about it. Stretch your old tired ethics.

There are incredibly tawdry "instant gratification" sleezy palaces like the Mitchell Brothers Theater, the Lusty Ladies (where peeping perverts feed quarters into slots that activate windows opening into a garden of naked dancing women), and the Crazy Horse lap-dancing saloon. Why can't there be, just as easily, comfortable places of solace and support where suffering souls on their last prayers could receive critical help and referral services?

Granted, there are scores of AA meeting places and drug crisis prevention centers for the addicted and the afflicted, but there is a stigma attached to these sites for many people too reticent and wrapped up in denial to make the first step toward recovery.

Many times, souls perched on the precipice of desperation are equally close to the embrace of hope; one is frequently the narrow flip side of the other.

Think how innovative this would be for the world's most beautiful city to adopt a plan of such magnanimity. Consider how many cutting-edge, progressive schools of thinking and behavior there are scattered around the Bay Area, with its wealth of major universities, medical centers and human behavior institutes.

In the early days of the hippie phenomenon, there was the Haight-Ashbury Free Medical Clinic in the heart of the Flower Children's playpen. There was nothing embarrassing or taboo about this heroic venture, and people in crisis flocked to the ramshackle office with all the fervor of approaching another fix.

Under the guidance of Dr. David Smith and his devoted staff, the clinic saved thousands of lives and steered whacked-out souls back to sanity. The thing is, Americans have this panic about pain, mainly because they don't properly understand it. People cover it with pills that last for hours, alcohol, which deepens the hurt and drugs that create additional trouble.

If people learned that dealing with pain in the proper way was truly the only way to proceed with their lives, we'd be a nation on the road to wellness. And what is the proper way? To understand pain is the first step.

The simplest explanation is to examine the pain of separation from mother, which in its cruelest form can be considered abandonment. Attached with the umbilical cord to all the warm and fuzzy comforts within, we are shocked at birth into a loud, messy, scary world, and we are suddenly alone. That is pain.

We will never again be able to have that maternal bonding, but we must also understand that we need not do harmful things to our system in order to attain bliss. Alcohol is a very brief and destructive antidote to loneliness, as are drugs.

Once we understand as adults that there are options for survival—nay, for actual *thriving* as individuals – we can then finally unleash the enslaving claws of addiction and reach instead for the liberating embrace of freedom.

This experience must be felt and experienced to make it intoxicating enough for suffering addicts to welcome its relief. Victims of various addictions must learn and can learn to crave health every bit as much as they once craved their drug, their escape of choice.

And those of us with the resources, imagination and full-blown sense of human compassion must put ourselves in a position of assistance to urge our fellow citizens toward wholeness.

Story 36

"I was lucky enough to find a great sponsor, although I choose instead to call her my mentor. It basically means the same thing, but somehow it sounds more weighty, lofty, significant."

The Alano Club is a recovery house on Lincoln Avenue in San Rafael. Its doors are open to anyone suffering from alcohol and drug abuse, and the facility has been a life-saving haven for untold thousands of afflicted Marinites striving to work through the pain of their diseases.

A well-worn building pleasantly shaded by overhanging trees, the Alano Club provides relief and refuge for countless suffering souls, seeking comfort from their debilitating afflictions.

Janet is a hip-looking 30-year-old waitress who's been clean and sober for almost two years. An alcoholic and crack cocaine addict, she came to the place on her knees after she saw her life spiraling out of control toward, insanity and death.

"The Alano Club was my last stop before heading for the bridge," she says, pointing vaguely in the direction of the Golden Gate, a mere 15-minute drive away on Highway 101. "I was absolutely in the throes of despair, primarily from my crack addiction. I had lost everything—jobs, relationships, money, cars, and, worst of all, my self respect."

"I was a complete basket case spending my days trying to figure out whom to rip off next. I'd wander the streets on the verge of a total breakdown. I came to the Alano Club weeping, and my life has been restored to me."

One of the basic tenets of AA is that new members seek and find a "sponsor," someone with substantial time of sobriety and a willingness to lend comfort, guidance and support to the "sponsee."

"I was lucky enough to find a great sponsor almost immediately," says Janet, "although I choose instead to call her my 'mentor.' It basically means the same thing, but somehow it sounds more weighty, lofty, and significant. Although I was so physically sick when I first got clean, I recognized soon after that what I was really suffering from was a giant lack of self-love. I'm the middle of five children, a genuine doormat and people-pleaser. My role in life has been to give, give, and give until there was nothing left for me. "I'll never forget the first night I told this to my mentor. She grinned broadly, and pulled this tattered old sheet of paper out of her briefcase. It was titled 'Ways To Love Yourself.'

"Now, you've got to see some of the humor in this picture. There I am in serious withdrawal from a crippling addiction, hating everything about the world, life and myself, and there's this angelic, beautiful woman trying to teach me how to 'love' myself. That was a thought that had never occurred to me. But, you know what? That piece of paper is today my proudest possession." Janet read aloud the 10 ways to love yourself:

1. Stop criticizing yourself. Talk kindly to yourself. Compliment, praise, thank yourself, and accept all compliments from others.
2. Forgive yourself completely, try to release guilt and fear, and live in the present moment. It's all you have.
3. Be your own best friend and treat yourself kindly. Do something special for yourself at least once a day.
4. Find support for yourself—partners, friends, a support group, a support person. Be around those who believe in you.
5. Have a life other than caregiving. Fun is part of life, too. Nurture your mind with healthy thoughts.
6. Take care of your body. What kind of nutrition and exercise is good for you?
7. Keep a sense of humor, live in gratefulness, and breathe deeply. Practice letting go.
8. Try to listen, and be there, without trying to fix the other person or the situation. Empower others.
9. Enjoy the simple things of life—silence, music, nature, a good book.
10. Love yourself, set limits, feel your feelings, and express your feelings in nurturing ways. You are *special*.

"I had never seen or read anything like this in my life," Janet says, a sense of awe creeping into her voice. "I was like that cartoon character—a dehydrated desert nomad parched from the sun and crawling on her last legs toward an oasis. I drank and drank from this list like I was drinking alcohol on one of my famous binges. Only this time I was drinking for my health, not to my health! I can't believe the miracles that are coming my way, and all because something got me to my knees long enough to crawl into the Alano Club. And then the magic happens where I find the perfect mentor. It's all a mystery, and I don't ever expect to know just how it works, but I do know it does work. And, as they say, in AA, "I'll keep coming back."

37

Story 37

Regina Neu says that as a mentor she has learned how to parent more effectively because she discovered through mentoring what is important to young people—honesty, realistic thinking, pragmatic direction, and a sense that there is indeed a place for them in the world.

Real-life people leaping with their hearts into real-life situations—this is the engine that drives mentoring.

As a true believer in mentoring, I am constantly awestruck by the heartwarming individual tales of involvement that are collectively rebuilding our state one child at a time.

Perhaps if I share some of their experiences with you, the attraction to the California Mentor Initiative will spark some degree of commitment from you as well.

Ellen Reays noticed 11-year-old Chris in the halls of Sutter Middle School in Sacramento. She noticed he wouldn't look people in the eyes, his shoulders were rounded, and he wore the same clothes to school every day—when he would show up at all.

Reays invited Chris into the Student Buddy office and learned that he, his brother and his emotionally abusive Mom were living on the street. Once involved with the program, Chris finally had something to call his own—the office, his new friend Ellen, and his "buddy."

Chris started attending school every day, his grades improved dramatically, and he cherished the time he could spend with his new support system. Although his own mother abandoned him, fleeing across the country, Chris' buddy has decided to become a foster parent to Chris until he graduates from college. Chris is now a confident young man in the ninth grade with a 3.6 grade point average and a future he can see.

At 16, Cindy met her mentor Judith Brown through Sacramento's People Reaching Out Program. Cindy was missing a lot of school, had terrible problems at home, and had moved into a garage with her drug-using, car-stealing boyfriend.

Mentor Brown says her major concerns for Cindy were pregnancy and drug abuse. She didn't tell Cindy what to do, but asked her to examine her choices because she had her entire life ahead of her. Brown repeatedly told Cindy that she deserved to have a better life and that she didn't need to accept her current plight.

Cindy became a leader in the alternative high school she attended. After graduating from high school, Brown and Cindy continue to see each other.

Cindy attended college classes for awhile, but her need to make money became a priority. She got a job at the Sacramento Bee in the collections department, and has since become a supervisor of the collections department with a Sacramento financial company.

Regina Neu of Big Brothers/Big Sisters in San Francisco says as a mentor she learned how to parent more effectively because she discovered through mentoring what is important to young people—honesty, realistic thinking, pragmatic direction, and a sense that there is, indeed, a place for them in the world.

Martin Jacks of the Oakland Mentoring Center and a seasoned leader in the statewide mentoring phenomenon says mentors become better people themselves because "It's impossible to walk someone else through their issues without dealing with your own. It's a continual process of self-evaluation and self up-grading."

Mentoring accepts people for who and where they are in life. Mentoring is not judgmental, it is not controlling. Mentoring is a human dynamic that inspires individuals to make choices that will breathe fresh hope into their lives. Mentoring is in place to assist people re-start their dreams, re-shape their hopes.

Mentoring gives purpose and meaning where once there was only lifelessness and despair. I think the brief examples cited also show the kind of profound ripple effect that mentoring has had upon so many of its participants.

Story 38

Mentoring provides the screaming, out of control, at risk teenager with a caring, calm, compassionate hand of an adult giving unconditional love, support and commitment to this worthwhile soul, who somehow tragically lost its way.

If you've ever watched in fascination as a school bus unloads its cargo of inner city kids upon a sandy white Pacific beach, you will get a sense of what it's like to be a participant in the California Mentor Initiative.

The kids emerge screaming in awe, squealing with delight at the sheer newness and freshness of the experience. It's not like they are being released from a kind of prison; it's that they are being released from a kind of prison.

The irony of living in squalor merely a few miles from a breathtaking world of hope cannot be lost on even the most casual observer. The same metaphoric distance exists between bad choice and good choice—damaged lives are frequently paper-thin differentials from lives enhanced.

This is what the California Mentor Initiative is all about, closing that distance between darkness and light, fear and love, despair and opportunity, and yes, the ghetto and the ocean.

All of California can be proud that we are the first state to build a mechanism whereby troubled teens can find the people to help turn their young lives around. That is the goal of the California Mentor Initiative.

The epidemic of youth crises—educational failure, drug and alcohol abuse, teen pregnancy, and violent gang involvement—is so overwhelming, it's downright heart wrenching. These are our children, for God's sake, the same babes we used to protect from open electrical sockets, discarded safety pins, and overheated Christmas tree lights. And now they're playing with loaded Glocks, unsafe sex, hypodermic needles jammed with crap, and gangsters who could never perceive how we once cuddled them in awe mere hours after their entry into the world.

We don't really have time anymore to ask what went wrong. In an epidemic, the first rule of procedure is to provide medicine on an individual basis, then worry about the pathology when the disease has been eradicated.

This is what CMI provides—medicine on an individual basis. Somewhere, somehow between the crib and the hood, the backs we once rubbed to sleep are now tattooed with defiance. Too many of us overwhelmed and oppressed with our own divorce, dependency or dollar problems, tragically abandoned these babes during the most critical times of all—adolescent crises when every drama is a five-alarm urgency, every cry for help an ultimate primal scream.

CMI heals our mistakes. Mentoring provides the screaming, out-of-control, at-risk teenager with a caring, calm, compassionate hand of an adult hand giving unconditional love, support and commitment to this worthwhile soul who somehow tragically lost its way.

The California Mentor Initiative is a triumph of the human spirit over the grim realities of life that have deadened our nerves and dulled our senses. CMI has unleashed an army of savvy, caring Californians upon this sea of confused, alienated, betrayed young teens who are battling the epidemic's demons and who know they can't do it alone.

There is room and the need for you in this army. The life you have lived, enriched by the way you have handled your own challenges, needs to be shared with young adults eager to mature but lacking the vital know-how. This is your best chance to take part in the greatest American experience of all—helping the young save themselves.

Story 39

This is the essence of mentoring, to stem all the needless destructive manifestations of a life gone awry, and to restore as quickly as possible, the feelings of self worth and love that had been left to wither so early in that person's development.

If you've seen the TV ads calling for mentors to come to the assistance of California's troubled young citizens, you know that the mechanism is in place to restore sanity and dignity to their tumultuous lives.

Since the inception of the California Mentor Initiative in 1995, we've been able to isolate and highlight the hot spots that have caused teens so many problems.

In fact, we've discovered, that an epidemic has been raging for some time, an emergency situation with four major symptoms—teen drug and alcohol abuse, educational failure, and gang attachment and teen pregnancy.

On paper, these sound like neatly packaged sociological divisions, but the truth is their boundaries are blurred and smeared, like a flood-stricken river that has swollen over its banks, spilling disease, chaos and physical destruction indiscriminately and often without warning.

But sometimes the most complicated issues are evaporated by the simplest of solutions. This is where mentoring comes in to play so perfectly.

A teen in crisis may turn to a gang for help and identity in a last-ditch cry for survival and recognition. Any kind of parental direction, interest and leadership at home is absent; the young person finds solace, acceptance and a kind of love in a venue that is temporarily satisfying, yet ultimately destructive.

Had there been one adult human being somewhere in this person's life, one solid, caring, responsible role model who could help him channel his anger, manage his rage, and direct his talent, he would've seen that his attraction to a gang was absurd and futile.

Time after time, case after case, we've discovered that new gang members are seduced by the short-term sense of fulfillment. Vacuums attract, and the overpowering void of parental instruction in this person's young life is quickly replaced by the even greater emptiness of purpose displayed by gang engagement.

If the beginning of rage exists in the simplest of notions, for example—Why didn't my parents love me?—the direction of that rage can be so simply managed by the introduction of a mature adult role model in that person's drama of a life.

This is the essence of mentoring, to stem all the destructive, needless manifestations of a life gone awry, and to restore as quickly as possible, the feelings of self worth and love that had been left to wither so early in that person's development.

The flood of hurt and abuse resulting from drug and alcohol use can be prevented in the same fashion. Thankfully, AA groups and rehabilitation centers are peopled in large numbers by aware, recovering teens who have already taken the first step to sobriety and sanity, but there still needs to be a significant parent, solid sponsorship, that will seal the recovering person's fate in a positive, life-enhancing path.

There is nothing more refreshing or joyous in a participatory society than to witness one solid citizen voluntarily coming to the assistance of a suffering fellow citizen.

Mentoring is not complicated. It is a very direct process whereby one experienced individual merely introduces the protege to himself—there is no greater power in life than to unleash the potential that resides within a temporarily struggling, yet always hopeful, human being.

Mentoring is that experience which gives soul to democracy, heart to our Founding Fathers' vision of a free Republic. The exciting thing is that it is something you can do simply by being yourself. We need you to be the next mentor.

Story 40

What Jake did not get from Trudi was her life, which she is slowly rebuilding. Trudi has an indomitable spirit, and she is making plans to go on a series of school lectures to talk to teenage girls about the dangers of an obsessive relationship.

If parents only knew what little effort it takes to shed love and self-esteem upon their children, there would be fewer problems among adolescents in America today. Hear it from Trudi, an 18-year-old Novato woman who's fearful of using her last name because she's just come through a harrowing court ordeal with her ex-boyfriend.

Trudi lived with Jake (not his real name) for the past two years, and she's still quaking with disbelief over the nightmarish traumas she had to endure. Currently staying at her aunt's house in Corte Madera, Trudi is nursing her wounds, reflecting upon the damage that scarred her young life, and trying to figure out what to do next.

She and Jake were madly in love, but after they moved in together, he began to exhibit behavior that should have set off major warning alarms in her system.

"Maybe if I'm able to talk about some of this stuff, then possibly other teenage girls can avoid the kind of mess I got into," she says, staring out the window toward the gray mass of the bay. "To show you how insidious and difficult it is for me to extricate myself from this relationship with Jake, I should tell you that even after all the trouble, I'm still directing my rage toward my Mom and Dad. If they had just loved me the way I needed to be loved; if they had just told me I was a worthwhile person; if they had just given me the kind of esteem that would have made my life a success, then perhaps I wouldn't have chosen such a jerk like Jake."

In quick sum, Trudi became Jake's obsession. He made her a prisoner of their home, he forbade her from going out with her friends, he invaded her privacy by reading her mail and listening in on phone conversations, and he beat her savagely.

"Jake was such a sweet, caring, loving guy," she says, shaking her head slowly. "Good-looking, too. You'd never believe in a million years he was capable of these kinds of things. Soon after we moved in together, he lost his job as a chef. Most of his restaurant pals were into drugs, so one of them introduced Jake to their dealer, and pretty soon Jake was dealing himself. He became a speed freak, and would be up two or three days at a time.

"He became totally paranoid and absolutely obsessed with every minor detail of my life. I thought I was going crazy. I mean, he actually thought I was a drug informant from the CIA or something. Weird, low-life people started coming over to our apartment, and I was scared to death we'd end up on an episode of COPS or something even worse. I felt like my life was spiraling out of control, and I didn't have a clue as to what to do. This may sound nuts, but I actually thought I could change Jake, as long as I never gave up or bailed on the relationship. I was under his spell, and it was as powerful as any drug I've ever heard of. "

"The jealousy was unbelievable. I still don't understand a jealous person, because once I'm committed to someone, there's no chance I'd ever cheat on him. But I couldn't even talk to a cable guy, the mailman, anybody. Jake suspected me of sleeping with everyone, and it was breaking my heart. The first time he slapped me, I was in such a state of shock; I felt every nerve ending of mine just shut down. I walked around in a numb daze, like a corpse. The beatings continued, and I felt like a worthless piece of dirt."

"The terrible irony of what happens to a woman who's been beaten is that, instead of reaching out for help, she starts working desperately to make herself more appealing, and that just infuriates the beater even more. What finally ended it all was when he tied me up and locked me in a closet one day. I started screaming, and that's when a neighbor came to my aid, broke down the door, and literally dragged me off to a woman's shelter."

"I even resisted that. I was in terrible, sick denial. The power he had over me is something I cannot even describe in words. I see now what an ill, awful coward he is, but when you're enmeshed in this cycle, it's almost impossible to break away. Plus, he had this charisma with people. He could get anything he wanted from anybody, trust me."

What Jake didn't get from Trudi was her life, which she's slowly rebuilding. She has an indomitable spirit, and she's making plans to go on a series of school lectures to talk to teenage girls about the dangers of an obsessive relationship. Trudi has a counselor, and one of the things they're exploring is how she fell prey to such an addiction to a person.

"I simply didn't get what I needed from my parents, but I'm discovering now that it's OK to forgive them and to become my own parent. I am my own mentor, if you will, and if anyone has experienced firsthand the urgent need for a strong, healthy role model in life, it's me. Now that I know how to avoid the sick, obsessive monsters, I think I'm going to be all right."

Story 41

If natural mentoring does not exist, if the so-called rare bird of American culture, the functional family, is not in place, the best and most effective measure to call upon is mentoring, which replaces broken parenting with stable, enhancing and ongoing relationships with adult role models.

Although Marin County may seem light years away from the ghettos of South Central and the street violence of Los Angeles, our kids are grappling with the same monumental struggles on the road to adulthood.

Teen years have a way of making everything seem melodramatic and larger than reality. It is with the multi-headed monster that's stalking their path to maturity—educational failure, drug and alcohol abuse, teen pregnancy and an inclination toward gang involvement that these demons leap into young people's consciousness like carnival madmen, tempting them into a life of ruin and away from steady personal growth.

In this regard, Marin kids are no different than the kids from real-life ghettos. There are ghettos of the mind and soul, too, and the journeys into these various forms of hell are quickened by irresponsible, ill-informed experimentation of drugs and alcohol.

The best preventive measures are those that replace wayward, negligent escape routes like substance abuse with positive, healthy, esteem-enhancing avenues of integrity. Drug use, after all, is nothing more than a frantic, desperate attempt to feel good. What if we were able to offer our kids the replacement for destruction, something that would genuinely make them feel good without tripping them up in the pitfalls of life?

Actually, we can do that. We can introduce them to themselves. And we can do that through mentoring.

You see, kids who have healthy self-esteem and a sense of identity do not make catastrophic life choices because they have had the benefit of natural mentoring—parents and extended family members who have blessed them with personal confidence, love, rock-solid direction, and a sustaining kind of maintenance apparatus that makes the kids feel welcome in the world they travel.

The overall sense of well being these kids feel and taste is infinitely more of a rush than any drug yet invented, and they are pointed toward life, not death. Getting into the stream of productive life choices is an addictive high that poetically replaces any metaphor about injecting artificial highs into the stream of one's veins. The pivotal point is showing less fortunate kids the availability of such highs.

That pivotal point is mentoring. If natural mentoring does not exist, if the so-called rare bird of American culture, the functional family, is not in place, the best and most effective measure to call upon is mentoring, which replaces broken parenting with stable, enhancing and ongoing relationships with adult role models.

The cynics might say those hot-button issues like gang violence, drug rampage, teen pregnancy and educational failure need something far more radical than an idea whose roots harken to the ancient days of ancient Greece. But, in actuality, mentoring is the most radical and effective concept currently in use to heal the wounds of dysfunctional family life.

Hear it from Lilly Manning, a Detroit native in her late 30's currently working as a mentor in Oakland.

"It's basically the old concept of either giving a kid a fish or teaching him how to fish. It's easy to see which one is better."

"The key is finding out what makes someone *want* to change and to become a better, happier person. This is what mentoring helps unlock, that desire to be a productive citizen."

The talent and energy and creative drives of youth should never be underestimated. Everything is at its peak in the tumultuous teen years. To a young person embroiled in these frothy waters, nothing could be more refreshing than a warm and stable adult influence, calmly reassuring the kid that not all these impulses need be acted upon—abstinence, for instance, has its own rewards, and waiting for the right time to give up one's virginity is actually quite a noble act.

What an incredible sense of relief such hands-on soothing can be for a confused, troubled teen—relief that will give the young person time and confidence, hope and determination, security and tools with which to re-chart the direction and construction of his newly discovered life.

And it's not so much the adult influence rescuing the young person in peril, as it is reaching within that young person's soul to highlight the potential that resides there already.

This is how communities like Marin can build coherent prevention efforts by galvanizing a local mentoring recruitment drive, thus restoring hope one child at a time.

Story 42

The lack of self-esteem is precisely the reason why many youth have run amok. Every child is a gift. It is just sad and tragic that some children never hear that expressed from their parents' lips.

There are roughly 500,000 gang members in the United States today. This is the harvest of "Dysfunctional America."

Most sensitive observers know the answers to why the country is not working for these young outlaws—it's easy to point to statistics like drug and alcohol abuse, teenage pregnancy, and high school dropout rates and weapons violence.

All of these hallmark flash points are manifestations of an underlying serious social disease sweeping the nation today, an illness that's really not that complicated. It's low self-esteem.

Remember fifteen years ago when Northern California State Assemblyman, John Vasconcellos, became the laughingstock of press pundits and social cynics alike when he proposed a controversial commission on self-esteem? He was ridiculed roundly as a soft-brained dupe who had been conned by New Age purveyors of California psychobabble.

Today, because of what's happened in the ever-widening gulf between gang members and mainstream America, Vasconcellos should be hailed as a visionary unfairly pilloried by his peers. The lack of self-esteem is precisely the reason for youth that have run amok.

Hear from Ben. He is a 45-year-old Mill Valley mentor who works with a former Mission District gang member, Carlos.

"The first misconception most citizens have about gang members," says Ben, a Caucasian who works on Montgomery Street as a financial consultant, "is that they are ignorant losers who live like savages in chaos and turmoil

"Through Carlos and his homeboys, I have come to know the opposite. The gang members I've met are some of the most brilliant, creative, resourceful and witty human beings I've ever encountered. If we let them loose in the Financial District, we'd all be in trouble!"

"Why they joined gangs has nothing to do with lack of intelligence. On the contrary, their survival instincts bring their wits to high levels of artistry, if you will. Con artistry many times, but artistry, nonetheless."

"These are the people who, given a few simple strokes of support and love in the formative years, would easily be leading corporations today. I am not joking."

"I take Carlos out to Candlestick Park to watch the Giants play every now and then. He was a fabulous athlete in high school before he dropped out to join a gang, and we frequently talk about role models while watching these well-paid stars on the field."

"Carlos is a very reflective young man, and he rarely says anything before thinking things through long and hard in his head. He has told me he doesn't think it's an evil power or a case of low morals or anything terribly complicated that led him down a very dangerous path into drugs and gang violence."

"He explains very glibly that he never felt a shred of human warmth from his father, who was a drunk who deserted the family when Carlos was nine years old. His father never hugged him, he never told him he loved him, and he certainly never expressed anything, or even approached his confidence in Carlos' ability to make something of himself."

"Carlos simply didn't feel worthy. He had above-average intelligence, but he displayed little confidence. He had little motivation to succeed at anything, so he funneled his hostility toward his father into acts of lawlessness that would at least get him some kind of attention."

"You see, I think it's incredibly simple. My wife and I have three children we absolutely adore. Sure, we had rough times in the early days of our marriage, but I'll never forget a talk we had with my wife's minister during her first pregnancy."

"The minister told us that parenthood was a great challenge, yes, but if we remembered one thing all the time, it would make our jobs extremely easy. That one thing was this—every child is a gift. I have lived by that simple rule every day of my parenting life, and I am extending the same spirit to Carlos. It covers everything, from showering the individual with affection to learning to communicate honestly on all levels; from never trying to control the person to always being mindful of his needs; from accepting the person for who he is to learning how to share tough-love pearls of wisdom."

"And, when you enjoy the presence of a gift, you show your emotions in a fair, even-minded, healthy fashion. You take pleasure in his company, and you are not afraid to hug. The truth is Carlos is a gift, just like every child who's ever been born. It's just sad and tragic that some children never hear that expressed from their parents' lips."

43

Story 43

"Mentoring offers the support so desparately needed by our emerging youth."

As an enthusiastic supporter of mentoring, I have some great news about America.

We are a nation in recovery and the prognosis looks good.

With commitment of both political conviction and public funds, former Governor Wilson embraced the phenomenon of mentoring as not only the most effective means to restore esteem and sanity and purpose to the lives of our young people, but also because it is the right thing to do. Governor Gray Davis has continued this commitment in California.

Mentoring has proven to be the most radical and workable solution to the multi-headed monster of youth disenfranchisement, a complex malady whose symptoms include teenage pregnancy, gang enrollment, drug and alcohol abuse, and a soaring dropout rate from schools.

Boiled to its purest form, mentoring is the introduction of a reliable, mature adult role model into the life of a damaged youth to heal the scars of alienation, loneliness, dwindling esteem and the self-inflicted litany of wounds that lead the victim into the downward spiral of drug and alcohol abuse.

This new relationship of mentor and mentee is not a short-lived, frivolous bond that resembles babysitting or weekend escapes into hobbies or sports. It is, rather, a fusion of spirits that is long-term, mutually sustaining and ultimately a healing bridge that spans the gulf from the wreckage of the past into the brightness of the present.

Through such organizations as Big Brothers/Big Sisters, individuals for years have been quietly reaching out to kids in crisis. These unsung heroes, offering countless volunteer hours of goodwill, are the backbone behind the structure of the California Mentoring Initiative.

What we have learned from these mentoring pioneers is that kids crazily hunger respect and recognition, especially in today's super-sophisticated world where once-predictable chronological boundaries have become hopelessly blurred. An 18-year-old youth grappling with today's intricate social problems simply bears no resemblance to an 18-year-old from the 60's or 70's.

But the antidote for alienation is a simple, serene mix of respect, acceptance, love and a guiding sense of direction. In our experience with "recovering" gang members, for example, we have discovered and documented the reality that a youth's initial attraction to a gang closely resembles the same magnetic draw to virtue. For a kid with a foggy sense of identity with little or no direction from a responsible adult, a gang looms on the horizon as a clearly marked family—there is a strong sense of community, there is a definite uniform and code of behavior, there is a purpose and a set of goals, however criminal or ethically skewed those endeavors might be.

We have come to learn with mentoring that with a few Zen-like twists of conscience and awareness, former gang members bring the same heightened zeal to a life of goodness and productive health that they once offered their gangs. Mentoring works and it works in a ripple-effect fashion that spawns miraculous results. First, you have the kid who comes from a hapless, dysfunctional family. Once mentored, he will turn to his peers, show them through quality living what this new level of structured rectitude is all about, and they in turn will rush to the same well of righteous behavior.

Then in turn, the mentor will find his life enhanced, spread the message to fellow office workers, many of whom will decide to try mentoring themselves. And, as a poetically correct completion of the cycle, the mentees will become mentors, returning back to society what they have gained from the program.

This is not to mention all the side benefits of the mentoring phenomenon, which include the sudden absence of crime from the individual's life, the inclusion of the person into actively productive segments of society, and all the ripple-effect sparks of goodness that will shine upon everyone in his circle of living.

California's mentoring plan is ambitious and explosive. With already $76 million earmarked by the governor to generate 340,000 mentors for 1 million kids by the year 2005, the Mentoring Initiative has become a burgeoning movement with a life of its own. One of mentoring's shining stars, Kay Coffin, former director of Fresno's Big Brothers/Big Sisters, puts it succinctly: "We are rebuilding society one kid at a time."

She also swears this work is what makes her happiest in life, and claims she would do it for free if she had to. Hers is the same kind of infectious satisfaction we hear from scores and scores of mentors across the state.

The groundswell is substantial, but it's going to be enormous in the next couple of years thanks to the awakening involvement of the corporate world, which is sponsoring, advocating, exhorting and supporting employees who want to give their time and talents to the experience of mentoring.

There is no limit to the possibility of hope that occurs when an adult shepherds a child through the pitfalls of life, shares his experiences with that mentee, advises and suggests life choices to the once-confused youngster, then stands by that individual for however long it takes to achieve maturity and independence.

Mentoring goes to the very core of civilization in the truest sense of the word. When life was simpler, more had the benefit of solid families with extended role models like uncles, aunts, grandmothers and grandfathers.

With substance abuse skyrocketing, with absentee parenting on the climb, the sorrows of youth and the holes created in their souls grew as cavernous as the Grand Canyon.

Mentoring offers the soothing installation of those extended families we all so desperately need to find our way through life's challenges. Mentoring offers substance and solutions to fill that gnawing void, instilling hope and choices on the path to personhood.

One of our mentors in Oakland talks about a 14-year-old girl she has been mentoring for months now. A former gang member and substance abuser, this mere child now waits on her front stairs' stoop a full hour ahead of her mentor's arrival, playfully bouncing a basketball and clutching her paper-bag sandwich as she anticipates her next step into a future with light and hope.

Your chance to join in the campaign to change society one child at a time is at your fingertips. Simply become a mentor.

Story 44

The best thing a mentor can do for a child searching for identity is to be a true friend. One who had no fear about showing genuine affection, but also one who knows how to maintain appropriate distance.

Scenes from a mall...

If you have any doubts that many of our young people find themselves in a state of languid stupor during the summer break, visit your local mall—Northgate, The Village, perhaps. Sit yourself in an unobtrusive location, say, the food emporium, and pretend you're a fly on the wall.

Merely watch and listen. Make no judgments. But keep in mind that these incredibly fascinating creatures might just need a little more, shall we say direction and guidance from their adult role models. You will observe their volcanic energy and talent, but you will see that they need mentors—strong, heroic people of conviction and courage who would be capable of steering some of these youngsters through the icebergs of life.

One girl with green hair, scrawling incredibly detailed and fine-lined sketches in her notebook says to her friend, "I saw Gerard. He was busted for crack, and he's in juvy. It's so bogus—he's just gonna get wired into more dope fiends out there."

A shaved-head boy around 15, toting a skateboard and about a dozen-pierced accessories in his body complains, "My Dad's so tight, man. He makes about $600,000 a year and he won't even buy me a CD player. And he wonders why I don't wanna do anything with him..."

A beautiful 14-year-old girl with waist-length blonde hair, blue eyes and a stoically drop-dead look right out of the pages of Vogue is in a vehement discussion with her mother about the appearance of some of her friends.

"It's so sick the way you judge them," she scolds her Mom, "just because [of] the way they dress."

"I'm not judging them at all," argues her Mom, sipping from a Coke. "I just want you to know that if someone wears 'grunge' outfits and slouches around looking disinterested, that's the way they're going to be perceived—as negative slackers with a bad attitude."

"That is so shallow and lame," rebuts the daughter. "I know what's in their hearts and minds. They have beautiful thoughts and ideals, and they resent very much being judged by externals."

The mother smiles wanly, biting back the urge to scream.

"This is a very cold, difficult world," she warns sternly. "If your friend presents herself as sloppy, messy and rebellious, then that's what people will attach to her insides, as well. Do you think people in this life are actually going to take the time to look beyond someone's appearance, and say, 'OK, I know you look like a pig, but I'll bet you have a beautiful soul?'"

The daughter lapses into facial lockjaw, her eyes glazed upon a frontier not in her mother's immediate vision.

Mom continues: "It's just like spelling. Nobody seems to appreciate that lost art anymore. But I'll tell you something. If you present your resume to an employer with a few words misspelled, just see how tough it's going to be to get a job."

The look on the daughter's face could freeze a flame. She stands up, adjusts her overly laden backpack, and tells her Mom she'll be home later that night. Through teeth that appear to be grinding, Mom says, "You'll be home when I tell you to be home, young lady."

"Whatever," the girl seethes, using that infamous one word which could easily stand as the anthem for this generation. As she shuffles away from her mother, she espies a group of friends lounging outside a video arcade. Looking backwards to see that her mother is no longer watching her, she catches her friends' attention, and sticks a finger down her throat in a gagging gesture. Not a pretty picture; gloomy, in fact.

But this is the reality of a generation gap that's at least as wide as the one felt by current parents when they were the young rebels back in the 60's. The sad truth is—no matter how cool or "with-it" a parent may attempt to be the communication gulf is destined to widen. No adolescent is going to modify behavior unless he or she truly wants to alter a life style, and what adolescent in the tumultuous throes of teenage discovery wants to be like the parent?

The best thing a parent/mentor can be for a child who is searching for identity is to be a true friend—one who has no fear about showing genuine affection, but also one who knows how to maintain appropriate distance. Mistakes should not only happen to be made but need to be made.

As long as the parent retains sanity and conviction about their own life choices, as long as the mentor lives well and shows by example how to attain happiness and serenity, then that example will have an untold impact upon the child's life. For a mentor, the best revenge is not conflict, but living well. That is a message, which will always be heard.

Story 45

45

We who are in the position of being effective mentors need to instill in the young a deep and lasting appreciation for things historical. Then they can advance more effectively toward full empowerment, lifting their dearest causes and issues safely away from the youthful pitfalls of drug addiction, teen pregnancy, educational failure and gang involvement.

One of the oldest and wisest political truths in America is the time-tested anthem: Real power is seized, not asked for.

From women's rights to Gingrich's New Right, from the Black Panthers to the Grey Panthers, from Gay Pride to the Christian fringe—the one thread binding groups like these into a common profile is that they don't meekly request the opportunity to be heard.

They aggressively assert and seize every opportunity for political advancement.

The same can be said of the nation's most amorphous and yet unlabeled power group in the land—the young.

The scary thing is that the young have little idea how much power they actually possess.

America is a country born of rebellion and activism. Boiler plate issues that bubble up from the underbelly of freedom's furnace, from the emancipation of slaves to the elevation of women. This is what formulates public policy, and that is how America works.

But the great massive body of youth as a power element remains largely untapped. Like the somewhat passive status of senior issues in America, it's a crying shame that these two polar-opposite social groups are not more evenly woven into the fabric of America's richly textured cultural quilt.

We're not without the tools. Never in the history of this great republic has youth been more effectively poised to conquer great challenges and to rise to heady heights.

Well-educated, streetwise, savvy and cool, this is the restless so-called Generation X. They are cutting-edge and impatient, instantly hip and opinionated, and incredibly sophisticated and plugged in to the greatest leaps in technological computer advances.

However, the lack of power and self-realization are real concerns, but not beyond the realms of hope.

What youth need from those of us who are older and wiser is not permission to grab the future, but a sense of history and leadership, both of which can be provided by effective mentoring.

We who are in the position of being effective mentors need to instill in the young a deep and lasting appreciation for things historical. Then, they can advance more effectively toward full empowerment, lifting their dearest causes and issues safely away from the youthful pitfalls of drug addiction, teen pregnancy, educational failure and gang involvement.

In this sense, mentoring does not mean some kind of vertical imposition of validation. It simply indicates to the young that this is the way the world spins. In order to be tomorrow's leaders, you must grasp yesterday's lessons.

We wouldn't be trespassing youth's precious boundaries by insisting on full knowledge of practical ideas. On the contrary, we'd be showing love of the most genuine kind, demonstrating that, in life there are no free lunches. Instead, the banquet of life comes from hard work and an open mind.

The "loop" of youth's endeavors has already begun to be complete with the enhancement of such technological wonders as e-mail, the Net, and all the other cultural accessories they have amassed. But the loop is nothing without heart for then it is senseless without a purpose.

The shrewdest mentor of all is the person who lets the protege be his own true self. Adult role models are merely that—they don't have time or energy to be full-time guardians and rescuers. But they must let the young people know that the most genuine power of all comes from within, and, unleashed will set them free.

Wise and effective mentoring will elevate solo acts of inanimate techno-wizardry into a climate more conducive to a meaningful global village.

Story 46

One of the strengths of mentoring is exposing a child to new experiences, to get him/her outside themselves. Exposure to nature for a city kid, for example, can be a wonderful experience.

As a social tool, the brilliance and genius of mentoring creates a life of its own. To hear mentors express in words the ongoing, ever-changing dynamics of mentoring is to witness a breathless, enthused and extremely vibrant ripple effect that is, in one word, miraculous.

Be a fly on the wall at any gathering of mentors sharing experiences together, and you will hear a whirling, kaleidoscopic exchange of life enhancements—an event of the human spirit that is at once educational, uplifting and vital.

Dr. Grace Massey speaks about mentoring with all the zest and vigor that 25 years worth of youth work has earned her: "We need to recognize that mentoring is a national issue," says the eloquently spoken educator. "We're dealing with the development of multi-cultural young people. In a changing society, they come in all types of colors, sizes and shades of youth—we get clear glimpses of the full spectrum of young people."

"The issues are common, yes, but we must learn to recognize the unique cultural factors that go into mentoring. All blacks, all Asian-Americans, all American Indians are not alike! We must focus on the internal diversity of each group if we are to be effective mentors."

Ramona Wilson is an American Indian from a tribe in Washington state. A published poet and activist, she fine-tunes her experiences as a mentor to troubled young American Indians:

"The biggest problem seems to be the ongoing identity issue that has plagued our people for years—just who am I? We agonize over this question as a throwback to the original landing of the Europeans, and it's worsening. We are a people forever in conflict—from things like armed warfare over fishing rights, the Indian wars continue, and it's passed on to each generation. The Federal Relocation Act yanked Indians forcibly from their roots, and there's this sad sense of alienation.

"As a mentor, knowledge is a weapon. I go to the library, get information, and bring it back to my mentees. The particular uniqueness of our culture is that our value system is so different from the mainstream. We place low value on financial status, for instance, and the young people don't seem to have the kind of get-up-and-go that other kids demonstrate.

"It's an antithetical idea—American Indian culture gives itself away—give, give, give. We place value on respect, not on outward status. We honor the connectedness of things, so we need to give the child the time to make these connections."

Mentor Janine Williams, who deals with black mentees, sees the roots of the problem all the way back to the end of slavery:

"It began with the Emancipation Proclamation. We may have been freed physically, but we started this downward spiral when it came to the mental processes."

"Mentoring is an enormously important tool to fill in those gaps to solve the real problems that are addressing us, and we need strong solutions. It starts with education, of course, and a vital sense of history. It's not very exciting to read history if you're never mentioned. For education to be effective, it has to teach you something about yourself. It doesn't mean anything if it doesn't involve you."

Martin Jacks is a veteran mentor whose voice is a booming instrument of advocacy for California's hard-pressed youth. Using an ancient African adage, one that could easily be the anthem for the mentoring movement—"It takes a whole village to raise a child"—Jacks speaks about his experiences as a mentor:

"It's crucial to let the kid know he's here with you, not because he's done something bad, but that he's in a natural, positive evolution. We reinforce that this is not a negative thing, but rather a natural, family-oriented experience. With this attitude in place, the kid will rise to excel in the programs you offer. You simply have to be in tune with the different developmental stages of youth, that's all."

"And one of the strengths of mentoring is exposing the kid to new experiences, to get him outside of himself. Exposure to nature for a city kid, for example, can be a wonderful experience. It's like, 'this is where eggs come from, a hen? I thought they came from the corner grocery store!'"

"Mentoring is helping them walk and grow by walking with them. Mentoring is all about introducing them to themselves. If we can make them believe in themselves, then we are doing our job. And school is not the only place for education. The school of life is the best school of all, and once your mentee sees his place in that big classroom and comes to enjoy it, the sky's the limit."

Story 47

All the stuff you read about gangs and drugs, guns and killings then this pops out of the bay to greet you out of nowhere.

★ ★ ★

The Berkeley fishing pier is a straight, narrow, seemingly endless snake of a structure aimed from the East Bay mudflats toward the middle of the distant Golden Gate Bridge.

On any given day, the pier is a lively united nations of walkers, tourists and anglers—people of all races mingling on this long finger of wood dissecting San Francisco Bay.

On this particular Sunday morning, streams of sunlight pierce the overhead haze. There is a small group of five black men in their 20's dangling fishing poles over the sides of the pier. Walking towards the group, one can hear the clearest, most pure and mellifluous sounds of choral singing emanating, presumably, from a sound box of high quality.

Approaching closer, however, one realizes there is no radio or tape recorder or portable CD player. No, there are five young black fishermen singing joyously and in carefree unison—a cappella—some of the sweetest sounds imaginable, gospel hymns and early American anthems.

This is a moment etched forever in the observer's mind. The pastel yellows and oranges of the Golden Gate Bridge form a natural stage backdrop for this most awesome and spontaneous performance.

Swing Low, Sweet Chariot, *Old Man River*, and *Nearer My God To Thee* are some of the melodies arising like heavenly mist from the sun-filtered bay waters. Is this a dream? Has the observer died and been swept away in some sort of Fellini film? Is this 1998? It is all quite real, yet pleasantly unbelievable.

The men are East Bay blue-collar workers. They fish at different Bay Area spots every weekend, and their singing draws goggle-eyed spectators from all around. Indeed, a great part of the show is to watch startled onlookers stop slack-jawed in their tracks and gaze in rapture at their sweet singing.

The guys are "just friends," and they used to be street thugs in Oakland. They were gang members who would sing Motown and Barry White in the streets. Somehow, through individual and various acts of redemption, they found themselves singing in East Bay choirs.

While they've never sung together professionally, they've come up with a name for themselves. They call themselves Impulse, which sort of captures the spontaneity of the moment.

Did you enjoy the music of *Les Miserables?* Did your hearts lift softly skyward when you heard lyrics like, "to love another person is to see the face of God"? This was the feeling of exultation these five former street toughs created on the rough-hewn, splintered boards of the Berkeley fishing pier.

Two 13-year-old wannabe gangster-dudes shuffled toward Impulse warily, their young bodies overgarbed in dark parkas buttoned only at the top, knit watch caps shoved low down their foreheads. Other pier-goers scoffed at the two boys to turn down their boom box which was loudly blaring unintelligible rap lyrics. The two young men complied, and then froze in their tracks, transfixed by the mesmerizing five-part harmony.

"Those brothers are *bad,*" one said to another in reverential tones. The boom box teenagers took a seat against the pier railing, and pretty soon a mixed-bag gathering of other listeners clustered around them. Overhearing the snippets of conversation from the impromptu gallery was like a peep inside modern-day wisdom and pop philosophy.

"Man," said one grizzled fisherman in stained-blue overalls, "if I could get my grandkids to hear these guys for five minutes, they'd learn more about life than they would from five hours in a classroom."

"Isn't this just a picture?" crooned a middle-aged lady in a sunny dress. "All the stuff you read about gangs and guns, drugs and killings, then this pops up out of the bay to greet you out of nowhere. Pretty cool."

"I've never seen anything like it," remarked a young Asian fisherman. "This must be how stars get discovered in America!"

Stars, indeed, but not the movie celebrity variety.

At the risk of squeezing the juice out of a perfect, sacred moment in time, what Impulse did for the crowd this wondrous spring morning was something 100 sermons and 1,000 lectures could never accomplish—provide a blueprint for the celebration of life through the gift of song and communion.

The two young men with the boom box may never realize what hidden power may move them toward maturity some day, but what they witnessed with Impulse is exactly what mentoring is all about.

Story 48

We can't legislate motivation into higher pursuits, but perhaps we can create the apparatus whereby the young rebels can willingly aspire to productive, self-satisfying pursuits.

It is a fairly reliable law of journalism that cab drivers make great sources. They have plenty of time to think and observe, that's for sure.

A cabbie in San Francisco was driving past St. Brigid's Church on Van Ness & Broadway, and, without being prompted by his passenger stated, "Ain't it a shame the Catholic Archdiocese is closing down all these parishes? Just look at that beautiful old structure."

He was referring to the Vatican's recent edict handed down to the San Francisco Archbishop that several local churches needed to be closed due to budget constraints.

"It's bad enough that all those good people don't have their regular place of worship anymore," continued the cabbie, "but what's even worse is that these beautiful old buildings are just sitting there unused."

"Now if I were Mayor," he chuckled, adjusting the rear view mirror to get a better view of his backseat passenger, "I'd take the next Concorde to Rome and meet with the Pope about turning these abandoned churches into youth centers for the bored and troubled kids of San Francisco."

"Why not?" he continued, warming up to the subject in controversy. "Take a look around this town. Excuse me, but it smells like a toilet. That's what happens when people live on the streets. There's trash everywhere, graffiti has taken over, aggressive punks are panhandling like crazy, and tourists are scared to death to walk anywhere."

"I mean, we all know the church is a cash cow, and these buildings are all sitting there pretty much paid for. Why not put them to good use? These kids are strung out and sick. They need a place to eat and sleep, to congregate, mingle and do constructive things together. Maybe they could do arts and crafts in the vacant buildings, learn how to do something with their skills, and make something of themselves. Or maybe they could be turned into counseling centers, something along the lines of a halfway house.

"I mean, I don't pretend to be a great theologian or anything, but my opinion is that if Jesus Christ were alive today, He'd be more than happy to run all the Big Money people out of the churches and turn them instead into shelters for the homeless and disaffected."

This cabbie was underrating himself. He is a great theologian and he would not be too bad as a city planning commissioner either.

Here is the truth. It's going to take exactly this kind of radical thinking to begin the recovery of cities like San Francisco, which is after all, The City That Knows How.

"Thinking Big," whether it comes from the mind of a cab driver or from the drafting board of an urban consultant, is precisely what we need to get to the root of the problems of disenfranchised youth. When you consider it took the entire four years of one mayor's administration to get a fleet of self-scrubbing public toilets installed on city streets, you have a foretaste of how difficult it might be to transform Catholic churches into community centers.

But the wheels are already in motion, on a similar scale, to convert buildings at The Presidio of San Francisco into mentoring centers for city youngsters in need of role models, thereby enhancing both the quality of life in the city and the edification of a former military base into a force for life.

What the metropolis needs no longer are endless complaints without positive answers. We must move from bemoaning the sorry plight of the present into an active mode of what we are willing to do for the future.

It used to be said by great liberals like Ted Kennedy during the Civil Rights Act debate: "It's true we can't legislate morality, but to stand by and do nothing in the heart of a crisis would be tantamount to even worse prejudice and hatred."

It is true about youth in gangs. We can't legislate motivation into higher pursuits, but perhaps we can create the apparatus whereby the young rebels can willingly aspire to productive, self-satisfying pursuits.

To stand by and do nothing would be the most fatal flaw of all. Using everything at our disposal—empty churches, available military bases, think tanks disguised as taxi cabs—is what we must do to show our young people that recovery, like hope, always springs eternal.

Story 49

The best mentor a drug-afflicted victim can have, is that person who can instill a sense of self-worth and esteem back into the veins that once received drugs of death.

In a way, it's strange and sad that drug abuse among the nation's young became a political football in the last presidential race. Strange and sad, because, according to Washington D.C. reporter David Whitney, "the politicians' reinvigorated rhetorical war, itself a replay of previous presidential campaigns, hides the views of most crime experts, conservative and liberal, that there's not much a president can do to fight (drug) crime."

"Others add that knee-jerk reactions from politicians often have alarmingly unanticipated consequences. According to the Heritage Foundation, 98% of violent crimes fall under state and local jurisdiction, not federal."

"The principal impact of the White House in fighting crime is through federal programs to target crime and drugs, and the appointment of federal judges who oversee prison crowding and rule on the constitutionality of crime laws."

There are painfully too many solutions to this complex problem eroding the undersoil of American life, but the sad truth is that the only way to steer users away from drug addiction is to provide something of alternative and long-term attraction that provides the same kind of happiness and euphoria.

This is hard work, and this is why treatment centers have eternally revolving doors. As long as presidential aspirants are playing the drug card, perhaps they should steal a page from the appeal of a man named Kennedy. You don't have to be too old to remember the early days of John F. Kennedy's administration, a short-lived epoch that raised the veil of gloom and boredom of the generic 50's.

Kennedy's lasting legacy is that he made Americans feel good about themselves again, which is an achievement worth far more than any number of ill-fated promises and empty-headed rhetoric being bandied about by two expert political football players in today's presidential sweepstakes.

In 1961 Jack Kennedy proposed that Americans get in better physical condition by pledging to partake in 50-mile hikes. For reasons not fully understood at the time, these were magic words. They served as a wake-up call to long-somnolent citizens lolled to sleep by the passive, conformist 50's of the Dwight Eisenhower presidency.

Even more than the attraction of his longish hair, his toothy grin, his clipped and brittle Bostonian accent, his endearing wit, and his seemingly boundless energy, this clarion call of Kennedy's was an enormously successful nudge in the butt to Americans of all ages. They responded in waves, and the nation was on the move, both literally and figuratively. It was the first time in memory the ages-old political oath, "I'll get this country moving again," was taken to heart.

Helping people feel good about themselves is the best antidote to drug abuse. Whether it's from a personal therapist, a support group, a drug treatment center, a relative engaged in an intervention, a lover, friend, or spouse—the best mentor a drug-afflicted victim can have is that person who can instill a sense of self-worth and esteem back into the veins that once received drugs of death.

What this is about is not a massive rescue mission imposed from above; it is a radical mission of hope seeded from within.

In this regard, the president of the United States can be the best mentor imaginable. But it's not as an announcer of myriad programs, not even as a sword-wielding hero taking on mythical enemies that his role as mentor is showcased. Like with so many other role models that have the charisma and the right stuff to pull it off, you either have it or you don't. Having helped former Governor George W. Bush establish the Texas Mentoring Initiative, I firmly believe that now President Bush is sincerely dedicated to insuring that every child who needs one, should have a mentor. The ultimate test is in the "actions" to realize this worthy goal.

Story 50

Mentoring made me what I am today—a good person with positive, concrete ideas able to make this world a better place to live. The difference is living in fear or living with hope.

In today's America—when kids are afflicted with emotional confusion, economic depravity, psychological chaos and an overall feeling of angst—mentoring is seen as the most effective tool to restore our youth to sanity.

DeVone Boggan, 28, has been on both sides of mentoring, and he can speak for its effectiveness. A full-time mentor at Oakland's Mentoring Center, the Detroit native is a fiery, charismatic, extremely articulate spokesman for the healing aspects of his profession.

"Mentoring came to me when I was 13. I can't imagine how badly my life may have turned if I didn't have someone to broaden my horizons and to offer choices when I had conflict," he explains. "My father left when I was 9. My two younger brothers and I went from middle class to very lower class within a year's period. Things fell apart when Dad left. Mom gave the responsibilities of being a man to me."

"Sure, it was exciting to be 'the man of the house,' but what nine-year-old can handle that pressure? Soon enough, as her frustrations grew because of the breakup, I found I couldn't do much to make her happy. I got into using and selling drugs, falling way behind in school. My life was a mess. I got into lot of bad habits. I was fragile as a kid, anyway, and felt I had done something wrong because Dad had left. That is a horrible guilt trip for a kid to carry."

"Luckily for me, I met my mentor, Andre, who showed me patience, resilience, and fortitude. He showed me around his campus, Michigan State, and I was in awe. He showed me that I was worth something, and he instilled in me the desire to make something of my life."

"The dynamic is fairly simple. When you're a kid, you have such a limited view of the world. Many kids come from families that don't have a lot of positive models. Or, if they do have them, there's not a lot of quality time, with both parents working. And kids desperately need attention, love and discipline.

"If they don't get it, they put the burden of not getting it on their own shoulders, which hurts self confidence and self-esteem. Until Andre came into my life, that's where I was. Through mentoring, he empowered me to see that I was somebody and that my past wasn't my fault.

"He showed me I can do a lot of things, and I have a lot to offer. Just meeting his friends and colleagues at college made a huge impression on me. He was a profound influence just letting me know I was worth the trouble. Andre put himself in a vulnerable position with me, peeling off the adult facade. As a kid, I couldn't wait to be an adult, because I thought adults had all the answers."

"But Andre showed me if he didn't have an answer, that was OK. That was mind-blowing. He'd say let's find out together. He became, in essence, a real, genuine person, and that's the key that kids are looking for.

"He'd tell me just to be honest about stuff, don't put all this stress on myself for not knowing how to deal with life. He was also the first man to tell me he loved me. He made me understand that was OK and appropriate."

"The energy I gained from him as my mentor propelled me into college. I went to Berkeley, and graduated with my degree in Political Science. That's when I learned that mentoring is a two-way street, a circular thing, and that's why I decided to devote my life to giving back to kids who need it the same way I did."

"When you grow up, you understand that people are human. And humans make errors. But you move on. Admit the mistake, and then grow from it.

"Look at gangs. I have a brother who's transitioning from a gang into something more meaningful. But gangs have distinctive clothing, they have a sense of community and belonging, they have initiation rites and rules. Basically, gangs are all about this hunger to be a person. It just takes the right kind of positive reinforcement from an adult to show a kid in a gang that he can gain the same sense of self-doing more constructive things with his life."

"Adults too often use blind faith in their dealings with kids – "do this because I said so," with no rational, compassionate explanation. This turns off kids. Mentors are extremely effective when they sit down and develop a relationship built on trust and mutual respect.

"Mentoring made me what I am today—a good person with positive, concrete ideas how to make this world a better place to live. The difference is living in fear or living with hope."

"I choose hope. I choose mentoring."

Story 51

51

I desperately needed to find myself, and mentoring helped me discover the true me.

Mentoring makes miracles.

Okolo Thomas, a 19-year-old young woman from Oakland, can attest to the sea of changes mentoring can make in someone's life.

"When I was seven," says the articulate African American, "my mother and father separated, and I couldn't understand why. I put it all on myself, even though my father was addicted to heroin, weed and cocaine."

"Drugs made him so violent toward my mother. I remember him twisting her arm until she cried. And then he'd come back, knock on the doors, break the windows and cry for me. It was emotionally very damaging. He'd come to the door with coke in his moustache, give me hugs and kiss me. He became a monster to me."

"Then, when my mother got a boyfriend when I was 13, I felt like she was abandoning me. Up to that point, I had done really well in school, but now my grades really started to slip. I was supposed to be at Berkeley High, but what I did was ride BART trains all day."

"At the start of ninth grade, I stole my older sister's car, wrecked it and then wrecked four other cars. I was selling drugs, beating up kids, running with a gang of 10 other girls. I pulled a knife on someone, shot at someone else, and narrowly dodged being shot myself. I was smoking weed and drinking. Basically, I was trying to get my mother and father back.

"I was sent to Washington High in San Francisco, but got thrown out when I beat up a Chinese boy, cracking open his head against a locker. So I went back to Berkeley High, but got into a racial fight with a girl, knocked her out and gave her a black eye.

"I was going nowhere, and I felt so rebellious. Somehow, some very strong teachers—mentors,—really took an interest in me, and showed me they believed in my potential. They gave me confidence, and I got interested in the Black Studies Program, which led to my involvement in African dance and public speaking."

"My mentors gave me specific things to do, and I was focused on positive activities instead of robbing someone or smoking dope. I gained confidence and started enjoying life and its challenges."

Thomas, who works full-time at the Oakland Mentoring Center, says she's had many mentors in life. All it took was going through the pain and taking a risk to find a better path."

"I accept my past," she says, "and I wouldn't want to go back and change anything, because all the things I've experienced are what makes me who I am today. I try to learn from my past, don't make the same mistakes, and then move on."

"I give so much credit to mentoring, guiding me from one situation to another, whether that situation is positive or negative. In school my GPA started rising dramatically. From tenth grade, when my GPA was 1.8, I got it up to 3.8 by the time I was a senior. I got into the Alta Bates Hospital internship program, where I was assigned a mentor and worked toward my certificate to be a nurse assistant. I learned how to take pulses, how to do blood pressure."

"I've always dreamed of becoming a scientific doctor for NASA, and this basic medical work is preparing me for that. I have a great curiosity about the universe. When I was young, my mother bought me a telescope and a chemistry set. What NASA would offer me is an avenue for exploration. All of life truly amazes me."

"At Alta Bates Hospital, I gave a speech one day about my experiences, and a lot of important people who were there—like the Mayors of Oakland and Berkeley—gave me a great ovation. I received a $400 scholarship and a job offer from Martin Jacks to work at the Oakland Mentoring Center, where I work on the Mentor Advocacy and Recruitment Campaign.

"The biggest miracle so far is that my father has beaten his battle with drugs, and he now owns and operates Christian rehabilitation centers. I have a great relationship with both my father and my mother.

"Even though I have had very specific mentors over the years, I want young people to know that mentoring exists in all forms. If you're tired and sick of your life, it is very easy to just open your eyes and reach out for the kind of help that is healthy and life-saving. You just have to want it and be open to it."
Okolo Thomas is only 19, but she's lived several lives already. In her recovery from gangs and drug abuse, she is devoted to her artistic pursuits—she raps professionally, and she is coming out with a tape and a music video in the summer of 1996.

"I desperately needed to find myself," she says, "and mentoring helped me discover the true me."

Story 52

52

Mentoring is the potent wave of stimulation that drives the ripple effects of the reflecting pool.

In the movie, *Dangerous Minds*, actress Michelle Pfeiffer portrays a struggling young schoolteacher whom, for economic reasons, finds herself in the unenviable position of educating a highly dysfunctional band of unteachable barrio students.

The role is not an original one for motion pictures. In fact, it's become something of a cliche-riddled format—young, pretty white woman finds her upright morals splayed against the turmoil of the ghetto: instant conflict, sudden mayhem.

But what makes Pfeiffer's role so unique is that she "gets" to the young rebels not through emotional thrashing, but against-all-odds gargantuan efforts of will.

She achieves success by letting go of the obviously Herculean task in front of her, deciding instead to simply be herself. Her simple message to the students is—if you want my respect, earn it. If you want to be responsible for your own lives, just do it.

The ever-serene and super-cool Pfeiffer creates miracles within the minds and hearts of her students by instilling in them—*through her example*—the desire to be whole, healthy and functional. She doesn't impose anything from above in an authoritarian, vertical fashion. She doesn't badger, flail, panic or threaten. She merely sets a standard.

Moving smoothly and without fear through their lives and psyches, Pfeiffer makes friends with the students and in the process, learns to care for their welfare. It's genuine and it works.

What makes her role even more exciting is that, in its simplicity and clarity of motive, it is the very personification of what it means to be a mentor in today's kaleidoscopic blur of societal problems like drug abuse, teen pregnancy, school dropouts and gang violence.

She brings to her role no great liberal agenda of political reform or social revolution. She's just a working stiff barely able to keep her own nose above the poverty line. But, because of her candor and her purity of purpose, every seemingly insignificant act becomes a bold stroke of courage.

She dazzles the kids, not because she's so different in skin color and background, but because she merely does the next thing, showing them in the process how glorious it can be just to show up—that's all. Her life as portrayed on the screen literally defines mentoring.

When a grief-stricken student gets in Pfeiffer's face, screaming, "How are you going to save me from myself?" Pfeiffer does nothing more than listen to the anxious face with all her heart.

This is enough to resolve the conflict at hand. The dynamics are simple. She shows she cares, she somehow instills in her student charges the hunger for self-change, and then she enjoys the rare satisfaction of a teacher actually witnessing the evolution of a person through education.

When she goes to visit a student at her home, the parents are instantly defensive and guilt-stricken, thinking that this authority figure has made a special trip to demean or diminish their child. But, in one of the film's special moments, the parents positively beam with a flood of facial pride when Pfeiffer dismisses their fears and, instead, tells them what a wonderful job they have done raising such a fine young adult.

The gratification and self-esteem she elicited from this impoverished family packed a mighty wallop in this movie's rising dramatic crescendo. Pfeiffer is walking proof that mentoring need not be complicated, overly organized or too difficult.

What it boils down to is this: If someone can muster enough passion about their own life, and if they can impart the undying notion that it is vitally important that everyone do the same with their own selves, then virtually everyone can become a mentor.

We live in an age when nobody really likes to be told what to do or how to live. But we also live in a highly intense "reflective" age of media, mirrors and MTV. Young people may hate to admit it, but they are masters of imitation. "I'll do what you do, but not what you say" could easily be their anthem. Mentoring is the potent wave of stimulation that drives the ripple effects of the reflecting pool. It's as simple, sweet, sexy, and brilliant as the serenity of Michelle Pfeiffer's face.

The ultimate test of mentoring is to live your own life so well that someone in crisis will be motivated to do anything in their power to have what you have, to enjoy what thrills you, and in the end, to be themselves thoroughly and well.

Story 53

Being a mentor for a kid is something that comes in variety. Mentoring's essence imparts to the kid the message that anything can be done.

Inspiration often comes from unlikely sources.

The movie *Independence Day* was a power-packed special effects thriller that blended state-of-the-art high tech pizzazz with cutting edge-of-the-seat dramatic intensity to forge a true blockbuster of epic proportions.

But, if you are one always on the prowl for how movies affect society, you should have seen the movie in the heart of a big city—San Francisco or Oakland, for example.

Kids raced from the doors as if from a revival meeting of major dramatic parameters. Their gait revealed a surge of adrenaline pumped with the renewed vigor of patriotic fervor. Inner city kids live in a world blurred with mixed messages. Con artists, street hustlers, role models of dubious character, and an entire array of low-life scammers, schemers and scoundrels surround them.

Independence Day was a breakthrough experience for kids like these because it paints themes like courage and heroism in loud, bold strokes. There is no subtlety, incongruity, ambiguity or confusion in this movie that is for sure.

Of course, the comic book-type simplicity of plot underscores the science fictional flavor of the movie, but there was a great deal to be said for the nearly titanic impact of individual bravery exhibited by the principal characters who are swathed in mythological auras.

Again, look at the faces of the inner city kids. Black comedian Will Smith, for instance, steals the show as a fighter pilot who unconditionally stares down a villain from outer space, punching the daylights out of this nefarious demon, risking his own neck for the sake of democracy.

Smith is the face of "No Fear". He has a girlfriend and a precious little boy to protect, and no slime-oozing gremlin is going to come between the pursuit of happiness and Will Smith. In a perfect mix of comedy and bravado, Smith bursts upon the scene as a no-holds-barred warrior of virtue.

Even the President of the United States himself, played with restrained panache by actor Bill Pullman, jumps into the cockpit of an attack jet, Eagle I, to lead a squadron of bomb-laden alien-fighters into spatial warfare.

Now, none of this is to suggest that big city kids should embrace Star Wars-style fiction as true life. The reality is, their lives are so torn by broken promises and daily struggles that the last thing they need is one more dream-dashing delusion.

But their reaction to the movie did suggest that they have a gaping-hole of a need that's simply not being met by the humdrum existence of their lives—the need for a larger-than-life true hero, a mentor, if you will. This is a need that's common to us all. For those of us who are older, the need may have been met by the celluloid images of Gary Cooper, Gregory Peck, or, in some cases, John Wayne.

It's not that we replaced the reality of our lives with the mimicking of theirs; it's more to the point that screen heroes gave us the fetching notion that there was something much bigger than ourselves out there, that there was indeed, a resting, a nesting place for our fondest ideals, goals, dreams and fantasies.

In a word, they legitimized for us the most profound yearnings of our hearts. This is as basic a human need as food, water, affection and shelter.

What harm can come to a kid who idolizes someone who is able to conquer evil? How bad is it for a child to know that the forces of light are infinitely superior to the shadows of darkness? And, just as a matter of relief, how terrible is it to provide relief and entertainment to a potentially free spirit who's usually bombarded with ennui and despair?

To be a mentor for a kid is something that comes in variety. Whether it's the fantasy of film or the magic of print; whether it's in-person quality time or by example of heroic acts, the essence of mentoring is that it imparts to the kid the message that "it can be done."

And, it's about empowerment and emancipation—the ability to free someone from whatever shackles enslave him to enable that person to become the full person he is capable of becoming.

When that happens, it's *Independence Day* in a very real sense.

Story 54

It is better to light a candle than to curse the darkness. CMI provides citizens concerned with the ongoing plight of the nation's young a clear chance to steer youth away from the shadows of fear toward the dawn of opportunity.

The genius of the California Mentor Initiative (CMI) is its simplicity.

Sometimes I am afraid that many of us in the public policy forum unwittingly complicate already-complex issues by our accumulated wisdom and well-intentioned enthusiasm.

Our backgrounds and education make us optimistic and eager to make this world a better place to live, but we sometimes get tripped up by high-minded ideas, overly intricate position papers, and staggering blizzards of statistics and studies.

The California Mentor Initiative, in stark contrast, honors democracy in that it gives power to one individual who wants to help another individual. It's that simple.

CMI, by its very existence, admits that there is a terrible problem of youth alienation ravaging California in epidemic proportions and on four raging fronts—educational failure, drug and alcohol abuse, teen pregnancy and violent gang involvement.

But instead of worsening the situation by heaping Band-Aid solutions onto main arteries gushing with blood, CMI goes to the heart of American democracy by simply making it possible for one caring citizen to come to the assistance and sustaining comfort of another.

Lives are saved, futures ensured, families re-fashioned, careers resurrected, hopes revived, and faith in democracy restored. This is a fact of life happening in California every waking moment and the sheer brilliance of CMI shall remain untouched by anyone who'd dare tinker with its genius.

Anyone who wants to participate in democracy can become a mentor. It is better to light a candle than to curse the darkness, and CMI provides citizens concerned with the ongoing plight of the nation's young a clear chance to steer youth away from the shadows of fear toward the dawn of opportunity.

We get reports from mentors up and down the State—average, everyday Californians who simply want to return something of value to the way of life that has treated them so well. Over and over again, we hear one resounding theme—kids are absolutely starving for the kind of attention that will spring their dormant abilities to life.

Maybe it's about a young man fascinated with guns only because he had no idea he could use his substantial mechanical skills studying at his city college's vocational development school. Or perhaps it's about a 16-year-old girl who got pregnant because she didn't have anyone to tell her she'd be a great Montessori instructor. And too often it's about an affection-starved kid who drank himself into a nearly fatal car accident because there was no adult in sight to take him to Dodger games.

The only special skills needed for the prospective mentor are the same skills that have gotten him through the different levels of his own adulthood, plus a willingness to share those talents as a way to prevent his protege from stumbling in the pitfalls of life.

Never has participatory democracy been so accessible. And nowhere else are the rewards of a job well done more visible and plentiful. Troubled kids need mentors, and the special secret of the movement to date is that mentors are getting more out of this commitment than they ever dreamed possible.

Story 55

Mentors and proteges alike are engaged in very real, nuts and bolts dynamics of living that create paths leading to healthy options and away from toxic, poisonous life choices.

The social epidemic of drug and alcohol abuse among California's youngest citizens has caused heartache, lawlessness, violence, despair and turmoil for an entire generation of youth who find themselves derailed before they have been able to board the train.

Launched in 1995, the California Mentor Initiative (CMI) is a successful social revolution of hope and recovery that has proven effective in giving fallen youth a second chance.

In its short life, CMI has triggered a massive movement of direct, positive action guiding young people away from fatal choices and toward alternative lifestyles of constructive decisions.

Mentors and proteges alike are engaged in very real, nuts 'n bolts dynamics of living that create paths leading to healthy options and away from toxic, poisonous life choices.

Both mentors and mentees are richly rewarded:

Karla Vargas of San Jose was a 16-year-old unwed mother living in a foster home when she met her mentor, Susan DuVall. Overwhelmed with motherhood, school and finances, Karla had repeated nightmares about past family relationships, and she suffered from health problems.

DuVall encouraged Karla to finish school, taught her to take actions that would change her life, and gently persuaded her to accept the things that couldn't be changed. DuVall also helped with Karla's one-year-old son, Rudy, allowing Karla much-needed time alone. Karla has now graduated from high school, trained to be a medical secretary, and has started taking classes in police training at San Jose City College.

Karen Lessman was an award-winning businesswoman in Sacramento when she started mentoring with the Student Buddy Program. Lessman says her buddy Alyse gave her far more than she could have given the young girl. "My relationship with Alyse kept my life in perspective. When I was with her, I'd let go of my worries and just be with her in the moment." Lessman now works full-time with the Student Buddy Program.

Rogello Morales was in junior high when he got his mentor through Big Brothers/Big Sisters in San Jose. Rogello was living in a single-parent home in a low-income area with high gang activity. But Big Brother/mentor Tom Esch provided both a father figure and a role model, encouraging Morales to volunteer 100 hours to feed the homeless, 50 hours to learn a new hobby, 50 hours to physical fitness, and a commitment of three weeks with the Outward Bound program in the Sierra.

Mentor Esch says mentee Rogello demonstrated pride and enthusiasm in all his activities. Today, four years into their mentor relationship, Rogello is a senior in high school with plans to join the Navy and attend college. He owns a future.

Jing Redfern is a mentor with California One-to-One in Los Angeles, and she works with inner city kids who regularly hear gunshots in their neighborhoods. A successful advertising executive from Missouri, she says: "Even though I had seen TV reports and movies about life in the inner city, it didn't seem real until I experienced it myself. Now I can't consider going back to advertising. The world isn't going to change if the dairy industry sells another gallon of milk, but helping children to see their value in society and giving them the tools to rise above their environment will change the world."

Story 56

When something works as well as the California Mentor Initiative, trying to explain it only diminishes the phenomenon, tarnishes the miracle. We only want to nourish it and expand it, which will happen on its own accord because it works so well.

The California Mentor Initiative (CMI) has something special to offer California and the entire country.

CMI is growing as an effective social tool, which is stemming the epidemic hemorrhaging, brought on by teenage drug and alcohol abuse, gang involvement, educational failure and teen motherhood.

It is an effective social tool because it is a radical answer to young people's anguished cry for identity, beginning with the most basic yearning of all: "I need help." CMI offers young people that help in its most revolutionary form—an adult role model who fills the vacuum created by absentee or non-existent parenting.

This service we call mentoring, a phenomenon which has proven to be the most successful healing mechanism yet generated by the engine of human concern, where one's deepest wounds integrated become one's greatest powers.

To understand the genius of mentoring and why it works so well, it is vital to realize that it is not the latest political invention or cultural fashion craze.

Mentoring has sprung to the forefront of societal change with all the force of a volcanic eruption, spewing forth its heat and light from the depths of human pain and suffering. At its core, mentoring is the natural evolution of man's response to his own inner angst.

Mentoring truly is the opportunity for each of us to step forward and engage in the process of democracy. Mentoring is the contemporary equivalent of barn raising in America, the kind of communal inter-mingling upon which our country was founded.

Through our own individual labor and sweat and blood and companionship, we raised those barns, then we stopped and wrote a check, investing in a Government that simply cannot make those kinds of strides without basic human engagement.

The four social epidemics cited above—teen pregnancy, gang involvement, drug and alcohol abuse, and educational failure—all pivots around the central issue of isolation. Merely talking to kids in a vacuous classroom situation is not enough, and it certainly falls far short of the collateral gained by positive human interaction.

If democracy in America is waning, it is because Americans are not participating in its call, which is a clarion to be actively engaged with our children. It is no more complicated than that, and mentoring provides the apparatus for dynamic participation. Even a minimum involvement of two hours a week with a protege can have profound, everlasting effects upon a child's life. What this is about is the re-potentiating of American democracy.

Mentoring works because it provides solid answers to our yearning desire, "I need me." When the suffering person comes to understand that self-realization creates the path to salvation, that person has drunk from the most sustaining and intoxicating pond of all. We have discovered that mentoring is the map to that wellspring of life.

We all know what has been stirring and rumbling inside that volcano all these years. We all bare scars and war wounds from decades of toiling in the fields—Peace Corps, Vietnam, the New Frontier, the Great Society. We look back at these huge social ideals and events, we ponder the investment we sunk so dearly into their realization, and we are bewildered and anguished why the country suffers so much today.

In her brilliant book, *The Healing of America*, author Marianne Williamson fingers the core of American pain and paints a perfect backdrop against which mentoring emerges as the shiny new butterfly of hope newly sprung from the mud of our failures.

"This book," she writes, "is about the yin and yang of American history, the Great Duality of our miraculous beginnings, the ultimate tearing apart of our vision from our politics, and an effort that can now begin in earnest to repair the resulting wounding of our collective soul."

Her words evoke delicious memories of America's original and great ideals, the very soul of democracy that first breathed life into the American spirit. Williamson eloquently lays out the carpet of our downfalls and sins, and she leads us on a two-step through the patchwork quilt of our biggest mistakes.

The portrait she paints is a somber one, and she uses bold strokes of rhetoric and historical flashbacks to bolster her underlying thesis that America first got into trouble when it lost its pioneering spirit, the rage to discover.

"I think America at this time," she concludes in her introduction, "is like someone who has gotten tired of being sad, so has decided to go back to pretending to be happy. Our political options range for the most part from complaining about what's wrong to denying what's wrong. Such limited options for national recovery results in a psychic pain that has sent most Americans into an unconscious throwing up of our hands."

Without even mentioning the word mentoring, Williamson's words wash up against this glittering social phenomenon like so many fingers of waves tickling the shores of hope. While her writing portrays an America gone gloomy with sadness, mentoring is already in place as a call to action, as a natural alternative to all the problems she cites in her book.

A child trapped in a world of indifferent adults is a child without hope; he has not only been deprived of his innocence, but he is powerless to even consider charting his future.

As a fully engaged point player and enthusiastic champion in the ongoing construction of CMI, I have a personal anthem I utter as a daily affirmation, which is: "I dream that every child wakes up to hear the words 'I love you, I hold aspirations for you, that you go off for enrichment and education in the afternoon, and that I tuck you in at night to say I love you once more.'"

This is the reality of the American dream, that every child be comforted in the buffer zone of his or her own bliss, so that every budding potential within that child be cultivated to fruition in a climate that is loving, nurturing, supportive and liberating.

This is also the anthem of the California Mentor Initiative, and I hear daily scores of stories of personal recovery and re-engagement for the purpose of social responsibility.

Mentors and proteges alike are dotting the landscape of this state like California's picturesque official flower, the Golden Poppy, whose seeds are re-sodding the infrastructure with deep-rooted, long-lasting foundations of conscience and conviction.

I don't mean to overly romanticize reality, but in fact what we are about is romancing the self. We have witnessed dark days and nightmarish evenings of drug decadence and alcohol ravaging among—for God's sake—our little babies. We have seen our once cuddly tots turn to gang violence and street rampage. We have witnessed them desert schools because they have been deserted by families. And we suffer in silence as we watch babies themselves give birth to babies.

These are all shrieks for help, primal screams for personal mercy. The unenlightened like to seize upon these symptoms as political fodder, stirring the pot of fear to build more prisons, clamp down more strictly on drug offenders, use others' pain for their own agenda gain. To follow their empty clarion call would be utter folly, this we know for sure.

One of the most radical of all Americans, Thomas Paine, once wrote, "We have it in our power to begin the world over again." He expressed that notion at the peak of the American Revolution. Here in California, where we are in the midst of a social catharsis every bit as important and as explosive as the American Revolution, we like to say we are rebuilding the state one child at a time.

Mentoring is the engine driving that social force. We are loving our children back to full engagement in the California Dream. We are giving them direction and tools to achieve specific goals and dreams. One young man from an Oakland gang went with his mentor to the University of California at Berkeley, the famed institution a mere two miles away from Oakland's glass-shattered streets. The young man never dreamed a library was so close, a science museum so near his grasp.

A young teenaged mother from San Francisco's Mission District had never ventured out of her own sooty neighborhood. When a mentor embraced her dreams and praised them as precious, she went on a field trip one day to a downtown dance studio, where she discovered that the inner, burning desire to become a dancer on one of San Francisco's famed stages was not just an illusion. It's just that she had never experienced anyone who cared enough to show her the way.

In Southern California, a 19-year-old young man, burnt-out with drug abuse and a rap sheet for auto theft, learned through his mentor that his writing skills could be properly channeled by way of a writer's workshop on the outskirts of South Central L.A. That young man with a seemingly hopeless look at the future is today an aspiring scriptwriter currently employed by a film production crew.

Again, some telling words from author Williamson: "For such were times when the world was recreated, when ages of dust were swept aside and civilization renewed itself. This moment is such a time. These transitional periods are always chaotic; there is no amount of legal or political maneuvering that can limit the explosion of human energy bursting forth at such times."

When something works as well as the California Mentor Initiative, trying to explain it only diminishes the phenomenon, tarnishes the miracle. We only want to nourish it and expand it, which will happen of its own accord because it works so well. The ripple effects it creates—with proteges turning into mentors and mentors looking for additional proteges—has already re-crafted the look and feel of California as we begin the new millennium.

Mentoring is the spiritual and realistic force that is forging new life from the chaos of despair. Mentoring, unlike many doomed social programs, which tried to impose joyless rigidity from a base without a vision, is an attractive dynamism that is returning California citizens to themselves, thereby re-engaging young minds and hearts in the greatest experiment on earth—American democracy.

Story 57

Failing in school bereft of any older adult role models who might have guided her through the hazards of adolescence, lacey fell into a spiraling decline. She reeled into the world of biker strip joints and dilapidated crack houses.

A friend recently shared the experience of a weekend on the sunny white beaches of the Pacific in Montara, a scant 20-minute drive from downtown San Francisco.

Nestled in the cliffs above the roaring surf and squatting amid a field of prematurely blossoming ice plant flowers sits the Chart House restaurant, a classy, glassy edifice with heavenly views of the pounding surf below.

It is early February with a brief weekend respite from the treacherous onslaught of El NiÔo. Patches of white cloud dance with mists of moisture rising from the foaming blue ocean.

He talks of the Chart House, a very popular steak 'n seafood eatery whose bar boasts a sweeping panorama of this remarkable vista, a fact which heightens the irony when you consider the saloon becomes a meeting room for Alcoholics Anonymous on Saturdays afternoons.

A half hour before her weekly meeting, a beautiful young lady named Lacey walks barefoot along the gorgeous seafront, holding sandals in one hand and her six-month-old child in a backpack.

Lacey is 17-years-old, a mere child herself who's lived a lifetime of pain and hardship.

"I don't think people truly understand the tremendous amount of trouble and turmoil there is for teenaged mothers today," she says, wiggling her toes in the encroaching fingers of the Pacific.

"You read the statistics, you see the Sunday night movie of the week, and you listen to all the talk shows, with everyone having an opinion on the subject. But you can't really know how horrible this is until you've lived it yourself."

Sensing immediately that she may have offended her tiny baby, she rocks the boy gently, and lovingly sweeps a hand through the light wisps of blond hair. Looking off to the distant horizon, she takes a deep breath, and recounts some of the horrors of her young life. How her parents split up when she was seven, leaving her with ghoulish nightmares, a broken heart and a constant sense of impending doom.

How she started experimenting with marijuana and hard liquor when she was ten, an age when "normal" girls her age were taking ski trips with church groups, joining soccer leagues with their peers and enjoying weekend camping trips in the wilderness.

How she lost her virginity when she was 13 to a biker dude she met at a beer-soaked pool hall in a sleazy South San Francisco bar. How she lost the trust and love of her childhood friends, and how she felt swept away by the overall feelings of hostility and rage that engulfed her with all the vengeance of a great flood.

Failing in school, bereft of any older adult role models that might have guided her through the hazards of adolescence, Lacey fell into a spiraling decline. She reeled into the world of biker bars, strip joints and dilapidated crack houses.

She tumbled into a world of darkness, fear, disease and depression. Twice she tried to kill herself by slashing her wrists and mixing liquor with sleeping pills. Distant relatives got her into rehabilitation houses, but she always ran away.

In what she sees now as a final, desperate attempt to cling to life, she got pregnant by a drifter from Texas whom she met at a tattoo parlor in San Francisco. He skipped town, of course, when he heard about the pregnancy, and she's never heard from him again.

After she had the baby, a nurse encouraged her to attend AA meetings with her, and soon the nurse became her AA sponsor, her mentor. They are also best friends, and the nurse has become a second parent of sorts to Lacey's infant son.

"I'm going through a miracle now," says Lacey, "but it's not been easy. My recovery from booze and drugs and that rotten lifestyle has saved me, yeah, but now I'm struggling with all the dreams that have been trashed, my childhood that never was, and the grim reality I have riding on my back right now.

"I walk around every day feeling this great big fear that I have made a nearly fatal mistake. My mentor tells me to take things easy, one day at a time, and I'm getting pretty good at that, but I simply have to say something to the teenaged girls of the world—don't get pregnant. It's not worth it."

Story 58

58

We are awash in a social epidemic of destructive forces of poverty, drugs and violence. This epidemic manifests itself in teens in school failure, drug use, teen pregnancy and gang violence.

A midsummer study recently released by the National Household Survey on Drug Abuse paints a mildly improving outlook on drug and alcohol involvement among the Nation's young.

There was bad news, however, countering these encouraging numbers. More teens than ever tried heroin for the first time last year, and there was an alarming increase in the number of teens who no longer view cocaine as risky. In addition, the use of hallucinogens among teenagers increased slightly.

So how do we view these results—as vast improvement in the field of drug and alcohol prevention, or more soberly, merely as a sadly predictable shift in addictions of choice?

As an enthusiastic champion of the California Mentor Initiative, I naturally welcome any statistical dips as progressive signs of improvement in our relentless campaign to inform, educate and change the state's younger citizens' oft-perilous trek through adolescence.

But, as a realist who knows full well the insidious nature of addiction diseases, my pledge is to never be seduced by surveys and studies into believing that the plight of substance abuse has been eradicated. In a roomful of 100 kids, if nine are using drugs and 18 are drinking, that's more than a quarter of the room making choices leading to destructive behavior, not only to themselves but also in the negative ripple effects they are generating.

That's why our work is far from over. We are awash in a social epidemic of destructive forces of poverty, drugs and violence. This epidemic manifests itself in teens in four distinctly troubling categories:

School Failure: California is the 43rd worst state in the number of youth who are neither attending school nor working. The school dropout rate of teenagers was 15.3 percent. Of those youth that do finish high school, less than one-third were prepared for college.

Drug Use: California has high rates of adolescents who regularly use marijuana, inhalants and LSD. A staggering 21 percent of the state's 11th graders reported drinking alcohol at least once a week in 1994.

Teen Pregnancy: California's rate of teen pregnancy is 21 percent higher than the national average, ranking it as the 42nd worst state in the nation. *Almost 12 percent of all births in California are to teen mothers.*

Gangs and Violence: California is the 46th worst state in the Nation in the number of juveniles arrested for violent crime. There are between 175,000 and 200,000 criminal street gang members in California, including 55,000 in Los Angeles County alone.

These are overwhelming facts of life spawned largely by the breakdown of the family unit. More than half of children growing up today will live in a single household, deprived of healthy, fluid give-and-take with adult role models. This is why we have developed the California Mentor Initiative, which effectively addresses the problems of isolation and alienation among the state's young. Mentoring connects a caring adult with a young person in need of attention and support.

The early results from our mentoring programs are very promising, suggesting that positive, consistent attention from an adult, even one who is not a relative can change young people's lives. Not only does mentoring benefit individual youth, but it also weaves an important strand back into the community's net of adult support for children.

Story 59

With the California Mentor Initiative firmly in place, the seeds of recovery spread among troubled teens are beginning to sprout into a healthy harvest of hope and rejuvenation.

In California today, we are waging an all-out war against the multi-headed demon of drug and alcohol abuse.

The toxic poisoning that afflicts more than 25 percent of our State's younger citizens has reached epidemic proportions, and reveals itself in four basic manifestations of dysfunction—educational failure, drug and alcohol abuse, teenage pregnancy and violent gang involvement.

As the supporter of the California Mentor Initiative, I report that our war-room strategy against the ravages of addiction has been struck.

In the evolving path of understanding the negative influences of teenage alienation, we discovered long ago that, while well-intentioned, the rallying cry "Just Say No" fell far short of a lasting remedy.

We came to realize that for us to succeed in beating an illness, we had to implant a lifestyle. With the California Mentor Initiative firmly in place, the seeds of recovery spread among troubled teens are beginning to sprout into a healthy harvest of hope and rejuvenation.

Mentoring is the hinge upon which pivots the difficult voyage from despair to life. Mentoring is the vehicle whereby thousands of once-hopeless young Californians are rejecting a crutch and clutching a lifestyle.

In their brilliant 1996 book, *Mentoring*, authors Floyd Wickman and Terri Sjodin offer four reasons why mentoring works as an effective social engine pumping good citizenry into the hearts of the young.

First, they explain mentoring survived and thrived over hundreds of generations because "no one can argue that experience is the best teacher when it comes to teaching. A mentor is someone who has experienced what you are trying to learn. He or she knows the pitfalls." If a struggling, stumbling teen loses his way because there is no significant role model available in the immediate family, there is no better formula for rehabilitation than the firm, guiding hand of an outside mentor.

Secondly, mentoring works through synergy, which is the ability of two or more people to achieve an effect that each is incapable of alone. "Mentoring works," write the authors, "partly because two people, if well matched, can create more energy and accomplish larger goals than one person can alone."

Thirdly, the genius of mentoring has its roots in ancient civilizations, where great secrets of life were passed on from generation to generation in a time-honored salute to exercises in sacred bonding rituals. "The mentoring process," explain the writers, "allows the secrets, tips, and tricks of an accomplished master to be passed from one generation to the next. It provides assurances to the mentor that his or her hard-earned knowledge will be preserved yet not made available to everyone."

And fourth, mentoring works because it goes to the core of human nature that an experienced mid-career person actively seeks a worthy protege to pass on what the mentor has learned over the years.

In the State of California, we have pledged ourselves and a huge commitment of time, energy, resources and money to ensuring that both mentor and protege alike be granted the right atmosphere in which to play out these basic, essential human needs as we step up our efforts to win the war against youth disenfranchisement.

Story 60

In an epidemic of any scale, the first thing to be done is to stop the bleeding. These were our children, the heirs to our legacy, and we had no choice but to step up and lay our lives on the line.

Those of us who have worked on the California Mentor Initiative for the past seven years always knew we had our grasp on an attainable dream.

In strategy sessions and in executive roundtables, we used to ask each other, "What would California look like if mentors were available to come to the assistance of our at-risk children?"

Our dreamscape harkened to the days of ancient Greece when Athens initiated built-in cultural/citizenship workshops for the youngest of their charges, or in a village a continent away where they instilled the ethic of shared responsibility. In their vision, they instinctually knew that youth formed the building blocks for the future, so they nourished and cultivated the deepest yearnings of the young. Thus was born one of the finest civilizations in the history of man.

Our question is no longer what California would look like. Today, the Golden State is a model for the rest of the Nation; indeed, for the world.

The genesis for our idea came about in a naturally evolving fashion. California's young were awash in a social epidemic whose magnitude and depth never before had been experienced. Gangs were terrorizing the state's most impoverished urban shadows; schools reported declining attendance and academic records in astonishing numbers; dire statistics pointed to ballooning drug and alcohol abuse among California's youth; and unwed teenage mothers were giving birth to fatherless children at an alarming rate.

In an epidemic of any scale, the first thing to be done is to stop the bleeding. These were our children, the heirs to our legacy, and we had no choice but to step up and lay our lives on the line.

Mentoring came about because it simply had to come about. And we discovered something else about this most radical of all solutions whose roots go back to those sunny days in Athens and Sparta. That is, the solution was in the problem.

We examined the mistakes of the young, and, much to our relief and surprise came to realize that, in most cases, they were simply the victims of good intentions.

A gang, for example, is little more than a healthy yearning for engagement, involvement and commitment to a cause, a community, a society where one could gain attention, affection and self esteem. A gang has a code of ethics, a strict uniform discipline, and a regimen of commandments with consequences. A gang satisfied the natural urge for belonging that was stymied at every other juncture of the youngster's search for community.

Same with teenage pregnancy, where a child bearing children is a shrill cry for parenting needs never met in her own adolescence. Becoming someone else's mother is merely the flip side of an anguished cry for love and connection.

Educational failure, drug and alcohol abuse can be seen in the same ironic light. A student may know that a diploma is the first step to success in America, but if he's emotionally and socially challenged, the defiant lack of study habits earns him a quick-fix, albeit damaging, sense of identity.

Drug and alcohol use gets immediate thrills and kicks, along with the fake security that highs are achieved today instead of through the long, arduous journey through reality.

Mentors come to the rescue of our kids merely by being there and standing tall for their problems. Mentors are not dazzling, simple-solution geniuses. They are merely reliable, stable adult role models that have lived through life's challenges enough to be able to impart common sense and wisdom to those still struggling.

In a sort of Zen-like, overnight switch from evil to good, mentors enable the proteges to deflect sick behavior into healthy action and attitude. Mentors accept these troubled kids for who they are—sensitive, needy, basically sound persons bursting with opportunity that has too long eluded their understanding or grasp.

So that's what California looks like today, a modern-day "village" with an infrastructure of solid citizens helping through their experience those still struggling. This is an evolution of volcanic proportions that is already propelling this state with an army of recovering youth positively chomping at the bit to attain the challenges and rewards of responsible adulthood.

Story 61

61

If you come from a single-parent family and your parent does not help you interact with the same sex of the parent missing from the home, you will grow up with a key element missing.

The whole concept of mentoring goes right to the heart of reviving America.

Hear about it from Martin Jacks, the founding director of The Mentoring Center in Oakland. Jacks, 49, is a robust, glibly spoken, charismatic Afro-American who minces few words, and milks them for every bit of impact he can seize:

"It's very important to clarify why we're doing mentoring in the first place," he explains. "I get invited to a lot of meetings where adults discuss the fate of young people. They speak about them as if they've suddenly given birth to demons."

"What the adults fail to grasp is that something terrible has happened in the past 10 or 15 years, and that something is loss of community. And we need to look at how families are structured both long ago and now."

"When I was growing up, both parents were home, and so were my grandparents, aunts and uncles. These were built-in, natural mentors who instilled in my seven brothers and me a sense of responsibility. From them, we acquired our values, attitudes and behavior."

"In this regard, when you talk about mentoring, all you're describing is the human development process. None of us were born with that stuff in place. We had to inherit it from somewhere. On Saturday mornings, my Dad expected us to mow the lawn according to his standards. Then we'd go mow the lawn of the Williams family down the street. They were an elderly couple, and we did not do it for money. This was our learned sense of social responsibility."

"That's how work ethic is transferred to kids. When you're part of a community, everyone who benefits from it has a role to play. It's like when we borrowed sugar or flour from neighbors. There was a definite ambience in the community that made people feel comfortable borrowing from each other."

"And, most importantly, when my Mother would bake cakes and pies from borrowed ingredients, the first slice would always go to the neighbor we borrowed from. We had to defer our personal immediate gratification until we paid homage."

"Same with riding the bus. If a woman or elderly person boarded after us, you'd see eight or nine kids offering to give up their seats. These messages were passed on to us kids through the actions of the adults in our lives. It was simply a way of life."

"Contrast all this with today's world. Kids don't even know the other adults, and they're deprived because of it. Take single-parent families, for example. If you come from a single-parent family and the parent in the house does not help you interact with the same sex of the person missing from the home, you will grow up with a key element missing."

"This is the need that mentoring was designed to fill."

"One kid I used to mentor would watch me in amazement as I groomed in front of the mirror in the mornings. He grew up only with his Mom and two sisters, and it had never occurred to him that men groom. It was not in his bank or repertoire, so how could he reach in to grab that experience?"

"You could also deduce that this kid had probably never seen a man treat his Mom in terms of endearment—kiss her, tease her, play with her. It's just not in the kid's bank, so when he hears his street friends calling women bitches, he does the same thing. Then we say he's a bad kid, he ought to know better. What I'm saying is that he doesn't know better, and that's where mentoring comes into play."

"We've got to learn to stop criminalizing kids because of their environment, and that's the backdrop as to why there's a need for mentoring."

Jacks currently mentors Michael Gibson, a 20-year-old Oakland resident who spent time behind bars for dealing drugs, car theft and attempting to kill a policeman when he was only fifteen.

Mentoring saved Gibson's life.

The youth had met Jacks in a training session while incarcerated at the California Youth Authority, then contacted him upon his release after serving three years of a seven-year sentence.

Says Gibson: "I had developed a writing skill while in jail, so I hooked up with Martin when I got out, and he exposed me to a lot of positive things. I work now at the Mentoring Center in Oakland and at the Omega Boys Club in San Francisco.

"I attend Laney College in Oakland, and would like to transfer to Morehouse College in the fall, hopefully as an English or Linguistics major. I've witnessed horrible things in my life, and I was involved in all kinds of criminal activity, except rape and murder.

"But now, with Martin, I take it step by step, and eventually I'd like to be an attorney or a professor of Cultural Anthropology. I've been a mentee for three years now, and I hate to think where I'd be without the program."

Story 62

Mentoring not only provides a sense of meaning in the lives of young people, but it also provides the very tools essential for survival and self-actualization.

Mentoring works.

Mentoring is cheap, direct, real, and perhaps the single most radical approach to the restructuring of damaged lives in America today. Perhaps the best enumeration of mentoring's benefits comes from author Marc Freedman, who writes:

1. Mentoring appears *simple*. As the National Mentoring Partnership materials state, "[m]aybe you can't change the world, but you can make a difference in the future of at least one young person."
2. Mentoring is *direct*. The mentor has direct, personal contact with a youth without layers of bureaucratic red tape.
3. Mentoring appears *cheap*, because it uses volunteers. It is perceived as a low-cost alternative to public services.
4. Mentoring is *positively perceived*. Popular culture has made being a mentor or being mentored an admirable undertaking.
5. Mentoring is seen as *legitimate*. It is a sanctioned role for unrelated adults to play in the lives of youth, as reflected by the many stories that help maintain its honored place in our culture. Furthermore, Big Brothers/Big Sisters, as the premier mentoring effort in the country, is also one of the most respected social programs.
6. Mentoring is *flexible*. Mentoring has something for everyone. At one level, mentoring speaks to the American traditions of individual achievement, progress and optimism. It is connected to an improved workforce and economic competitiveness. At the same time, mentoring has another, more subtle allure. This aspect speaks to yearning for community lost, to a time of greater civility and responsibility for strangers.

The truly exciting thing about mentoring is that it brings the idea of personal resurrection to life. The avalanche of drug abuse and emotional alienation as depicted in motion pictures, modern literature and the nightly news paints a somber portrait of America as a nation of lost souls, especially among the youth of the country.

Mentoring restores those souls to sanity, not by means of shallow Band-Aid therapy, but through the total reinvigoration of self-esteem, confidence and social interplay. Therein probably lies the most essential requirement for an effective mentoring relationship: an adult attitude that views youth as resources to be nurtured and not problems to be fixed. Without this positive attitude, one cannot communicate high expectations.

Or, as Kaoru Yamamoto expands: "In mentoring, as in child rearing, this need to see on one's own has to be carefully, if subtly, preserved and enhanced so as not to deprive the individual, who is momentarily under guidance, of motivation and dignity."

Researcher Emmy Werner and others have found that adult relationships, that is, *natural mentoring*, not only provided by parents and grandparents, but also by neighbors, teachers and other concerned adults, are a protective factor for youth growing up in stressful family and community environments.

In her research of 700 youths growing up in high-risk environments, Werner discovered that the key to effective prevention effort is to reinforce, within every arena, the natural social bonds—between young and old, between siblings, between friends—*that give meaning to one's life and a reason for commitment and caring.*

One of the underlying principles of mentoring is the time-tested theory that humans tend to emulate the behavior they see in others they care for and admire. The critical importance, then, of caring adult relationships for successful outcomes for kids also makes the direct case for mentoring programs, which, by definition, attempt to create a one-on-one, adult-to-youth relationship that lasts over time and is focused on the developmental needs of youth.

Bernard Lefkowitz's book, *Tough Change: Growing Up On Your Own In America*, is based on interviews with 500 disadvantaged youth, a majority of whom credited their success to the support of a caring adult in their lives. Caring relationships that provide affiliation, that is, belonging and security, are the foundations of what programs provide.

Without the affiliation and security of caring relationships, youth hesitate to incur the costs or to take the risks that conventional success may require. Mentoring, then, not only provides a sense of meaning in the lives of young people, but it also instills the very tools essential for survival and self-actualization.

From alienation to a sense of community; from loss of identity to a solid grasp of personhood; from lapses into drug abuse to permanent steps toward maturity—these are the seeds of growth planted and nurtured by the dynamics of mentoring. In the final analysis, there is no better antidote for drug abuse than adolescents' beliefs that the world is a positive place, that they can accomplish what they want, and that they can gain satisfaction from life.

Story 63

Jennie Hudson is a mentor in the truest sense of the word. She brings commitment, unconditional energy and focus to her job.

Marin County in the 1950's was the archetypal California suburb. Post-war quietude and the giddy quest for material acquisition provided the backdrop for a playful, almost frivolous existence for the newly prosperous suburbanites.

The cliche was true—residents really did leave their doors unlocked at night.

Jennie Hudson was the lead majorette in the cheerleading squad at San Rafael High. Of Cherokee Indian descent, her specialty was twirling a flaming baton high into the tranquil Marin skies.

About the unlocked doors at night, Hudson recalls it wasn't until sometime in the early 60's when her family decided to locate a key to secure their home. Two prisoners had escaped from nearby San Quentin, and had made off with the Hudson's family car in the still of the night. It was a pivotal point in Hudson's perception of reality, jolting her into an abrupt realization that there was a larger, darker slice to life she had so far not experienced.

"Up until then," she explains, "I had no taste of fear. We were a big, thriving family—seven children, lots of aunts, uncles and cousins. We all cared for one another, and we were sheathed with a protective sort of coating. It felt good."

The Hudson family was functional and caring. If the parents couldn't respond to immediate needs and concerns, the aunts, uncles and grandparents were there instantly. And, if they weren't available, then the neighbors from the streets surrounding the family home would be there to lend a hand.

"We thought nothing of this kind of authority care," Hudson says. "We didn't know there was a name for it in those days, but the adults we looked up to were definitely our mentors. They gave us something solid and lasting, a seamless feeling that this was how values and traditions were passed on to the next generation."

When it came to career choices or how to be as a parent, there was no doubt, confusion or anguished deliberation in Jennie Hudson's mind. What she had been brought up with in childhood rang true and good to her, and it made her happy. No wonder, then, that she is currently celebrating her 26th year as a counselor at Marin Juvenile Hall. An employee of Marin's Youth Probation Department, she has held the post since raising her two children, who have in turn graced her with five grandchildren.

The remarkable thing about Hudson, also a professional dancer, is that she has maintained her youthful appearance and positive vigor through nearly three decades of service work.

"Call it my Indian genes," she laughs. "And you ought to see the faces of some of the fresh kids at 'Juvy' when they get smart with me and I tell them I have five grandkids…"

Jennie Hudson is a mentor in the truest sense of the word. She brings commitment and unconditional energy and focus to her job.

"It's very simple," she explains. "These kids didn't have what I enjoyed, and I'm just returning some of it to them. It's how I was raised—that there is much expected of those who have been given so much. I was such a tomboy in my youth; my Dad actually referred to me as his son! He brought me fishing, hiking, and told me all these marvelous stories about the real world."

With this foundation, her role in life as a good citizen was never up for debate. Reaching out to serve others is as natural to her as breathing.

"The key to working with kids today," says Hudson, "is to be a good listener and to never be condescending. They are extremely smart, and they can tell instantly if you are for real or if you're being bogus."

The kids of Marin are especially savvy. As inmates of Juvenile Hall, they are forever trying to outfox the authorities. Their little tricks and schemes are endless and clever. Friends on the outside, for example, have been known to hurl tennis balls stuffed with drugs over the fences. Hudson says the most satisfying part of her job is to have some of her charges return years later, their lives newly focused and re-charged.

"The fact that they remember me and want to thank me for turning their lives around is enormously gratifying," she says. "I've even had a few of them bring their own kids out here as a way to 'scare them straight' and away from trouble. I really think the key is to show them by example how to be a happy, functioning human being—that there is hope for a sane life in a world that sometimes seems like it's spinning out of control. I try to be their friend, but I also know they respond well to a firm, no-nonsense tough love kind of attitude on my part, as well.

"The ultimate compliment, of course, is when they come back after a few years to say they wanted to be like me. I guess that means I was a pretty good mentor to them."

Story 64

Mentoring programs across the country have demonstrated that not only are they beneficial to the individuals involved, but also to the ongoing health of a community.

In Bakersfield, California's country/western music capital, teenagers are doing a lot more with their summer vacation than strumming guitars, writing songs of heartbreak and dreaming of recording contracts.

They are tangibly making a positive difference in society today—they are mentoring kids even younger than themselves.

The *Bakersfield Californian* recently reported on the Elementary Mentoring program, which offers 15 high school students (the mentors) career training while, at the same time, providing 200 Franklin Elementary School students with 15 positive role models.

Kindergarten through fifth-grade kids were mentored in skills ranging from reading to basketball, the newspaper reported. This is certainly what is called a "good news" story, and it is far from boring.

As Dr. Nancy Young and I wrote in *Mentoring California's Children: A Concept Paper* early in 1995, many studies and experts agree that it takes only one person to change a child's life, and to help ensure that he or she will not be left behind in the desperate wake of poverty, welfare dependency and hopelessness.

The fact that this "one person" can frequently turn out to be someone just a few years older shouldn't surprise any of us.

For us to be a true role model means to offer someone not just a positive example, but a *relevant* one: The finest mentors are those who are able to empathize with their mentees—to truly understand what they're going through, possibly because they went through it themselves, and not that terribly long ago.

In bygone days of extended families, this usually meant an older brother or sister, aunt or uncle, still living nearby or under the same roof. Today, in our infinitely more complex and far-flung society, it could mean a mentor. If you are still skeptical about how mentors can make a difference, consider these depressing facts about California's young adults.

We have witnessed with great sadness the return of almost record-breaking overall drug use among young people in grades 9 and 11. Alcohol is the most popular drug for 21 percent of our 11th-graders who reported drinking on at least a weekly basis. With these staggering numbers, it's not surprising we have many young people ill-prepared to cope with their present life, much less their future, if they're going to be fortunate enough to have one.

Simply put, there is no place for them in the job market—not when, just three years ago, only 45 percent of fourth-grade public school students could read at or above a basic reading proficiency level, which awards California the dubious distinction of having the fifth lowest reading rate in the Nation.

But what if a young person met, early on, someone a little older, a little wiser, who had applied himself or herself to the tasks of self-improvement and the hard-earned trait of self-respect?

What if a young person knew that he or she had the emotional support of older people, as well as the affection and safety net of belonging to positive community and church groups? What if competence was rewarded, and sloth challenged?

Mentoring programs across the country have demonstrated that not only are they beneficial to the individuals involved, but also to the ongoing health of a community. It's a simple matter of investing in tomorrow—but making the currency time, not just money.

Remember that the next time you're driving through, near or to Bakersfield—a country/western mecca that knows the sweetest music comes directly from the heart.

Story 65

We may not be able to return family/community structure and functioning to what it was in yesteryear, but through mentoring we can create healthy, positive, effective environments for young people.

In the barrage of media reports on gangs and youth violence, very little attention is given to a sparkling undercurrent of social activism churning beneath the ugly exterior.

This healing glimmer of hope is mentoring.

In the seven-county San Francisco Bay Area region alone, the Oakland Mentoring Center is a clearinghouse currently serving 130 mentoring programs for youth who are experiencing personal and family difficulties.

Most traditional agencies and institutions—school districts, juvenile justice agencies, corporations, civic groups, colleges and universities—have begun to employ mentoring as a very effective means to stem the tide on youth academic low achievement, violence and other attitudinal/behavioral problems.

What does it take to be an effective mentor? If you're an adult, you qualify. If you're an adult with a social conscience, you are already a mentor. Sadly, most adults do not even consider mentoring as a choice because they do not realize how simple it is to become a mentor.

In the days when the word "dysfunction" was not commonplace, mentoring came naturally and undefined. Children grew up in households and lived in communities where there was an abundance of caring and nurturing adults. Adults gave freely of their spare time to actively participate with neighborhood youth. They gave advice, offered assistance, doled out praise and even rendered discipline.

This was built-in mentoring.

Today, young people do not grow up in environments like that anymore. With the rise of single-parent families and the disintegration of close-knit communities, many young people are taught to fear adults. Seeking counsel, advice or role emulation is simply out of the question. If we as adults are concerned about the behavior and condition of our youth, then we must assure that there are appropriate environments available to them.

We may not be able to return family/community structure and functioning to what it was in yesteryear, but through mentoring we can create healthy, positive, effective environments for young people. Mentoring, then, can be seen as a means of "artificially reconstructing the extended family." Mentoring is not missionary work; it's human development. Potential mentors must understand human development concepts; they must be able to respect cultural differences; and they must understand how different family and community lifestyles and circumstances require different kinds of approaches in working with youth.

Mentoring is nothing more than assisting youth to become the best they can be, or, at least, assisting them to understand, in a discerning kind of way, their options.

In his book, *The Ghetto Solution*, author Roland Gilbert (founding director of Simba, Inc., a nationally acclaimed adult/youth mentoring program) writes, "One of our major mistakes is that we focus directly on the children—what are their grades? What is their behavior? What we don't understand is that children are the result of someone else's modeling."

"As a result, children simply become like their models. Every child around you is going to unconsciously become who you are. So, by focusing solely on the children, we are not dealing with the very cause of their programming. We are dealing with the children after they have been programmed, after they have the belief systems and the thought patterns instilled in them by adults."

In today's rapid-fire world of sound bites, sensationalized TV news stories and on-the-spot coverage uplinking us to instant tragedy, we have come to view that the real problems for youth today are guns, crack, cocaine, violence and lack of jobs. These, however, are just the symptoms.

The real challenge for youth is the way they learn to respond to these things, not the things themselves. Mentors must teach people how to take responsibility for how they think, feel and act. Mentors must teach people how to get the results they want in their lives, and give them the dignity and responsibility to be able to make good choices.

Mentoring is a vehicle, which can facilitate this effort. Effective mentoring is designed to solve the problem, not how we feel about the problem. And mentors must first directly teach children that intellectual development is something they can achieve through effort. "Think you can. Work hard. Get smart!" is the message mentors must convey.

Mentors must build up children's confidence through their belief in and emotional support for the child by communicating the following positive, nurturing expectation, "This schoolwork I am asking you to do is important. I know you can do it. And I won't give up on you." That is mentoring in its purest form.

Story 66

If unhappiness, misery, crime, mental illness and an overall sense of alienation are any indication, then a whole lot of mentoring is not taking place.

The idea of mentoring is not the exclusive property of the poor, the disenfranchised, the violence-prone or the gang members. Actually, everyone on earth needs a mentor of some kind at some time in his or her life.

The simplest, most natural form, of course, are the birth parents acting as mentors to their offspring. The troubles in society, however, vividly point to the fact that this doesn't always work out.

If unhappiness, misery, crime, mental illness and an overall sense of alienation are any indication, then a whole lot of mentoring is not taking place. And it would be a serious mistake in judgment to think that mentoring is confined to a certain social class, as well.

Take the case of a 45-year-old white male named Tim from Larkspur, who lives in a leafy apartment complex with a gorgeously sliced view of Mt. Tamalpais. Tim had heard about mentoring from a conference on the subject that was held at Mills College in Oakland in the fall of 1995.

At first, he had thought about becoming a mentor himself. Semi-retired and a single father, he wanted to find a way to do something more meaningful in his life. After reading the literature and hearing a few speakers, Tim realized with a cold splash of reality that he was more qualified to be a mentee, not a mentor.

"I've not had a very happy life," he explains, "although, on the surface, most people would think I'm relaxed, settled, well-adjusted. I was born in San Francisco, the middle of three boys, to a well-known, long-established family. My father was in the media and my mother a full-time housewife. To outward appearances, we were the perfect, upwardly mobile American family."

"But there was always a dark cloud surrounding me. I just felt like there was a sense of impending doom about to crash down upon me at any time. I had great athletic skills as a young man, but I never felt worthy of this talent, because my father wanted me to pursue other interests. I didn't want to be anything else but a major league baseball player, but I didn't have that fire in my gut. Maybe with a little support from my father, a little confidence and faith, I could've pursued my dream."

"But no, he had his hands full with his own life. You see, my mother had a lifelong affair with another man, and it was the big family secret. Crazy thing is, it wasn't even a secret. All my friends and their parents knew about it, but my brothers and I kept up this facade that it wasn't there. Talk about denial..."

"Anyway, my father was always locked up, totally unavailable emotionally. The closest he ever asked me about how I felt was, 'How's your apartment?'"

"Now, I know he's a good man, and he's worked hard for his family, but I have such low regard for how he handled this affair, I walk around like a time bomb of hostility. And, of course, I can't talk to him about it, so I, in turn, focus that anger upon myself, and I get paralyzed from doing anything. I'm an alcoholic, but I have somehow put 10 years of sobriety together."

"Prior to my recovery, I was a mess—in and out of treatment centers, declaring bankruptcy, experiencing divorce and separation from my kids, whom I adore, the whole nine yards. But now, even in sobriety, I still feel enslaved by this inability to talk with my father. He's told me if I ever 'cross the line' and try to deal with my mother's affair, he'll never talk to me again, so I'm really trapped."

"I desperately need to be free of this, because I don't feel that I'm living. I feel numb all the time, and, even at the age of 45, I haven't even begun to tap my true potential as a person. Discovering that such a concept as mentoring exists does give me new hope. I have asked someone I respect very much to be my mentor, and it's turning my life around, slowly but definitely."

"I'm learning how to unlock all the blocks that have kept me from being my own self. I'm learning how to focus my hostility onto something positive and life enhancing. And, most importantly, I am learning how to come to forgiveness, especially where it concerns my father. Letting go of people and things has always been extremely painful to me. In AA, there is a great saying—'Alcoholics don't make friends, they take hostages.' And I am learning how to deal with how this sad reality wreaks havoc in my life."

"My mentor—much like an AA sponsor—is always there for me. He knows how to listen, he points me in the right direction, and, instead of assuming responsibility for my troubles, points to my own strengths so I can learn how to deal for myself."

Story 67

67

Like a comforting arm soothing the shoulders of a victim, an adult mentor reaches out to a suffering protégé, and the first step to full recovery has been taken.

Isolation is the single most damaging ailment suffered by California's disenfranchised young people.

The social epidemics afflicting our state's young—educational failure, gang involvement, drug and alcohol abuse and teen pregnancy—have created a vacuum of loneliness and despair wherein dwell the aching hearts of rebels without a hope.

Magnifying this sense of alienation and hopelessness are media accounts of America's economic prosperity. To young kids who have no piece of the pie at any level, this is a nose-rubbing reminder of how lonely and lowly they actually are.

Boiled down to its barest essentials, the purpose of government is to help its own people. When its youngest citizens who are the heirs to the nation are lost and hurting, government and its most inspired social architects have a duty to create an apparatus designed to lift the minds and hearts and bodies of suffering citizens into the mainstream of opportunity.

Such a social apparatus is the California Mentor Initiative, which has been thriving for more than seven years as the most effective weapon in the war being waged against these social epidemics.

In many ways, the California Mentor Initiative is the purest form of participatory democracy yet revealed—a responsive citizenry rallying in a compassionate fashion to the cries of the needy who so often merely require the slightest nudge toward recovery.

The essence of this apparatus is simple and brilliant, and it harkens to the earliest dawn of Jeffersonian democracy. Citizens with varying degrees of success and experience voluntarily extend their support and wisdom to a fraction of the populace scratching and clawing their flimsy grasp on survival.

The young's social epidemic is a nightmarish vision of ongoing psychological damage, deep emotional hurt and bruising, physical and spiritual scars. First, the California Mentor Initiative stops the bleeding.

Like a comforting arm soothing the shoulders of a victim, an adult mentor reaches out to a suffering protege, and the first step to full recovery has been taken.

The mentor is someone who has not only *survived* the pitfalls of life, but also thrived in the process. The mentor is a mature, caring role model who can reach deeply into the well of positive experience and share unselfishly with a mentee starving for the most primitive steps that will guide him to a new life.

If you examine the dynamics of the epidemic's grip, what you see are desperately voracious embraces of the wrong stuff. One of life's most primal physical wisdoms is that vacuums attract.

When someone young and hungry and starved for attention and a sense of significance opts for drink, drugs or gang engagement—a bad choice will spiral downward to include educational failure and teen pregnancy—it does not take much study to see that this is a natural urge badly aimed.

The mentor-mentee relationship re-directs that craving, this time in a healthy, progressive, liberating fashion. If a gang satiates the young person's hunger for community and a strict code of ethics, then the healthy embrace of a caring mentor satisfies that same yearning in a remarkably healthier style.

Mentoring is a miracle in the ever-revealing phenomenon of recovery. That it has come about through the much-maligned machinery of government makes it even more miraculous, but the fact is CMI is the brightest jewel in the diadem of state government.

CMI has unleashed armies of human potential to engage in the war against this epidemic. Soldiers in this battle are ambassadors of mercy. In one-to-one encounters with their afflicted charges, they first of all stop the bleeding with words of kindness. They tell them they are worthwhile persons who have only slightly gone astray. And they give them positive direction to worthwhile life choices.

Once pointed toward colleges, trade schools and financially rewarding job opportunities, the proteges can shed the dead skin of their previous bad choices, and begin to rejoice in a sense of new life. The mentor is an agent of hope who will sustain the friendship in an ongoing fashion. This is how we are rebuilding California one child at a time.

Story 68

In families where there is a vacuum of leadership, love and direction, the simple lesson of consequences gets distorted, twisted beyond recognition, and never learned.

Of the many phenomenal experiences reported by California mentors working with the state's afflicted and disenfranchised young people, one of the most striking common threads is the news that so many of our youth know so little about life's inevitable consequences.

Absent significant role models in their formative years, this is probably fairly predictable, but the astonishing thing is the almost universal lack of knowledge concerning consequences on all the little things so many of us take for granted.

Grasping consequences to one's actions is a lifelong process, a progressive evolution that begins at birth. If a child is brought into the world amid chaos, indifference, poverty, ignorance or rampaging dysfunction, his fate is usually sealed before his first breath.

Consequence is a large word with a simple definition. It denotes how one thing leads to another. In families where there is a vacuum of leadership, love and direction, the simple lesson gets distorted, twisted beyond recognition, and never learned.

Martin Jacks, who operates the Oakland Mentoring Center, is fond of speaking in the simplest terms to his proteges about the flow of consequences.

He remembers how Saturday mornings were as a child. His job was to mow the lawn. If he didn't do it just right, including sweeping up the clippings and trimming the edges perfectly, he'd have to retrieve all the equipment from the shed and start the job all over again.

In his mind, there was no questioning the authority. This was a fact of life as commonplace and as accepted as food, water and sleep.

Then, after finishing the family's lawn, he'd take all the equipment a few doors down the street and mow the lawn of his neighbor, an elderly woman whose husband had died. Back at home, Martin's sisters would be baking cakes for the family's Saturday night supper. Their first duty was to bring this same widow the first cake baked before they even thought of having a piece for themselves.

In Martin Jacks' family, thus was born a sense of social awareness, duty, selflessness and a lifelong sensitivity to consequences.

He's also fond of talking about natural mentors, adult role models who extended beyond his mother and father. Aunts, uncles, grandparents and godparents, all of whom took their extended parenting roles very seriously, surrounded him. If, for some reason, something got by Martin's parents, he swears there was no way he could get through the natural mentoring radar screens in place throughout his large family.

Many kids today have no such apparatus in place hence there is a vacuum of consequences eroding their actions. They can't grasp the concept of investing in study, for instance, because nobody has ever told them that the way to attain a college diploma is hard work and daily reading.

They never get the idea of using their God-given skills to enhance a trade talent because no one has ever reached out to tell them they are gifted in a certain fashion.

Not one person has ever pointed them toward a library, concert hall, fitness gym or trade school, they are left alone, whirling in the vacuum of their own mis-directed devices.

They make choices geared to instant gratification, seeking the results without the process. Hence, drug experimentation to make themselves feel good, irresponsible sex to fulfill the emptiness within, gang attachment for the gnawing sense of community left unattended, and, of course, school absenteeism because there is simply no time left for education.

Awareness of consequences is what the deepest blocks of our underlying personal foundations looks like. Without them, we are lost as people.

Mentoring, the insertion of adult role models into the dire vacuum in the lives of our youth, is the key to restoring sanity and worth to the hearts and minds and souls of kids throughout California and the nation.

Story 69

In the summer prior to Jake's senior year, Romy heard from a friend of hers about the concept of mentoring and how enlisting the help of a mentor had helped her friend's daughter who was in a 12-step recovery program.

Romy Miller is a young Sacramento single mother who can attest to the miracle of mentoring.

Her son, Jake is a high school senior who's always been the most sensitive of her four children.

When she was divorced 10 years ago, Jake withdrew into himself much more deeply than his siblings did Romy naturally focused most of her attention on his welfare.

She was primarily concerned because Jake was such a happy child. Photos show a tousle-haired young boy constantly beaming with delight and joy, and he was very popular with his young friends.

It worried her sick that the trauma of divorce had killed something inside her young son. His was the first name on her lips when she said her prayers, and she diligently took him to counseling sessions with a reputable professional.

Yet, if he wasn't depressed, Jake was behaving somewhat differently, for lack of a better term. Often sullen, frequently hostile and verbally explosive, occasionally silent for long periods of time, he was behaving in a fashion that gave all the signals of someone in distress.

Some of his more upbeat, clean-shaven, personable companions were replaced by a moodier group of downbeats—lots of wary glares toward adults, much mumbling and grumbling, and far too much lounging around in front of the TV watching dark and dreary videos.

During his sophomore and junior years, Jake ran with a crowd of guys known for their heavy drinking and dope-smoking ways. He'd swear up and down that he wasn't involved in substance abuse of any kind, but Romy often worried that he was merely in the stubborn grip of active denial.

There were a few incidents reported by school authorities, mostly boyish pranks that didn't result in suspension or expulsion, but indicative signs, nonetheless, about a possibly troubled youth. As Romy's prayers increased Jake's attitude and grades continued to decline.

In the summer prior to Jake's senior year, Romy heard from a friend of hers about the concept of mentoring and how enlisting the help of a mentor had helped her friend's daughter who was in a 12-step recovery program.

At the time, Romy was going through another breakup with a male friend, someone who had spent considerable time with Jake, and she was really worried now that Jake's anger would reignite itself into some kind of dangerous behavior.

She was genuinely terrified that this latest breakup would lead to her losing Jake for good consequently she made some phone calls and contacted a potential mentor.

The man came with great recommendations from Romy's minister, and she got some relief when she watched Jake greet the mentor with warm, albeit cautious, eyes.

She decided to turn her experience over to God and the mentor, who'd meet with Jake once a week at the start of his senior year. She fought every compulsion to urge information out of her son, but she decided to concentrate on her own life and trust in this new phenomenon of mentoring.

Several weeks passed, and Jake seemed to be doing just fine. He was still quiet and somewhat moody, but there was a new sense of steadiness and balance to his behavior. She was determined not to pry, but she was really curious about Jake's senior perk, which stipulated he could leave campus at lunchtime.

So, during the Parents' Night program when teachers mingled with mothers and fathers, Romy asked one of Jake's teachers about his lunchtime activities.

"Oh, hasn't he told you?" answered the young woman. "He has the choice, as you know, of leaving campus with his friends, who usually hang out at Burger King, but Jake's been volunteering his lunch hour each day at Easter Seals, helping the developmentally disabled people with their work."

Romy stood in rapt silence. She had never felt such a thrill of pure joy and relief.

"I can't believe he hasn't told you," echoed the teacher. "I think it has something to do with this mentor he's been seeing."

"You know," said Romy, choking back tears, "I like it much better that he hasn't said anything to me. Much, much better!"

Story 70

Without judgment, ridicule, condescension or prejudice, Jasmine's mentor accepted this woman for who she was—a struggling young person who desperately needed a listening compassionate ear.

The Public Market in Emeryville is a vast, sprawling amalgam of food concessions and shopping kiosks, a veritable melting pot of multi-cultural American consumerism.

The Market, featuring spicy and lively foods from around the world, is abuzz with international languages, laughter and all of the chaotic sights and sounds of a modern-day mall.

Amid the din sits a 19-year-old East Bay woman named Jasmine, a strikingly tall, slender African American with wisdom beyond her years. Spinning noodles with her fork and yarns with her fast-moving wit, she's talking about the experiences she's had in the past year with her mentor, a woman she says has not only saved her life, but enhanced it beyond her dreams.

She explains that her years from 13 to 18 are a blur, dulled by drugs, worse friends, and a downward spiraling sense of herself as a person. She says she felt invisible, worthless, totally lost without purpose. She remembers feeling totally bewildered that her life seemed so absurd before it had even begun.

And she vividly recalls thinking about ending that life were it not for the intense pain that went with that feeling of being invisible.

"There was this great big contradiction," she says now with a warm, sad smile, "that, at the same time, life seemed senseless and extremely painful. It was the pain that saved me, because I was sitting on a park bench weeping one day when my mentor approached me and held out her hand in one great big saving gesture of hope."

Jasmine's mentor is a retired Oakland teacher who had been walking through Lake Merritt's trails one day, and saw the young lady crying alone.

They hit it off immediately. Given the emotional trauma of the moment, they never lapsed into small talk. It was, after all, an emergency situation.

Without judgment, ridicule, condescension or prejudice, Jasmine's mentor accepted this woman for who she was—a struggling young person who desperately needed a listening, compassionate ear.

Jasmine is still in awe of their meeting, and she talks about how the encounter was brilliantly simple.

"We talked about little things," she says. "I was a basket case, all right, but we didn't dwell on great big issues. My mentor explained in the clearest, easiest terms possible how she once turned her own life around during a bout with depression.

"She talked happily about how she'd start each day on her knees, begging God for help and mercy. Then she'd make her bed. That simple task somehow centered her day, and she immediately felt better and stronger, able to take on the day's challenges."

Jasmine pauses long enough to let out a loud, crisp cackle. "It's funny," she explains. "But my own mother used to tell me that if I made my bed, I had to lay in it. I never knew what she meant until now!"

Jasmine goes on to rave about her mentor. She talks about how simplicity began to rule her life. She took joy in the smallest things, from washing dishes to taking walks to buying a library card.

Her mentor gave her a reading list, and urged her to read one book a week. She read *To Kill A Mockingbird* the first week and *Native Son* the second week. Both books awakened in her a long dormant sense of social consciousness, and they opened the floodgates for a voracious reading appetite.

Jasmine enthuses about how her life today is one endlessly surprising series of small joys—not necessarily an easier life, but a better, richer one that's rebuilding her esteem, resurrecting her spirits. She calls herself a lighthearted person currently under reconstruction.

She starts each day on her knees, and the first prayer of thanks is for her mentor.

Story 71

"I call Dr. Drew my mentor, because he led me to a safe place and made me feel good about myself."

Mentoring is frequently a means of salvation. The following vignette speaks to this phenomenon:

Angela is a 19-year-old Central California native. She's a part-time student who has a novel job—she drives cars up and down the spine of the state, the long gray line of I-5, for her father's leasing company.

"I deliver new cars to people leasing them for my Dad," she explains, "and I can't tell you how extremely boring it is to spend most of your waking hours on the most monotonous freeway in the nation."

Angela drives cars from Eureka to San Diego, from Ukiah to Santa Barbara. She's been doing this since she turned 16, and she boasts she's only had one speeding ticket.

"That was in Chowchilla, a demon speed trap. They nailed me going 90 miles per hour, and I spent most of my day's salary, about $100, paying off that crime!" she laughs.

But all was not always so humorous in Angela's driving experiences. Terrified that she might fall asleep at the wheel and find herself crushed beneath the weight of a big rig driving behind her, Angela fell into a speed trap of a different kind. She started taking speed as a way to stay awake.

"I won't name names or anything," she says, "but up and down the highway system, at any number of truck stops, you can find most anything you want to keep your eyes peeled. And me being a young girl didn't hurt, either."

The habit got pretty bad, and even Angela knew she was headed toward destruction.

"I know it's crazy looking back on it now, but once I made two round trips from L.A. to San Francisco in a 24-hour period. That's a lot of driving, and I was wired on speed the whole time."

Luckily for Angela, car radio reception is such on I-5 that the motorist can tune into just about any radio station in the West, especially late at night.

"It was late last summer, almost midnight," says Angela, "and I was listening to my favorite late-night show. It's a popular L.A.-based program featuring a medical doctor and a wise-cracking deejay. They're names are Adam and Dr. Drew, and they have a huge audience. Kids from all over the country call in with the wildest questions about sex and drugs.

"What I like about the show, besides the fact that it keeps me awake, is that it mixes serious medical information with the free-wheeling style of a smart-aleck personality. And they have all sorts of celebrities and musicians sitting in as guests to take some calls, as well. So, anyway, there I was on cruise control, doing about 95 on I-5, when something clicked big time in my heart and mind while listening to this show.

"A young girl caller about 15 had called in, practically sobbing. She was pregnant, and she blamed her condition on drugs. She was so naive about everything, particularly about drugs, but Dr. Drew was so kind and compassionate, it made me cry, too. What he said jarred me into pulling off the side of the highway and taking several large gasps of air. Very simply and still maintaining his cool, hip style, he explained that drugs are wrong, dead wrong, for this reason alone:

"Any changes the person might experience while under the influence are pharmaceutical and pharmaceutical only. Changes that come from within the person, on the other hand, are physiological and spiritual in nature, and, hence, the only worthwhile changes.

"The simplicity of it all hit me like a ton of bricks."

"I had been injecting all this crap into my system, blindly convincing myself that it was good for my body and my soul, providing me with the power to get my job done. And I realized with full force that it was all a smokescreen, and I was headed for disaster. I crave so much inner peace and serenity that I will take any measures to make this happen, so I stopped taking speed immediately. The withdrawal was not fun, but I kept visualizing how good I would feel in a few days when I'd be clean and sober."

"I call Dr. Drew my mentor, because he led me to a safe place, and made me feel good about myself. Not only that, but I'm taking it a step further. I've decided to set up a support group for kids my age who are dabbling in drugs and alcohol. I don't want it to be like A.A. or anything too severe. In fact, I'm kind of modeling it on this radio show—we're gonna have a good time while discussing the more serious aspects of life like sex, relationships, meaningful endeavors, and how to fulfill our dreams."

"Then, in turn—who knows?—maybe my good works will make me a mentor to someone else. And you know what? That drive along I-5 is a lot faster and sweeter now than it ever was on speed. I listen to self-help tapes, I talk into a tape recorder about my goals, and, of course, I listen to Adam and Dr. Drew."

Story 72

"I know I have the raw material and the basic tools, but I recognize that I need a nudge, a swift kick in the butt to push me to the next level."

What if mentoring had its' own TV channel? Consider the kind of mindless garbage currently being served up on daily talk shows.

Television looks like an abused medium, indeed, when you gaze upon the wreckage of these pathetic people's lives who, for God only knows what reasons, lay out their personal, twisted tragedies for the whole world to witness.

Actually, to say, "television is abused," is much too passive a term. Because of the infiltration of these daily freak shows, TV has become the abuser of its own potential, literally the destroyer of its own self. If it's true that most people only learn to use a tiny percentage of the human mind, the same sad statistic can definitely be applied to the untapped power of television.

Granted, PBS stations, science channels and higher-grade cable feeds offer a wide diversity of information, arts and cultural refinement, but then there are also the questionable options of shows like *Beavis & Butthead, Married With Children*, and the sexually explicit, drug-promoting exploitations of MTV programming.

Dissatisfaction with television doesn't necessarily come only from self-righteous reactionaries, authority figures from above the common man. Hear it, somewhat surprisingly, from a former gang member.

Julia is stirring her virgin Margarita wistfully, staring at the slumped shoulders of bar patrons from her table inside the La Barca restaurant on Theard Street in San Francisco. Spread before her are pages from her personal diary, etchings of a damaged life.

"There are thousands of kids like me," says the bright-eyed, raven-haired 24-year-old refugee from The City's mean Mission District streets.

"In these pages," she sighs, pointing to the mix of prose, poetry and pictures, "there could be another Jack Kerouac or, maybe, a Maya Angelou. We'll never know, because we are artists without direction, guidance and focus. I know I can write brilliantly, but who will ever read it? I know nothing about the real world of self-advancement."

The subject of TV is a raw one with Julia.

"I know people scoff at the notion that TV is a negative influence. Liberals, especially, are afraid to tackle the issue because of First Amendment fears, but I can tell you this—we are all influenced by the medium. It sets the standards, particularly for kids, and if they don't feel 'MTV' enough, they feel they're not cool. What we need are strong role models and real-life teachers, just like the movies need strong roles for women today."

"What if there was a channel devoted to nothing but role models—positive, life-enhancing people we would love to imitate?"

"Yes, I admit it, I need a mentor. Don't forget, we are the Sesame Street generation. That was our babysitter for years. Same with *Mr. Rogers*. You might say that I was raised by Big Bird and Fred Rogers. I may be in my rebel period now, but those early childhood experiences never leave you."

"So, what I'm saying is—what if there was a cable outlet devoted entirely to our self-improvement? Hey, I'd watch it all day, if need be. I know I have the raw material and the basic tools, but I recognize I need a nudge, a swift kick in the butt to push me to the next level. Believe me, I don't want to spend the rest of my life brooding away my potential in dank coffee houses and smelly bars.

"I survived the drug scene and the violence of the Mission, but I'm kind of in limbo right now. I really need to learn how to market my skills."

Julia shuffles through some papers, then brightens when she comes across a captioned illustration. It is a close likeness of herself, a drawing of a young woman in a black bikini, tattoos on her arms and shoulders, sprawled on a sunny beach with palm trees and crushed white coral sand.

The caption reads: "God didn't rescue me from the waves in order to beat me up on the shore."

The message is beautiful for its simplicity. Here is a woman who's taken steps to enact her own salvation, yet she's still trapped in a passive state. Another scrawled line from her eclectic diary reads: "Most people do 98% of what it takes to be successful, then quit when there's only 10% of the work left. Why?"

Julia laughs. "I heard Ross Perot say that," she guffaws, sticking a finger down her throat, "but hey, everything counts, right?"

Maybe a mentoring channel would fill in that missing 10%.

Story 73

In life, there is no mentor as powerful as the individual act of courage from a peer. This was mentoring at its finest.

It happened on a July evening in 1996.

The athletic event of the Summer Olympics stands as the anthem for the very definition of sport and patriotism in America.

A deceptively fragile-looking 18-year-old gymnast, Kerri Strug, needs a 9-plus, knockout performance on the vaulting beam to ensure the first gold medal in the history of American women's gymnast competition.

While the world watches, her first attempt is a botched effort, resulting in a severe ankle twist that leaves the pretty young athlete grimacing in anguish and limping in pain.

Incredibly, instead of rushing to her aid, her coach exhorts her to summon up the courage for the next and final attempt. His words are audible: "You can do it! You can do it!"

What happened next is so emotionally gut wrenching and inspirational, no Hollywood scriptwriter would have the gall to create something so … perfect.

Her eyes brimming with tears, her face contorted into a power pack of bravery, Strug starts racing down the exercise mat, plants her damaged limb onto the take-off spot, then launches into a soaring, spiraling leap that appears to last a lifetime, then completes it by landing on her wounded foot, which she quickly and gracefully raises before collapsing in a heap of raw pain.

She scores a 9.7, and nails down history—gold medal for the young American women's gymnastic team, which is the true Dream Team of these Olympic Games. This magic moment should be required viewing for every teenager in America. In life, there is no mentor as powerful as the individual act of courage from a peer. This was mentoring at its finest.

It was almost too divine a moment to imagine. The camera flashes to her emotion-wracked parents in the grandstand, and one can only speculate on the years and tears of discipline, commitment, exercise and devotion this family brought to young Kerri's talent and ambition.

That all her years of hard work and dedication would culminate in a symphonic moment of grace and triumph is almost too eerie to contemplate. Surely even the most jaded observer felt the goose bumps trickle up the spine. And then the sight of her teammates swarming to her assistance to help her climb up the stairs to receive the gold medal as a team—is this pure heroism, or what?

You want to seize every troubled teenager in America and watch the tape over and over again. You want to say—Look, *that's* what can be done when you put your mind to something.

that's what selfless dedication is all about, that's what heroism means.

that's what it means to be an un-complaining, courageous leader. That's how you celebrate your individuality and your uniqueness.

that's how you make a difference among your friends. That's the embodiment of the courage to be all that you can be.

This was viewed not by millions of Americans, but by *billions* of people around the globe—the impact this heroine had on the minds and hearts of the world's young people is incalculable.

The cynics among us may have snorted, "Another millionaire is born," and, in the final analysis, he may be right. Andy Warhol's 15-minute fame rule probably never anticipated such built-in wealth that will no doubt come this young lady's way from commercial endorsements and fast-track commercialism.

But, no matter what she harvested in financial gold, it should always be remembered that the power of her conviction and character induced her to the supreme heights while she was still an amateur, before she had even made a dime.

It makes you wonder about basketball professionals—with their $80 million salaries, would they have risked additional injury like this frail young songbird did on this July night in Georgia?

No, this is not in the slightest about money. This is about the surge of patriotism, honor and dignity that one tiny girl instilled in all of us with the performance of a lifetime. How many of us cried with joy as we watched these magnificent seven young ladies mouth the words to our national anthem as they received their gold medals, looking for all the world in their racial diversity like a living, breathing rainbow coalition?

Playing with pain. Putting the needs of the greater community ahead of one's more immediate needs. Acting on intuition, guts, glory and a heart of gold. Thank you, Kerri Strug.

Story 74

Stella has become my friend and mentor. She never takes one day for granted, and tells me to seize every opportunity that comes along.

One of the most annoying complaints a parent can hear from a child—especially in the summertime—is: "There's nothing to do."

Boredom is an insult to the bored and an irritant to those in the same vicinity. Among young teenagers, however, it's a distinct sign of lack of leadership from role models. Unsure of their own skills and talents, they need a little nudging into waters not yet tested.

Doing something for others, for example, is an excellent way to get a youth "out of himself" and into the process of maturity. If kids groan about a "Boy Scout"-type of activity that paints them too much as "goody-two-shoes," however, urging them toward social consciousness may, at times, backfire.

But they need to be informed that doing things for others is simply what's expected of someone in the maturing process. It's also what's expected of good citizens who are part of the American way of life.

Take the case of Tori, a South San Francisco high school sophomore who was facing a dreary summer of "hanging out" with her friends at the local mall and not much else. She saw a notice on a bulletin board at the Post Office about an elderly woman who needed assistance with light chores, some cooking and paperwork needs.

"I'm not sure what seized me," Tori recounts today, "but I just felt compelled to give this lady a call. It was probably because I didn't want to hear my parents nagging me about lounging around the house too much during the summer," she adds with a laugh.

"Anyway," says Tori, "it turns out this woman has changed my life. The instant I met her on the day of the interview, I knew she was someone special, but I had no idea at the time that she would open up whole new worlds for me."

Tori works for the lady three days a week, for about five hours a day. Not in her wildest dreams did she ever think a summer job could be so much fun—"And," says Tori, "I mean 'fun' in the broadest sense of the word."

Her new employer's name is Stella, who's an 85-year-old Russian-born former dancer with 50 years' worth of American citizenship behind her. Stella's husband died earlier this year of a stroke, and she found keeping up the details of her life were simply too demanding. Hence, her plea for a part-time worker.

Tori is at that difficult age between childhood and serious job-searching.

"I'm too young to be flipping burgers, which I couldn't stand to do, anyway," she says, "and too old to be playing on slides and swings. This suits me just fine. Stella has totally opened my eyes—she talks about growing up poor, in fear, and constantly looking for ways to escape from her homeland. I had absolutely no knowledge about life outside the Bay Area, so I listen to her stories with amazement.

"And she has this fabulous library at home—Russian novels, books on dancing, the Classics, and volumes and volumes of poems. I have always kept a diary, and think I'm a pretty good poet, and my ultimate dream in life has always been to be a professional dancer. Stella has become my friend and mentor. She's a stern lady because she's been through so much, but she's also like a little child at heart. She never takes one day for granted, and tells me to seize every opportunity that comes along," she says.

"Nobody in my life has ever taken so much interest in me. Yeah, she pays me for my work, but the real reward to me is the fact that she believes in my dreams and constantly goads me toward accomplishing them. Do you have any idea what kind of impact that has on a kid who usually doesn't feel very special? I mean, it's not that I have lousy parents or anything—they've always taken care of me and stuff, but they just don't take me very seriously," she says.

"I always had this nagging notion that there was something big missing from my life, and Stella is the key that opens the door for me. I mean, we talk about ideas, politics, art, people, life, God and what it all means. This is like the best thing that's ever happened to me, and my parents tell me they've never seen me so happy. Same with my friends—and a lot of them are really negative about a bunch of stuff, and a few years ago, they probably would've laughed at me if I raved to them about how much fun it is to do this work."

"I feel so lucky. There I was trying to make a little money, and it turns out to be this whole new experience. I feel like I hit the jackpot. And I'm putting a little money aside every week, because what I'd really like to do is buy Stella and me tickets to see a ballet in San Francisco. That's going to be my thank you to her for being such a great friend and mentor."

Story 75

75

I would love to have a hero, a mentor, someone I can dump all my fears upon and not feel guilty or bad about not being perfect.

If anyone doubts that teenagers today need—no, crave—solid direction from adult role models, they need to speak to young people in trouble.

The Rape Crisis Center of Marin is a 24-hour full-service support clinic that treats victims of sexual abuse. A recent rape victim whom we'll call Taylor is extremely grateful for the help she received immediately following a "date rape" she suffered after a night of binge drinking and marijuana smoking.

Taylor is 15-years-old, but she could easily pass for a 21-year-old fashion model from the cover of Vogue magazine. Born of well-to-do, successful Marin parents, she has all the external trappings of the good life—creature comforts like a multi-story home with a sweeping view of San Francisco, pet horses, cell phones, and, tucked in a garage, a little yellow sports car awaiting her driver's license.

Wily, savvy, sophisticated—some from the inner city might say spoiled, as well—Taylor looks to be the antithesis of someone crying for help. Frankly, the only thing that betrays her outward appearance of suave serenity is the teen-requisite backpack smeared with Grateful Dead stickers dangling crookedly from her shoulders, as she sips coffee in the courtyard of The Village, a swank, upscale Marin County shopping mall.

"OK," she says, a shy smile creasing her well-tanned face, "I don't want to use the language of victims, because I take responsibility for my actions, but I do know that I got myself into this mess for a reason. It may look like I've got it all together—I have more friends than you can imagine, I've never missed a meal in my life, I get to vacation in Tahoe and Maui, and I live in the most desired place in America, "

"But inside me is this gaping dark hole as big as the Grand Canyon. My counselor tells me this emptiness is where God lives, but I've never been too religious, so the verdict is still out on that one. What I do know is that I have never felt truly loved. My parents are part of that Marin 'Beautiful People' circle that desperately needs attention and approval from one another.

"In terms of cars, money, stock options, and status, we've got it all. But the truth is, I feel like just another possession of my parents. I'm just like their matching Jaguars, only I've caused them a lot more trouble. Neither of my parents has ever sat down with me for a good heart-to-heart. When it comes to hearing the facts of life from them, it never happened. All I know about sex I learned from the girl who does my hair, and she's not much older than I am.

"I walk around feeling hurt all the time because I can't for the life of me understand why they neglected me so much. Aren't I worth just a simple 'How are you feeling?' in passing?"

Taylor's gimlet-colored eyes glaze over in a mist of self-pity and sadness, then she suddenly jerks to a fully upright state of angered awareness.

"What I desperately need is someone older than me to talk to me about my feelings, my dreams, my confusion, my identity. I know I have something extremely worthwhile to offer the world, but I feel so uncomfortable and worthless about it all the time. I would love to have a hero, a mentor, someone I can dump all my fears upon, and not feel guilty or bad about not being perfect.

"The night of the rape, it was all so clear to me where it was headed. We had smoked some grass and done some heavy flirting, then we got into some expensive wine, and I felt warm and fuzzy and excited all at the same time. But when it got physical, that's when I definitely said no and drew the line, only he didn't stop. I felt so terrible and dirty and used, and I am so ashamed of myself that I put myself through this ordeal."

"Sex isn't that important to me, and I truly believe that people my age should not be active sexually. What would really turn me on in a healthy way is to have someone in a mentor-like capacity show me love and guidance, directing me in practical ways to learn about my abilities and my place in the world.

"Now that would be orgasmic!"

Taylor looks momentarily embarrassed by her candor, hiding her face in the palm of one hand while scratching her long hair with the other.

"I mean," she says, scrambling for clarity, "what I really want to do is turn this bleak experience into something positive. I want to 'get underneath' what it's all about, try to understand it, avoid any repetition, learn to love myself, and start living life for me, not as a trophy for my parents, but as someone who wants to make a mark upon the world. Right now, I hunger for a mentor. I recognize that I need help of that kind, and I am ready to start feeling good as a person."

Story 76

76

I am there for them in every facet of their lives—from relationship confusion to career choices, from trouble with their parents to peer pressure, from advice on se to strong, strong counseling on alcohol and drugs.

Gabriella is a strikingly pretty Hispanic woman from San Francisco. As she strolls along the newly coined "Herb Caen Way" on The City's Embarcadero waterfront, shards of sun glitter against her shiny raven-colored hair.

"*There's* the reason I became a mentor," she says, pointing in the direction of a group of grunge-garbed teenagers skateboarding past the Ferry Building. "They're a lost generation, starving for a sense of direction and purpose, and I think I have what it takes to steer them in the right path."

Gabriella is a recovering addict, but you may be surprised at the form her addiction took.

"I was addicted to a person, my ex-boyfriend," she explains, tossing a handful of sourdough crumbs to a squawking band of San Francisco seagulls. Whirling toward her visitor and flashing eyes of steel upon his somewhat startled gaze, Gabriella says, "I can tell you this: addiction to a person is every bit as paralyzing, debilitating and enslaving as any other addiction to drugs, sex or gambling. I was an obsessed slave, and it was so unhealthy, it nearly killed me—emotionally, spiritually and physically."

"We were together nearly 10 years, and it had started out beautifully. We were both deeply in love for the first six years, but then things got weird. I forgot who I was except in terms of who I was with him. I was nothing except one half of the 'we.'"

"The roots of this, I think, came about because he helped me through my battle with alcoholism at the beginning of our relationship. He was so wonderfully supportive of my fight against booze—going to meetings with me, talking through my cravings, even coming up with fun 'rewards' for me whenever I conquered the next urge to drink. Sadly, in total opposition to all that Alcoholics Anonymous stands for, he became my Higher Power, my god. I turned to him for everything instead of to the Almighty, who, in AA, is at the basis of the program's spirituality, whomever it is you choose as your Higher Power.

"So, you're probably wondering what does all this have to do with being a mentor," Gabriella smiles, pointing once more to the sidewalk skateboarders. "Well, it's extremely important to realize that every form of addiction squeezes the life out of a person. It's the false coating of personal identity that literally robs the victim of freedom.

"There's a great saying in AA—first, the man takes the drink, then the drink takes the man, then, in the final stages, the drink takes the drink. The same is true of every obsession—you absolutely lose your freedom and your chance at happiness.

"Now, I'm not saying that every teenager is going to fall into an obsessive cycle like I did. But what I am saying is that I have made a choice to turn all my sick behavior into something positive and constructive—and the central thrust of my message to teens is to shape your personal freedom and hang on to it at any cost under the sun."

"There's another great saying in AA—God didn't pluck you from the waves of misery in order to beat you up on the shore. In other words, God saved you from being a drunk, and now He offers you something new and refreshing to contribute to the world."

"By the way," she chuckles, "I used to be so put off by those corny AA sayings that are plastered all over the walls like beer signs in bars. After all, I'm a college grad from an East Coast university. I should be above all those pithy sayings. But you know what? They work better than any lofty philosophy book I've ever read.

"Anyway, about my choice to be a mentor. I have never been happier in my life. I have taken three teens under my wing—two girls and a boy, and I invest in them all the wasted, sick energy I used to put into obsessing over my boyfriend. With him, I thought it was love, when it was really just a few shades away from genuine stalking. But, with my mentees, it is the real thing, and it feels so good.

"I'm their surrogate Mom and their best friend. I tutor them, play with them, go on hikes with them in Marin and out on Ocean Beach. We go to concerts together, ballgames, and have beautiful picnics in East Bay parks. In a word, I am there for them in every facet of their lives—from relationship confusion to career choices, from trouble with their parents to peer pressure, from advice on sex to strong, strong counseling on alcohol and drugs.

"To think I used to spend so much time and effort on a dead relationship that had run its course—it amazes me how I allowed myself to get so trapped. Of course, the kids don't know this, but one of the best parts of this experience for me is that I never think about my ex-boyfriend anymore!"

Story 77

Stripped of my ego and those fake, malfunctioning crutches of addiction, I was free to become my son's role model.

This is a story about how a wayward husband became a magnificent mentor to his two sons. Patrick McKenna (an alias for reasons of privacy) of Stockton is a 40-year-old San Francisco Bay Area product who, visibly, looks like a centered, successful white male.

But he grins shyly when he talks about the turmoil that was once festering just below the surface of his skin.

"God moves in mysterious ways, that's for sure," says McKenna, stroking his chin in nervous reflection of his past. "I was married when I was 21, and didn't have a clue as to what I was doing. My wife got pregnant right away, so we didn't really have much of a life together before the reality of raising a child hit us smack between the eyes."

McKenna worked for the State of California in a Stockton field office in the early days of his marriage, and he fell into a bad crowd of drinkers and drug users who'd party very heavily after work.

"There wasn't much else to do in the outlying areas of Stockton," says McKenna, "and I always rationalized my behavior as something I deserved after a hard day's work."

By the time the couple's first son arrived, McKenna had developed a hardcore drinking problem, but he somehow managed to keep his job and family intact.

"My own family's upbringing didn't teach me a thing about being a hands-on father," he says, "but I adored my child so much, I did whatever I could do improvise this parenting thing. Because of my addiction to drugs and alcohol, my wife and I had long stopped connecting on any level, but we were both so enthralled with our son, we thought we were doing OK."

"But I had this huge dark cloud hanging over me, this awful feeling of impending doom, that somehow I just wasn't living right. I felt like a fraud, like the whole thing was going to unravel, that someone was going to discover the fact that I was an evil person, and my life would be over. I was feeling the paranoia."

McKenna recalls those first few years of his son's life were fueled by a massive outpouring of love toward his child even while he felt the fabric of his own character being stretched toward destruction.

"When my son was four, my wife became pregnant again, and I had what you might call a spiritual awakening that changed my life and my family's life for good."

McKenna's wife, who had been praying for her husband in her church group, invited the pastor over to dinner one night. It's now been 15 years, but McKenna remembers the evening like it was today.

"I had come home from work pretty drunk, and there was this huge, imposing minister in our living room. Since then, I've heard of interventions that happen between family members and people who are drunks or addicts, and I knew instinctively that something was going to change me forever. He was a no-nonsense guy—large, gruff, with enormous eyebrows and piercing eyes. But, oddly enough, he was extremely gentle. He talked to us about our upcoming big event with the second child, and he said something that has been etched in my memory ever since.

"He told us that there was only one thing we needed to know about childbirth, and that was the simple fact that the baby was a gift from God—*a gift from God*, not a possession to be controlled, not a trophy to be shined. A gift. This was the moment that turned me inside out. Everything I had done to this point was futile and self-destructive. I stumbled at every turn, even though I had been given great skills and opportunities.

"After hearing these words and letting them sink into me, a great load was lifted from me. I felt a sense of peace I hadn't experienced in years. I would no longer have to apply half-baked, ill-conceived 'strategies' upon my marriage and parenting. This was the event of my life—kind of like Saint Paul being thrown off his horse! I felt free at last.

"I know it sounds simplistic, but I entered the process of maturity at that moment. When my second son was born, I embraced them both with this new spirit of humility and gratitude. I treated them every day as though they were the most special gifts I had ever been given, because that's what they are.

"Stripped of my ego and those fake, malfunctioning crutches of addiction—I entered treatment and have been clean and sober since that night—I was free to become my sons' role model in life. But I was able to do this not by how I had first anticipated, but by losing myself and my old tired notions first."

"I play with them because I want to. I guide them through school because it brings me joy. I never miss a play or concert, because it would be robbing me of great pleasure and enhancement if I did. From my struggles, I have become their mentor. I feel their love and respect back to me. And I am happy and free."

Story 78

The kids are so hungry for a sense of direction it is really a cakewalk helping them out. All it takes really is to give them a message of hope, bolster their self-esteem, make suggestions about career choices and probably most importantly, make them feel really good about themselves.

The beauty of mentoring is that sometimes the mentee becomes the mentor. Not only is this a satisfying occurrence, but it also gives final validation to the fact that the mentor is truly doing his job—imitation being the most genuine form of flattery.

Jim Dwyer (an alias for his choice of privacy) of Los Angeles gazed out the window of the commercial jetliner streaking toward San Diego, where he was headed for a business conference. A 40-year-old executive with a software firm, Dwyer was speaking of his years working with Big Brothers/Big Sisters.

"I'm in my fifth year of working with kids from all walks of life in the Los Angeles area," he explained, sipping a soda and shielding his eyes from the glare of the Pacific Ocean to the west.

"I first got into it because, frankly, I was bored with my adult friendships. I was hanging out with a lot of people from work, and they would get into this negative, badmouthing mode of behavior—bashing fellow employees, people of different races, bosses, elected officials, basically anyone who breathed."

"It was really disgusting. I mean, who do they think they are? Mostly white, upper-middle class members of the workforce, they should be grateful they have a job in the first place. I was always raised to believe that to whom much is given, much is expected. I think it goes back to my Kennedy-inspired, Peace Corps-training days."

"At any rate, associating with this crowd kind of created a vacuum in my life. There was a hole in my soul, if you will. I just knew there was something missing, and I couldn't take the negative energy any longer. I've always looked upon kids as a blessing. I have two grown teenagers myself—a boy and a girl—and I think I was fairly successful at raising them."

"They're both great personalities with their heads screwed on right. My son is in management training at a restaurant chain, and my daughter is learning how to work on a cruise ship line. So I went into Big Brothers/Big Sisters with an attitude of trying to share some positive parenting principles, and, for the most part, I've been very successful.

"There are so many kids out there who need so much from those of us who 'have it made.' I simply can't understand why there aren't more adults spending a few hours a week trying to turn someone's life around. As a mentor, I do the usual things—take my mentees to Dodger games, the museum, air shows, walks on the beach. It's not a high-pressure job. I just make myself available to listen and to give witness to the fact that he or she is a worthwhile human being."

"The kids are so hungry for a sense of direction, it's really a cakewalk helping them out. All it takes, really, is to give them a message of hope, bolster their self-esteem, make suggestions about career choices, and, probably most importantly, make them feel really good about themselves."

Dwyer's eyes began to shine as he settled back to recount the best part of his story.

"It's extremely satisfying work, but one time I got a huge surprise from one of my kids that served as a major life lesson. It was around Christmas time last year, the winter of 1995. I was going through a break-up, and it was definitely having a bad effect on my performance at work.

"It was as though I was moving through mud—like in one of those nightmares where you can't run away fast enough from a demon. My life was flattened, and I started acting and thinking like those negative people I was describing before. Well, a few weeks before Christmas, I met with one of my Big Brothers/Big Sisters kids. We were going to meet for lunch, then go to the mall to hear a church group sing Christmas carols.

"The young man I was mentoring, Jamaal, is one of nine kids from an inner-city African American family. He immediately sensed my discomfort and sadness, and asked me if I'd like to talk. At first, I shrugged it off, dismissing my bad mood as something work-related, but he wouldn't buy it. He told me he could read people pretty well, having observed all his siblings for the 'many' 15 years of his life. Before I knew what was happening, I was spilling my guts to Jamaal, telling him all about my relationship woes and how I was developing a bad attitude at work."

"He listened to me better than I had ever been listened to before. He was just starting a job as a busboy at a steakhouse, and there I was, a white-collar executive, taking advice from him as he said: 'Just remember, all work is honorable, even if your heart isn't into it. And, about your breakup, just hang in there. Explore your feelings, and understand what they are trying to tell you. Accept them, don't let them destroy you, then move on.'"

"That was it. Something huge was lifted from me that day. I felt like a new man. My mentee had become my mentor."

Story 79

The appeal of mentoring as a prevention strategy lies in its linkage with the core resiliency efforts—the development and sustenance of a caring relationship between an adult and a young person.

If you read the statistics carefully about problems facing California youth today, the impact is staggering. Merely a cursory, flash-point glance at some of these dire numbers is enough to make you reel in despair. Imagine how tough it is for a child to survive stress like this:

- **Alcohol and Drug Use:** Among in-school youth, California experienced a dramatic rise in use rates of various illicit drugs in the 90s. The state exceeded the rest of the nation with intake of marijuana, inhalants, stimulants and LSD. Among dropouts, usage of alcohol, tobacco and other drugs rose sharply. Drug involvement for dropouts began at an earlier age and contributed to a wide range of personal, school, social and health problems.
- **School Failure:** In 1999, 52,000 California students in grades 10 through 12 dropped out. These kids will be less able to get a job, have a great likelihood of becoming parents, and, in the case of girls, drift toward the welfare system. With the inability to secure employment comes a built-in gravitation toward the drug culture.
- **Teen Pregnancy:** California, with the highest teen birth rate in the nation, averages 186 teen-mother births *every day*. That figure represents 11.7% of all live births. In 1998, there were 68,000 births to teens aged 15 to 19. Compounding this problem is the fact that over 10% of teen mothers test positive for alcohol or other drugs at the time of birth.
- **Gangs and Violence:** There are roughly 200,000 criminal street gang members in California. In Los Angeles, there are more than 500 gangs with more than 55,000 members. By the turn of the century, there could be a quarter of a million gang members in our state. *Gang members shoot at law enforcement personnel, deal in drugs, intimidate witnesses, victimize communities and deluge the criminal justice system.* In 1999, over 20,000 youth were arrested for violent felonies; 25% of all homicides in California are gang-related.

Add to this mix the sad fact that our nation faces a crisis of absentee fathers, with nearly one in four children living in fatherless homes, and you begin to see a clear relationship between the litany of problems and the lack of role models. Children who grow up without fathers are five times more likely to be poor, twice as likely to drop out of high school, and very likely to end up in foster care or juvenile facilities.

In the 1980's, it was popular among prevention programs to cite, identify and seek the underlying causes of social problems. This "risk factor" approach, while unveiling the linkage between drug abuse and social disorder, actually had the curious effect of making matters worse.

The practice of labeling youth as "at risk" in order to help them created its own sense of stigma and alienation. This "ostracism" even led to expulsion or exclusion from school programs and activities. Because of these adverse results, research shifted away from the "risk factor" method and toward more practical strategies for solution.

Several studies found that, contrary to expectation, individuals immersed in adverse conditions—such as children living with alcoholics or in poverty—frequently emerged as normal, well-adapted people. These individuals displayed certain "resilient" elements, including social competence, the ability to solve problems, autonomy, and a sense of purpose in their lives.

Prevention programs utilizing this perspective came to be known as resiliency efforts.

Critical elements within such resiliency programs include a caring and supportive relationship with another person; the clear communication of high expectations; and the opportunity to participate in and contribute to the social environment.

From this positive, head-on reality grasp came the phenomenon of mentoring, which is basically what healthy life should be were it not damaged. Mentoring programs are spreading rapidly and becoming more viable as effective strategy. Researcher Emmy Werner's studies of youth in high-risk environments identified that the presence of an adult relationship in a child's life was a vital factor in their ability to survive.

Extensive interviews with 500 disadvantaged youth indicated again that the supportive relationship between the youth and an adult was a key factor in their success. The appeal of mentoring as a prevention strategy lies in its linkage with the core of resiliency efforts—the development and sustenance of a caring relationship between an adult and a young person.

The combination of a strong theoretical base and a potentially plentiful supply of adult mentors provides a sound rationale for increasing governmental and public support of mentoring efforts.

Story 80

Enter the concept of tele-mentoring. View it as a cleansing solution surging through the satellite beams of television and the micro-thin channels of energy that fuel the internet.

It's truly wonderful the way the word "mentor" has crept back into popular usage. Not that it's one of those trendy, instantly contrived words, mind you. After all, its origins date back to the beginning of civilization.

So it's doubly refreshing that a word with genuinely timeless roots finds itself once again in the lexicon of the aware and the newly enlightened. It appeared on a recent episode of *Seinfeld*, for instance, that wacky comedy which prides itself on being about "nothing."

One of the zany female characters introduced her lady friend to someone as "my mentor." It wasn't used as a throwaway phrase or as a dig at a culture of old—it was uttered casually and sincerely.

And, laced throughout the seemingly endless menu of daytime talk shows, the word has taken on bold new significance. Psychological experts and counselors for the dysfunctional are frequently paraded onstage towards the end of a show to prescribe therapy, medicine or a guiding hand to the emotionally wracked panelists who have been chosen as guests.

Many times, these experts emphasize that what this child needs in life is a mentor, or what that recovering alcoholic/dope addict/sex fiend should seek out is a mentoring center. This is a marvelous experience to behold—it's just the genesis, a sneak peek, if you will, at what America would look like if mentoring became as commonplace as, say, TV watching.

Speaking of which ...

Baby boomers who were born roughly at the same time as the TV was conceived are the same people who used television as a babysitter/mentor while raising their own kids. Just think about *Sesame Street*. Here was a show that offered education, advice, values, entertainment, knowledge and opportunity—all components of a model mentoring program.

This is not to say that *Sesame Street* was a seamless package of everything a viewer needed to succeed in life.

On the contrary, real life always has a way of rearing its ugly head, and the kids of baby boomers are subject to the same kinds of emotional and maturity problems everyone in history has faced—even without "Big Bird's" all-embracing tenderness.

What "Sesame Street" couldn't provide was that ongoing, tactile, tangible, sustaining sense of continuation that's so carefully built into the most effective mentoring programs modeled after the Graeco-Roman civilization. If *Sesame Street* was the training wheels for the new kid on a bike, so to speak, then mentoring is a two-wheeler without the extra assistance.

Perhaps what's needed for an entire generation of videophiles, perhaps the thing that will provide the key missing ingredient is something we can refer to as ... tele-mentoring. It's simple. Where have the kids gone now for information, play and knowledge, those same kids that used to sprawl on the living room floor, hands cupped under chin, gazing slack-jawed at Bert, Ernie and the Cookie Monster?

Well, they've gone to two places, actually—the TV screen and the computer screen. Enter the concept of tele-mentoring. View it as a cleansing solution surging through the satellite beams of television and the micro-thin channels of energy that fuel the Internet.

Imagine tele-mentoring as a heroic savior dashing to the rescue of two media that are strong in information, weak in value. Conceive of tele-mentoring as the PBS of the Superhighway, offering role models and value systems that will offer fundamental, foundational options to empty-headed, vapid entertainment.

Think of the questionable material currently spewed by both TV and the Internet. One of the great arguments of the 90's has been about censorship, whether or not to install a so-called "V" chip that would monitor and delete offensive material. But where are our great thinkers? Instead of controls bordering on censorship that will ultimately fail, how about coming up with better, loftier, classier options?

Tele-mentoring could be simple and basic—it could teach young people how to balance a checkbook, where to search for work, how to get involved in church groups and social occasions. And it could be more complex and profound—it could visually display true heroes of history, genuine role models whose lives would lead the viewer from despair to hope, modern-day mentors that could easily trigger points of greatness currently dormant and passive in the viewer's mind and body and spirit.

The ancient Greeks and Romans had their forums and amphitheaters. And we would have tele-mentoring, as accessible as the nearest electrical outlet.

Story 81

She talked about her starving hunger for a mentor who could lead her down a righteous path for once in her life.

The Delta King hotel/restaurant in Old Sacramento is probably the least likely place in California you'd expect to find a quartet of gang members sipping drinks, but this was the scene one night in early September.

The ancient paddlewheeler is a grand old fixture of California lore. For decades, it used to sluice through the delta waters between San Francisco and the capital city, toting rowdy boatloads of Prohibition-era revelers, fancy Society matrons and erstwhile riverboat gamblers. Today, it sits permanently berthed on the edge of the Sacramento River, a shrine to a more gilded age, and tourists flock to view what has become a landlocked museum.

The Delta Lounge is a small, cozy bar finely detailed in mahogany and brass, its ambience clubby and exclusive. It's a quiet refuge on the top section of the boat usually frequented by politicians, lobbyists, and self-anointed movers and shakers. On this balmy, moonlit night, streaks of an orange sunset smudge the sky to the west. Four young black gang members have somehow found their way from the streets of Sacramento to this exclusive enclave, raising more than a few eyebrows.

The two guys sported bandannas and leather jackets. The two young women wore bare midriff outfits with liberally inked tattoos and a wide array of jeweled piercing. One could only wonder how the whorish ghosts from the boat's speakeasy past would look upon this scene.

"Four shots of tequila, barkeep," snapped one of the ladies. "We're holding a wake in memory of Tupac Shakur."

To the uninitiated, Shakur was an outlaw black gangster rap musician fatally gunned down in Las Vegas late in the summer of 1996. Long considered to be the baddest of the bad, his death at 25 surprised hardly anyone who knew of his self-destructive lifestyle. Three of the four gang members clinked their shot glasses together, but the fourth, a young lady in skin-tight jeans and smartly cropped raven hair, quietly slipped off her bar stool and headed for the piano in the far corner of the room.

"What's she up to?" snarled one of the male companions, who gestured to the barkeep to pour another round of tequila.

"Guess she's gonna rap somethin' out for Tupac," answered the other young lady.

"I didn't even know she could play the piano," laughed the second male, swiveling around in his seat with his elbows planted firmly on the shiny bar top.

But if they seemed surprised by their friend's brave move toward the piano, they were in for yet another jolt. Posing dramatically over the keys for several long moments, the young lady slowly began to play some of the sweetest classical notes in history, a medley of Chopin and Bach. The look of wonder on the faces at the bar was incredible. Rapt silence.

After about a half an hour of play, the sprinkling of other guests gave her a hearty applause, and then she wandered shyly back to the bar.

"Wassup, girl?" asked her stoolmate. "You never told me you could do that."

She stared solemnly into the untouched shot glass of tequila, then said: "You never asked."

"Well," laughed her friend, "let's drink to Tupac."

"No," snapped the newly discovered pianist. "He's dead, and, as my sweet mother used to say, good riddance to bad rubbish."

Now her friends were really intrigued. It was as though she had violated a basic Mafia tenet, and flashes of her sleeping with the fishes in the Sacramento River no doubt crossed her mind. Then she embarked on a long soliloquy "dissing" gang members, violence, bloodshed, and just about everything Tupac Shakur stood for. Hers was an act of brazen guts and courage her outlaw friends could only dream about ever acquiring.

The gist of her story was that Tupac's life was nothing, he stood for nothing, and he was the embodiment of evil. She talked about the need for good, solid, healthy role models in life—like her ailing grandmother who had taught her piano for years—and she talked about her starving hunger for a mentor who could lead her down a righteous path for once in her life.

"You guys glamorize Tupac's death like he was Martin or Malcolm or something," she concluded. "For me, it was like a giant weight had been lifted from my shoulders. He's gone, and he's left nothing, *nothing,* for me to learn from, except that I never want me or my kids to be like him."

This was a moment from the movies. She gulped down the tequila, slammed the empty shot glass on the bar, and walked off the boat alone, but her head held high.

Story 82

82

Mentoring has proven to be an effective device for transforming homeboys into heroes, for elevating failures into functional young adults.

San Francisco Mayor Willie Brown, in his first week of office, made a boldly original announcement that he'd like to see gang members on patrol inside some of The City's most beleaguered and violence-riddled public transit buses.

Even longtime Brown watchers snickered at his plan as a futile exercise in outrageous posturing. One gang member was heard to chortle on TV, "That's a lot like putting a rat in charge of the cheese factory, isn't it?"

But Willie Brown is a lifelong survivor of rough-'n-tumble, hardboiled politics, and he hasn't made many stupid calls. This particular tactic—though admittedly brushed with classic Brown flash—is far from stupid.

In fact, if you examine its roots, it is mindful of the entire mentoring movement that's sweeping the state. We are a nation in recovery, let's face it.

From 12-step programs to prison rehab efforts; from Big Brothers/Big Sisters to reality-based self-help outfits like San Francisco's Delancey Street Foundation; from Alanon to Adult Children of Alcoholics to Curtis Sliwa's Guardian Angels—we are a country of the walking wounded determined to heal.

Resuscitating America is what life in the new millenium is all about. We need not fear the kind of thinking that propelled Mayor Brown's gang statements; we need, on the contrary, to understand gangs so that we can do something to turn self-destruction into self-esteem.

A gang, in its purest form, is simply a longing for community gone awry. Gang members unify around rage when, in fact, given the tools and the attitude, they could just as easily unify around hope. This is where mentoring becomes a dynamic for change. Mentoring has proven to be an effective device for transforming homeboys into heroes, for elevating failures into functional young adults.

In an extensive paper on barrio gangs in Southern California, researcher James Diego Vigil listed the nature of peer influence in gangs into three types: friendship, direct confrontation and psychological disposition. Friendship was the most commonly cited reason for joining a gang, and entailed a desire to be with associates one had made earlier. This desire underscored a strongly felt need to be with peers that made an individual feel socially comfortable.

The second category, direct confrontation, involves a peer helping another to make a decision to become apart of the group, even though other conditions are also operative.

The third factor, psychological disposition, denotes fear or a tendency toward "loco" behavior stemming from a need for respect or protection.

Heavily sociological those terms may appear to be, the vocabulary is almost synonymous with healthier life choices that meet basic human cravings—sense of belonging, self-respect, social interchange, active involvement in a cause for greater good of the community. Searching for a social niche is one of the most basic human needs. Gangs, flawed and dangerous, fulfill that craving.

Take the case of Chuy, an 18-year-old male from Ontario, who reported: "The vatos made me feel like they cared. They really stick with you and back you up. When you were called 'Homeboy,' you felt good because you were one of them."

Or, hear it from Sam, a 16-year-old from Norco: "It got to the point where 'You back me up and I'll back you up!' You get respect by not backing down."

Larry, 20, from Chino, said that when he joined, "I never thought of us as a gang, we were just friends. As I got older, I knew that doing things like stealing was what they expected me to do. I didn't want to go against my friends."

Consider mentoring, then, as a zen-like flip-side approach to righting wrongs. Change through mentoring comes about not by badgering, but by showing a better way to the same basic needs. In the case of the youths cited above, what if they had met, early on, someone a little older, a little wiser, who had applied himself or herself to the tasks of self-improvement and the trait of self-respect?

What if a young person knew that he or she had the emotional support of older people, as well as the affection and safety net of belonging to positive community and church groups?

What if competence were rewarded and sloth challenged?

Mentoring programs across the country have demonstrated that not only are they beneficial to the individuals involved, but also to the ongoing health of a community. It's a simple matter of investing in tomorrow—but making the currency time, not just money.

Story 83

83

Mentoring is a powerful social tool that unleashes a myriad of growth-oriented enterprises, and Theard has yet to meet an adult mentor who has not gained dramatically from personal involvement in the lives of young people.

Working with the California Mentoring Initiative it gives me great pleasure to spotlight the community leaders in our state who are ironclad devoted and committed to making this initiative successful as part of the very fabric of our society.

California One to One was a Los Angeles-based community catalyst organized to support mentoring programs and to leverage resources at the national and local levels to expand effective mentoring practices.

The non-profit organization was formed in 1990 as a field office of the national One to One Partnership, Inc. As an advocate, catalyst and convener, One to One's mission was to "promote mentoring and economic empowerment—two strategies that connect committed adults with disadvantaged youth—for the sole purpose of changing lives for the better."

The dynamic executive director of California One to One was Patrice Theard, who oversaw mentoring programs throughout Greater Los Angeles, perhaps the single most mentioned and focused area for kids in trouble in the entire nation. After a sabbatical Patrice is now back working with the L.A. Mentoring Coalition.

"Mentoring works," says Theard, who speaks with love and compassion and hope about kids in trouble. "I love kids, and there's so much work that needs to be done. I have been fortunate enough to have a job where I can help facilitate people coming together all for the good of youth."

Theard is a tireless, vivacious, totally committed worker who brings joy and light to her calling. It is an absolute pleasure to highlight someone like Theard, because her commitment to make mentoring work in our society is changing the very texture of our society's fabric.

"I'm very encouraged about what I see happening," says Theard. "There are large numbers of people from all sectors of the community—differing ethnic backgrounds, religious, socio-economic, responsible, caring people—coming to the table to address how we're helping our kids realize their potential."

Patrice Theard orchestrates hope in a world too often seized with despair; she offers light for kids swathed in darkness. And she has no plans ever to quit.

"This is not like a job for me," she explains quietly. "This is life itself. I am doing this for the kids, yes, but the truth is I have gained so much from my involvement, I couldn't imagine doing anything else in life."

Mentoring is a tidal wave movement that is mobilizing all the engines of society. Corporate honchos are sacrificing weekends with their families to spend more time with needy young people. Brave mentees are addressing political leaders, including the governor himself, extolling the assets of mentoring and singing the praise of their mentors.

Leaders from the world of entertainment and big business are searching for new ways to bring kids into the mainstream of the workforce, establishing job opportunities as a solid way to enhance self-esteem issues.

Theard smiles as she speaks of mentoring's widening influence: "There is such a ripple effect that happens with mentoring. The specific link, the reason we're all doing this, is to direct our youth, and that is our priority. And we could talk for hours about the success stories of kids from all socio-economic levels and backgrounds.

"There used to be a profile of those kids who need mentoring, but the truth today is that all kids need mentors. That's where I see the positive steps toward making mentoring a part of the fabric of society—it's not just for a targeted group of people anymore.

"The challenges kids are facing today are so great, all kids need mentoring for one reason or another. Mentoring is not a panacea, but part of a successful strategy that works in concert and complement with other resources for kids."

Theard articulates the full-cycle revolution of mentoring's impact. She admits starting out doing this for the benefit of the kids, but now she sees the phenomenon as an all-consuming dynamic that effects every part of her life, from adult relationships to business dealings and personal interplay.

Mentoring is a powerful social tool that unleashes a myriad of growth-oriented enterprises, and Theard has yet to meet an adult mentor who has not gained dramatically from personal involvement in the lives of young people.

Says Theard: "The goal, you see, is to make mentoring natural the way it used to be, symbolic of the African proverb, 'It takes a whole village to raise a single child.' The goal is to not craft and create relationships, but that they will happen naturally, because it's the right thing to do and because people will want to do it. It's all so simple, that's the brilliance of the program."

Theard is swift to point out, however, that youth do this in conjunction with a strong program, because there's still the need for a solid structure. But what gladdens her heart is that youth, instead of waiting for an adult to come forward to apply empowerment from above, are actively seeking out mentors, asking teachers and parents for guidance. That's when you know the program has taken root, when the kid wants it so badly, he'll take the first steps.

"We're rebuilding communities," says Theard, "and therefore rebuilding society. We create love, friendship and understanding. People are becoming more tolerant and celebratory of commonalities, and from there we can really do anything."

Patrice Theard is a vital agent for social change.

84

Story 84

My mentor did not lay any guilt trips on me, and she didn't hammer me with shame or accusations. In her own beautiful way, she made me take a look at my life, and I came to the realization that I was one very unhappy person who had a bunch of growing up to do.

After seeing her today, it would be impossible to imagine her as a jaded gang member. Victoria, 21, is a pastry chef at a tiny, upscale Sacramento dining establishment.

Her face a beaming sun of positive radiance, her rich black hair tied tightly into a bun, Victoria works in the midst of a bustling crowd of earnest young kitchen employees. The telltale 21st century aroma of garlic mingled with mesquite fills the redwood and glass interior with vapors of quiet, cool elegance.

Victoria's bearing is a model of serenity. It was not always so. Six years ago, at the tender age of 15, Victoria was a mean-spirited gang member with no hope of tomorrow. She was not only hanging out with the "wrong crowd," she was the leader of the wrong crowd.

During a break in the action from the noonday lunch bunch, Victoria sits hunched over a caned chair turned backwards, lights a clove cigarette, and breathes a deep sigh that's many years deeper than her 21 years.

"I was doing it all," she says, "breaking into homes in the middle of the night, smoking crack cocaine, stealing from my parents and their friends, conjuring up all kinds of hustles and scams. I got pregnant, had an abortion, got beat up by my so-called boyfriend, started drinking myself into oblivion, and, basically, didn't care whether or not I woke up the next morning. I was a walking shell of nothingness, and I have no idea how I stayed alive to talk about it."

"The moment of clarity hit me a few years ago when that famous hostage situation hit the airwaves over at the electronics store. I knew one of the gang members holding those people hostage in the store, and when I saw him on TV, I was shaken to the bone. It hit me all at once, and I knew I had to do something drastic. While the whole city was watching this drama unfold on TV, I started to shake violently and cry like a baby. There it was, pictured for me in all its simplicity, the very essence of good and evil, and I was on the side of the devil."

"It had a major, profound effect upon me. All at once, I realized the person I had deserted long ago. Me. The little girl in me sobbed and sobbed all through the night. The next day, I walked to the Sacramento River and threw away my guns and knives, and then I started to write in my diary, and I haven't stopped writing since."

"My dream as a very little girl was to be a poet, but my parents snickered at me and laughed at my ambition. My Dad would get drunk and very angry, scolding me for not having more realistic goals and making fun of me for being too soft, and my mother was too wasted on drugs and pills to offer any hope for me at all."

"In effect, I didn't have any parents, but I was suddenly in this vulnerable position—no parents, no gang members, just me and this huge hole of depression. I was walking in Capitol Park one day—feeding the squirrels, if you can believe that!—and I saw this very beautiful Hispanic woman writing on a bench. We started talking, and it turns out she's a published poet and a member of Alcoholics Anonymous."

"We hit it off immediately, and talked for hours. She brought me to this restaurant where I work, and, in effect, became my mentor. Just listening to how she turned her life around after years of alcohol abuse was enough for me. I wanted what she had today, and I wanted it now."

"She didn't lay any guilt trips on me, and she didn't hammer me with shame or accusations. In her own beautiful way, she made me take a look at my life, and I came to the realization that I was one very unhappy person who had a whole bunch of growing up to do."

"Now I see where I went wrong. I don't want this to sound overly simple or too full of blame, but the truth is I didn't have anyone to tell me the difference between right and wrong. It never occurred to me that using crack was not only unhealthy, but also wrong. It never occurred to me that lying and stealing and cheating and hustling was downright wrong, but it is crystal-clear to me now that it is wrong.

"Today I have a feeling of righteousness that's so much more powerful and good than all the bad things I was doing. It's intoxicating. Doing something good for another human being, for example, was something that had never occurred to me, but now I try to do it at least once a day."

"My poet friend and mentor told me that it's all attitude, but sometimes you have to change your behavior first, and then the attitude follows. She was right on target."

"I'm one of the lucky ones. There are gang members dying every day. I'm not quite fully healthy yet, but pretty soon I'll be in a good position to be a mentor to one of them, as well."

Story 85

Mentors teach the children, who teach the parents and their peers, who teach other children and other mentors, round and round.

Working with the California Mentoring Initiative, it gives me great pleasure to spotlight the community leaders in our state who are ironclad devoted and committed to making this initiative successful.

One such individual is Kay Coffin, former executive director of Fresno County's Big Brothers/Big Sisters program. Coffin, who holds a Master's degree in social work, lives by a simple principle: "We can change the world one child at a time."

"As an organization," she says, "we worked for a single purpose, to prevent juvenile delinquency. What I do is not just a job, but a passion and a commitment. This is what drives me on a day-to-day basis, seeing the changes that occur in children when an adult enters their life to give them a feeling of self-esteem and worth. The changes are immediate. Teachers tell us that when a 'Big' enters the life of a child, the school grades improve swiftly and dramatically, friendships become more solid, and atmosphere at home takes on a more positive, glowing note."

Coffin administered a vast population of troubled kids, and her organization was a conduit of change for children scattered from Stockton to the Tehachipis, from Fresno to Bakersfield. Since 1968, Fresno Big Brothers/Big Sisters has been of service to over 5,300 kids and their families. While there, the agency implemented a new program called EMPOWER, which is a workshop designed to inform their kids and their parents and the volunteers about child sexual abuse issues.

One of Fresno's local TV stations—KSFN-Channel 30—made a commitment in 1991 to produce a *Wednesday's Child* segment, which promotes the concept of mentoring. Hosted by local TV newsman Rudy Trevino, the show generated a 30% boost in the number of volunteers wanting to become "Bigs." As of July 1984, nearly 200 kids have been matched with "Bigs" because of this show's involvement.

"Every one of our kids," says Coffin, "attests to the fact that were it not for our intervention, they'd be out on the streets dealing drugs, engaged in prostitution, and rotting away in a prison cell somewhere. Sometimes we got bogged down by the overwhelming magnitude of the problem, but if we just take it one kid at a time, the ripple effect has enormous consequences.

"It's the cycle and circle we frequently talk about. Mentors teach the children, who teach the parents and their peers, who teach other children and other mentors, round and round. The numbers show that there are 250,000 mentors statewide currently committed to one million kids, but also consider the impact all of these have upon the one million-plus parents of these children—it's staggering, and we are changing society one brick, one child at a time."

Coffin's agency set up a model approach to actively engage disenfranchised youth into the mainstream of society. The organization not only screens potential "Bigs" in thorough background checks and evaluations, but it also looks for kids in the "middle," which is to say the younger brothers and sisters of gang members before they themselves get initiated into the gangs. Coffin's people completed home visits, they analyzed what the client's most pressing needs may be, they measured and identified progress with teachers, and they constantly monitored the matches to see that they are always fresh, vital and effective.

"We were constantly aware of the simplest things," explains Coffin. "Mentors took kids to the Fresno State campus, for example, and the kids were wide-eyed at this whole new world of possibility, which has always existed in their neighborhood, but they've never had an adult introduce them to this reality. Nobody has ever said to them, 'You can do this, you're good enough.' And kids love to perform for adults, it's in their nature. They just need to be shown the tools, to be directed toward the potential."

Coffin talks longingly of the child's yearning for structure and discipline, which is provided by the "Bigs." She tells of a youngster's hunger for attention and company, describing a touching scene about a young boy waiting on his stoop a good hour ahead of his scheduled mentor's visit.

"Universally," she says, "we had mentors come in with preconceived notions about all the great things they are going to accomplish, and how they're going to change the lives of children, which is all true and accurate, but what astonishes our 'Bigs' is how much they themselves get out of the program. We only asked for one-year commitments from our mentors, but we got everywhere from three-to-10 year commitments. It simply means the world for these kids to have someone enter their lives who is not going to stray or disappear. It's the solidity of this relationship that vaults the kid into a productive adulthood."

The mentoring movement statewide is a groundswell of hope and accomplishment. With leaders like Kay Coffin and with the thousands of great citizens who are reaching out to our children, we are making giant strides toward making California a more civil place to live.

Story 86

To diehard activists like Jacks, Mentoring works better than anything else to combat the multi-headed monster of drugs, booze, teen pregnancy and school dropouts.

As someone who has witnessed the ripple effect of the mentoring movement reach tidal wave proportions, it is an absolute joy for me to highlight the heroes who have helped weave mentoring into the very fabric of society. One such hero is Martin Jacks, a 49-year-old community activist and longtime youth leader who is founding father and executive director of the Oakland Mentoring Center.

Jacks is built like a block of granite with the voice of a boom box. The Oakland Mentoring Center is situated in a striking, polished Victorian in Preservation Parkway, a stone's throw from the city's government center. Jacks and his staff make themselves available to urban kids who are seeking positive, alternative lifestyles to the dead-end cycle of drugs, alcohol and gang involvement.

"I wouldn't do anything else," says Jacks, a Peace Corps veteran who's also worked as a project organizer in Union City and Marin City. "I would do this for free. This is what makes my heart sing, to furnish for young people an entire universe of services that meet their needs."

Jacks and leaders like him have their work cut out for them. In more than 100 programs in five Bay Area counties—Alameda, Contra Costa, San Francisco, San Mateo, Santa Clara—there are an estimated 16,000 young people on waiting lists for volunteer mentors. To diehard activists like Jacks, mentoring works better than anything else to combat the multi-headed monster of drugs, booze, teen pregnancy and school dropouts.

"With mentoring," he says, "we are trying to artificially reconstruct the extended family. But family means different things to different cultures, and we are trying to come at it through that lens."

For a man whose very presence commands respect, Jacks gives as much respect as he receives. He recognizes that one of the underlying ailments of youth today is the deeply entrenched starvation to be taken seriously. Kids in the 90's are enormously sophisticated—they have access to the kinds of instant information their parents' formal education never approached. Combined with savvy, worldly street smarts and all the energy and passion that drives the engine of the young, kids today are a boiling cauldron of possibility.

But the one vital element that's universally missing from kids in crisis is the steady hand of a secure, caring adult role model.

"We don't come out of Mom's womb with these understandings," says Jacks, explaining the dynamics of mentoring. "We don't intuitively know what our values are and how we should behave. These things have to be taught. Now, if the society I have been born into hasn't given me that, I must look elsewhere. That's where mentoring programs designed for kids come into play."

Mentoring is a radical solution to the vexing problems of youth—it works effectively and lasts a lifetime. Shining lights like Jacks can attest to its effectiveness and longevity. They will tell you it's all very simple—kids yearn for respect from their elders, even when the opposite appears to be the case, and, once that key is open, their course for the future is fixed for a smooth sail.

"This is not a rigid, militaristic thing," says Jacks. "We don't say, 'This is what you're gonna get, and if you get it this way, you pass, and if you don't, you fail.' Our attitude is if the kid doesn't get it, it's the school that fails, and the teachers who fail to teach. If we look at it this way, the onus is on the adults, the program operators. There is not one modality. The true teacher takes into account all sorts of diverse cultures and backgrounds, to serve all people. Genuine teaching, you see, is about drawing from within the student. It's derived from the Latin word 'educare,' which means to draw out what's already in there. This opens up a whole new area of doing business. For the kid, it's now my choice, and this is the only kind of education, the only kind of mentoring, that sticks."

When adults are so committed to a program, to a vision, like mentoring, that's when kids breathe a collective sigh of relief and know that a sturdy foundation for guidance, direction and love exists for them. The depth of mentoring is that it calls for a long-term, sustaining relationship between mentor and mentee alike, and it is that solidifying endurance factor that allows a young mind to absolutely flourish as a person for the rest of his/her life.

One final flavor in Jacks' recipe for success is this: "Mentoring is about sustaining relationships, yes," he says, "but once a kid gets served by this program, then it's incumbent upon him to become a mentor to someone else—this is where the cycle gets complete and where you see the beauty and effectiveness of this whole reciprocal program."

Former President George Bush used to be fond of describing valiant, patriotic Americans and their endeavors to strengthen our country in boldly stroked poetic terms—"a thousand points of light" was his way of commending citizens of good heart. Martin Jacks is one of those points of light, and his beacon illuminates the way for thousands of once wayward youths.

Story 87

"In a word, mentoring has pushed me to a new level of recovery, and, for Pedro, it has liberated him to follow his true spirit, which for now is an academic career majoring in art history."

Because he requested anonymity, we'll call this man "Jack."

Jack sat on a bench on the shore of Oakland's Lake Merritt, and the intensity in his blue eyes matched the shimmer of the water's sparkling surface.

A salty-haired former sailor in his mid-fifties, Jack has the face of a man a few drinks on the wrong side of movie star handsome.

"I've been dry as a bone for 15 years," said Jack in his South-of-Market native San Franciscan Irish tongue. "But a while back, I grew weary of AA meetings.

"Don't get me wrong," he quickly added. "AA saved my life, no doubt about it. I was drinking over a quart of vodka a day, and by noon I didn't even know who I was anymore. After years of denial and destruction, my family finally intervened me into sobriety. I am what they call a 'grateful alcoholic.' Happy to be alive.

"But the meetings were beginning to burn me out. I'd look around the room, the same room that brought me back to sanity, and I'd stare closely at all the faces. These were good people, struggling people, people I still pray for, but I wanted to make a radical change from all this sadness.

"In the program, there is a vital step called making amends. I decided one day that the best way for me to make my amends was to do something positive and constructive for another human being.

"I was certain I was never going to drink again, because I knew how to internalize the 12 Steps without going to meetings. But it was time for me to do something larger with my recovery. I just couldn't face another meeting and get mired in my own sense of remorse."

Jack stared across the lake, the lines in his face forming a craggy smile.

"This may sound crazy," he laughed, "but instead of going to a meeting one night last year, I flipped on the Miss America pageant. One of the finalists, a young lady from Washington, I believe, said that her burning issue in life was mentoring adolescents in her home state.

"Now, I knew what the term 'mentoring' meant, but I didn't know there was an actual way for a common citizen like me to become a mentor. In this weird, ironic way, a Miss America beauty contestant seemed to be speaking directly to me.

"Something clicked. A great sense of clarity and well being came over me. The next morning, I called my Catholic pastor and asked him if he knew anything about mentoring in California. Somehow, I knew that I should become a mentor. It would be the perfect way for me to get out of my AA funk and do something meaningful for another human being."

Jack sat in silence for a few moments, measuring his next thoughts with careful deliberation.

"I've raised five kids and put them through college," he said, "but I have to tell you nothing has given me greater satisfaction than becoming a mentor to a very troubled Southern California youth.

"My business brings me to L.A. a couple days a week, so I met this young man, my mentee, through an organization just outside of South Central. We'll call him 'Pedro.' He's a former gang member, a recovering addict, a reformed thief, and now, thanks to the miracle of recovery, an accomplished painter.

"Very simply, I applied the tough-love principles of the AA program to my relationship with Pedro. I am not an authority figure, and I am not condescending. I am merely an example. I share with him the agony I went through during my years of waste and sickness. I spare no details. I tell him that it is a very thin line between good and evil, that macho toughness is quite often a thinly disguised search for self-esteem and respect.

"In a word, mentoring has pushed me to a new level of recovery, and, for Pedro, it has liberated him to follow his true spirit, which for now is an academic career majoring in Art History.

"And if there's one further message I'd like to impart, it's that there are thousands of recovering, healthy people like me who might be treading water in their 12-Step programs.

"I urge them with all my heart to consider risking their newfound comfort and sobriety in something totally new and different. I urge them to consider mentoring.

"There is a tremendous sense of personal salvation and satisfaction I gain from my time with Pedro, and I am extremely happy that a light went off above my head just in time to do something useful for society, not to mention for myself.

"Mentoring is fun, meaningful, significant and very important in today's complex world. And it's a whole lot easier than the first phone call I ever made to A.A.."

88

Story 88

Mentoring is a radical, grass-roots phenomenon that should not shun any effective medium striving to disseminate the message.

Any effort to make young adults feel good about themselves has to be applauded, and sometimes these efforts can be discovered in the most unlikely places.

Television has never quite mastered its full potential as an influential medium for good, but an exception simply must be made in the case of *Loveline*, which is a fairly new production airing late every night on MTV.

How to describe this amazing show? Basically, it's a call-in production hosted by two vastly different white males, both 30ish. One is a prank-prone, wisecracking, street smart class clown named Adam, the other is a stern, avuncular medical physician named Dr. Drew. They sit next to each other on a sofa, and a loveseat next to them carries a different cast of characters each night—sometimes the guest is a comedian, other times it's a rock group, actors, actresses, writers, raconteurs, all of them young.

Nationally syndicated, the show is a forum for discussion on sex and drugs. Adam plays the eternal devil's advocate—he's irreverent, takes risks, likes being outlandish and daring and fearless, and he's very hip. Dr. Drew is a more conservative doctor. He's precise, clinical, compassionate yet tough, extremely well-informed on addiction and abuse issues, and he's the perfect straight man for Adam's knee-slapping hysterics.

The audience is made up of teens and twenties bristling with sexual curiosity and penetrating queries about drugs, booze and other addictions. There's both audience participation and calls taken by phone. Thanks to the straight-talking doctor and his outrageous sidekick, there's little mincing of words and dancing around subject matter. Sex and drug references are very open and frank.

What becomes very clear after watching this show for several episodes is that, perhaps unbeknownst to themselves, Adam and Dr. Drew are role models to the throngs of young audience members and countless TV watchers around the nation. The two hosts assert themselves without equivocation on most controversial issues. They display leadership and an unconditional sense of loyalty with their listeners. Many times they've re-stated their central intent for being on the show—they're here to help.

Help is, indeed, what they have to offer. One look at the young, beautiful faces scattered around the living room-style studio, and you're immediately convinced that connections are being struck, convictions fortified, breakthroughs executed.

It's an unusual, highly refreshing format, especially given TV's woeful track record on programs that are actually contemporary and effective. What *Loveline* does is shrink the global village into a comfy, overstuffed couch where conversation and plainspoken soul-bearing is played out in a safe, educational environment. This show has accomplished that parents have tried to do for years.

Now, we have come to realize that mentoring is more complex and sustaining than what can be produced in an hour's TV programming. There is, for example, the component of a long-term relationship between mentor and mentee alike that obviously doesn't exist on a video production, but there are qualities of character displayed by the co-hosts that serve as adequate guidelines for effective mentors.

First of all, they speak of what they know from experience. The kids in the audience are hungry for a solid sense of direction, and Adam and Dr. Drew are near enough age-wise to provide some degree of peer advice and support.

Secondly, the hosts' style is non-threatening and not in the least patronizing. Except in the rare case where a caller exhibits immature or inappropriate behavior, Adam and Dr. Drew treat each troubled teen with respect and a no-nonsense dose of tough love.

Thirdly, like a microcosm of a fruitful mentoring relationship, the hosts take pains to detail referral services for the suffering caller. They realize that a kid's problems will not be solved in a snappy, tidy three-minute answer on the air, so they're scrupulous about mentioning support groups, medical specialists and drug counselors who will continue to respond to this, the kid's initial plea for help.

In California's burgeoning mentoring movement, we frequently speak about the ripple effect that gives this revolution sustenance. Mentoring is a radical, grassroots phenomenon that should not shun any effective medium striving to disseminate the message. The message is one of hope, and that is precisely what is being dished up by *Loveline*, a show that's giving kids permission to be cool by subscribing to righteous behavior.

Story 89

Mentoring programs have become an integral link in schools, corporations and community-based organizations forming viable professional and socially responsible alliances that can only serve to benefit the greater community at large.

When 15-year-old David Sherman of Oakland looks around him, he's surrounded by bullet-riddled buildings, abandoned cars and many vacant-looking people who can't steer him beyond the block.

But he dreams of living in a neighborhood where the schools are safe, clean and challenging.

David talks of being part of a community where people grow flowers in the yard and invite neighbors over for barbecues. He also wants to do work no one else has ever done, and create something new that will make people's lives better.

Though not quite sure what that something will be, David is adamant that it will be great.

David and his mother long for people, especially men, who will guide him in making good choices that will put him on a better path.

She worries that his life will be so cluttered with moral, social and financial obstacles that he just might not get to create that something that will make people's lives better.

David talks of dropping out of school, and feels the "boyz in his hood" are the only people who can really be his friends.

Alvin Easter is an executive with IBM, and longs to play a significant role in the lives of young African American men.

Easter grew up in a community where his father, brothers, uncles, teachers and ministers provided enormous support and served as role models for both his professional and social life.

Easter wants to provide younger men with some of the same support that kept him on course to a professionally and socially fulfilling life.

Were it not for the wonderful mentoring projects so dynamically in place in communities like Oakland, David and Alvin may never have been linked together on a path of mutual need and support.

While no one project or program can address the myriad of issues impacting our children's lives, mentoring programs can offer new friendships, access to vital resources and exposure to opportunities that have life-enhancing possibilities.

When combined with solid educational experiences, substantial differences in student achievement have been noted, as well.

Mentoring programs have become an integral link in schools, corporations and community-based organizations forming viable professional and socially responsible alliances that can only serve to benefit the greater community at large.

According to Ervin Flaxman, author of a study of mentoring for the Educational Resources Information Clearinghouse on Education, "Mentoring has become a powerful way to make a difference for youth who are isolated from adults in their schools, homes, communities and workplaces."

Mentoring can have two important assets for youth: It can improve the social chances of youth with social, economic, and educational disadvantages by giving them resources they might not have had, and it can give them some psychological support for new behaviors, attitudes and ambitions.

Mentoring must offer a mode of behavior that takes into account personal rules and conventions, as well as those of family and community. All adolescents need modeling and cultural support to reduce the confusion of the conflicting paths before them.

The mentoring experience can provide linkages to an extended network of social resources in which they have access to ideas, influences, information, people and other resources that are at some distance from them.

A good mentor must do two things: 1) Make a connection with the young person that establishes trust and fosters mutual respect and 2) Through the relationship, convey the message that they are a valuable human being, and, by working with you, they can expand their horizons and increase opportunities for success.

Mentors do this through words and achievements.

The delivery of this message may be in taking a young girl to the museum for the first time or a boy to see his favorite team play.

It may be in tutoring a difficult subject, or visiting the mentor's office. It may be spending time away from school and work, or enjoying a nature walk together. The focus of the mentoring program will help define the activity—the message is the same.

Mentoring is effective—the one-on-one attention for a sustained period of time for children who need support and guidance can make a difference in their lives.

The mentor is a role model. Mentors are, almost by definition, successful and motivated. They can pass on these qualities to a young person simply by spending time with him or her.

The best mentoring experience not only provides the student with an important relationship, but also empowers the student to use the experience in planning and working for the future.

Story 90

In one outstanding moment in time for Blake Sr. all his insecurities about what kind of mentor he is been came to a final place of peace…

This is a father's dream mentoring experience:

In 1985, Blake Sr., a Northern California writer, went through an excruciatingly painful divorce with his wife of nine years.

Choosing the path of healthy recovery over bitter acrimony, Blake Sr. recommitted himself to being an excellent father to his two sons, then five and eight years old.

Never once did he express chagrin or anger toward their mother, a wonderful, devoted parent. He was determined to devote all his energies to being an excellent provider and guardian to his young charges.

His fatherhood blossomed, even though it was raw and painful to wait two weeks at a time for the every-other-weekend custodial arrangement.

Both he and his ex-wife absolutely cherish their children, and the boys benefited greatly from two sources of quality love, rather than a single source of fractured attention that would have occurred had the marriage continued.

Today, 11 years since the divorce, the two boys are doing better than fine, and the parents are once again close friends.

Francis, now 19, has won a scholarship to a college on the East Coast, and Blake Jr., 16, is flourishing as a high school junior in Sacramento.

No parents could have two more different sons. Francis is a risk-taker and a gung-ho organizer, a natural-born leader. Blake Jr. is more reflective and cautious, possibly more sensitive and meditative. Both earn high praise from their friends' parents, the ultimate adolescent compliment, who say they can't wait to see what career choices the boys will make.

Blake Sr., now 49, is a worrier. The divorce rocked him severely, and he's never been quite certain that his fatherhood has really taken deep roots. But, since this recent episode involving Blake Jr., he can finally take a deep breath and relax securely.

Neither boy has even been effusive or overly affectionate toward their father. They're boys, and Dad accepts that. In one outstanding moment in time for Blake Sr. all his insecurities about what kind of mentor he's been came to a final place of peace.

Blake Jr. had just passed his driver's license test, a zenith rite of passage in the life of a teenager, and he was ready to tackle the State's freeway and road networks.

His dad was less ready. In fact, he was flat-out terrified.

It was time for a father-son talk, which went something like this:

Blake Sr.: "I have to admit, while I'm extremely proud of you for the way you've handled school pressures and your social life, that I'm really nervous about you driving. I mean, you're still my baby." (Blake Jr., according to his new driver's license, is six-feet-three inches, 170 pounds.)

Blake Jr.: "Dad, you worry too much. We have driver training now. I've had my permit for almost a year, I'm very responsible and cautious. You have nothing to worry about."

Blake Sr.: "Yeah, but ... there are some really dangerous maniacs out there. All of a sudden, some lunatic appears in your rearview mirror going 90-100 mph., and, well, I don't even want to think about the rest"

Blake Jr.: "Dad, chill. I've been watching you drive all my life. Those trips between your house and Mom's, I was always in the backseat curled up with my blanket, but my eyes were open. I saw the way you drove so carefully. I saw the respect you gave other people in all your dealings. I learned from you, Dad, how to be a person, and you set a great example."

Blake Sr.: "Yeah, but ..."

Blake Jr.: "Dad, there are no 'Yeah, but's,' believe me. Francis and I know how much you love us. We watched you on weekends and during those great summers. We know how devoted you are to us. We know how much it hurt you to be away from us, but we were so proud of the way you always kept a cheerful face for us. We learned about how to handle hurt and stress from you, Dad. You are our teacher, you are our mentor. We will not let you down."

Blake Sr.: "You mean, you don't think I've come on too strong or been too overbearing?"

Blake Jr., laughing: "Well, you've had your moments! But don't think I'll ever forget those countless hours you played catch with us, those nights you gave up going out with dates or friends just so you could be with us. You've taught us that sacrifice is what fatherhood is all about. But now it's our turn to show you that those sacrifices were not in vain. It's time for you to let go, and not be worried. It's time for you to receive from us, Dad."

Blake Sr.: "Are you saying you really did see all the things I did for you guys?"

Blake Jr.: "We never missed a beat. And we always paid more attention to your actions rather than your words. You showed us through your relationships and business contacts how to make our own way in the world, and you gave us the tools to build our own lives. You've been our mentor, Dad. Thank you."

Story 91

It is in this mix of mentor and mentee, in this stew of positive, hopeful give-and-take that the bridge to the 21st century will be constructed with the firmest foundation of all—a resounding "Yes!" To youth's question: "Do we have a future?"

As we march as a nation into the 21st century, building a bridge from one incredible era to another yet unseen epoch, I like to think of mentoring as sign posts of progress that plot our path.

If America has ever been united around one central theme, it is that our finest investment as a country is in our children.

As proof of America's boundless sense of know-how, this fundamental tenet of freedom and democracy has moved from the passive state of cliche to an active mode of full-tilt community participation.

From an airline pilot in Flagstaff, Arizona, to a hardware store owner in Burbank, California; from a ballet teacher in Manhattan to an astrologer in Reno, Nevada; from a furniture manufacturer's representative in Dallas, Texas, to a Sunday school teacher in Boise, Idaho—these are American mentors nudging the nation's youth toward maturity.

No longer is it enough for middle Americans to sit around bemoaning the plight of their brightest hope.

Granted, the statistics swilling around the problems of youth today are billboards of disaster—gangs are steeped in guns and violence; baby-faced girls are struggling with the grim reality of pregnancy; treatment centers are swinging-doors for lost young souls laced with early scars of drugs and booze; and school dropout rates are astronomically high.

And yet ...

There is a new sense of pride bursting America's seams.

It is the realization echoed long ago by a President named Kennedy that ... to whom much is given, much is expected.

Call it the Peace Corps come home. Call it America's wayward foreign policy turned domestic and functional. Call it the essence of the American dream.

Call it what you will, but recognize it for what it is.

American adults by the thousands are sacrificing their lives and their much-deserved free time in dedication and devotion to troubled teens. It's that simple.

But, mind you, this is not empty-headed do-goodism, no hollow exercise of successful people "talking down" to less fortunate individuals.

If mentoring in the 90's has demonstrated anything pointing to the fact that it is a way of life here to stay, it is this:

Mentoring begins with a quiet acceptance of the youth in crisis. Remember that what got him into trouble in the first place was the loss of self—little or no self-esteem passed down from parents who often times have vanished; no foundation of confidence upon which to witness self-esteem blossom into self-awareness; and absolutely no clue about how to survive and thrive in a world that has become incredibly cold and closed to individuals' dreams.

The mentor of today is not a vertically situated dispenser of goods and services. That would be futile and short-lived.

The mentor of today accepts and embraces the culture from which the mentee has sprung, albeit crookedly. The mentor is not judgmental or authoritative, aloof or arrogant.

The mentor is, however, fiercely loyal, unconditionally supportive, open-minded, liberal with suggestion and direction, and, most importantly, every bit as positive, hopeful and loving as the mentee never saw from a parent who never was.

The mentor does not present himself as the only example of success. Rather, he accepts his mentee for who he is, emphasizes that he is a worthwhile person, and creates an attitude and an atmosphere in which the mentee can finally, within his own cultural heritage, begin to realize his dreams.

What is more wonderful than that?

Forget, if you can, the poison spewed forth from fat-headed radio hosts and mean-spirited political demagogues who disdain multi-culturalism, who blame the moral turpitude of youth for their own problems, and who have never done anything for anyone.

Dwell, instead, upon these inspired new couriers of hope, harbingers of courage, who have profited from the American experience and who now accept their role in the process as responsible givers of dreams.

It is in this mix of mentor and mentee, in this stew of positive, hopeful give-and-take that the bridge to the 21st century will be constructed with the firmest foundation of all—a resounding "Yes!' to youth's question: Do we have a future?

Will you cross that bridge with us?

92

Story 92

With the California Mentor Initiative, we are able to introduce stable, sustaining, responsible and caring role models for the young person suffering from neglect and isolation.

If you've ever pondered the truly awesome dynamics of the recent Sierra firestorm, you can apply the metaphor to grasp the impact of the California Mentor Initiative upon the state.

Think of the firestorm as the tempestuous, volcanic raging of teenage violence—out of control, unconditional damage, insane fury, wanton devastation.

These are, in truth, the consequences of the social epidemic ravaging today's teenagers—the dire results from drug and alcohol abuse, teen pregnancy, gang attachment and educational breakdown.

In the Sierra, chaos reigns. Once dignified spires of pine are reduced to sinister skeletons of their former selves. Once verdant hillsides, lush with carpet-like foliage, are now barren fields of dust and ashes.

Innocent young animals, recipients of the collateral damages of nature's madness, wander hysterically and without direction through their playgrounds turned to peril. Like members of a dysfunctional human family who are not directly responsible for the fire's origin, these poor souls inherit the symptoms of the catastrophic conflagration. No one is spared fire's furor.

When it comes to psychological holocaust brought on by the social epidemic cited above, the firestorm analogy is strikingly clear. Extend the metaphor to its positive, logical conclusion.

Shortly after the Sierra incineration, yellow-garbed forest workers dot the hillside like welcome spring poppies. Using the cinders themselves as nourishing fertilizer, the quiet workers plant sprigs of baby pines, sturdy bright green sprouts of new life and hope.

Reforestation has begun. We do not bemoan horrendous tragedy, and give up on life. Instead, we take the remnants of disaster and use them as tools of renewal. Thus is the cycle of life as old as Genesis. Hope springs eternal.

The California Mentor Initiative is playing a similar role of natural redemption with our state's younger citizens. Beset with a social epidemic whose perimeter of wreckage exceeds our worst fears, we do not shirk the responsibility to aid and comfort the afflictions of our young.

The rage of a young person under siege from within has to do with the neglect he's suffered from an absentee parent. We must understand this, because it goes to the heart of every misdirected act of violence, every bad choice eroding the core of that person's heart.

With the California Mentor Initiative, we are able to introduce stable, sustaining, responsible and caring role models for the young person suffering from neglect and isolation.

The adolescent doesn't need someone in authority dictating a laundry list of restrictions and regulations. Remember this is a wily, street-savvy wild animal who's already survived severe restraints and obstacles. This is a person starving for freedom, gasping for independence.

Sierra workers re-seeding ravaged forests don't need to hover around the new seedlings. They've provided faith, a sense of self-esteem, and the nourishment of the stable young sprig comes from deep within its own natural instincts to survive and thrive.

So it is with mentors and protégés. This is not a possessive, repetitive relationship. It is a friendship rooted in the finest interpretation of letting go.

The adult role model provides the mentee with everything he's never had—someone he can depend upon and turn to, someone who can provide solid direction and experienced advice, someone who recognizes the will to live throbbing with its own chosen pace and rhythm, someone, in a word, who will cherish that person's individuality and unique place in the world.

From the ashes rises the Phoenix. Mentoring is as simple as that. We have never had to argue its merits, and we have never had to rationalize its worthiness. Its success speaks for itself in the thousands of strong young pines dotting the hillsides of California's citizenry, a reforestation of respect and esteem.

Story 93

Those of us who have been working to implement the California Mentor Initiative for the past six years are making giant strides in re-sodding the once parched soil of adolescent development in this state.

Statistics can too often numb us into insensibility, but one fact of California life might just awaken in us a much-needed jolt of outrage.

It is this—70% of California's prisoners come from homes without fathers.

That is an astounding piece of data, not just because it explains the behavior of thousands of incarcerated felons, but also because it contains some good news as well.

The solution is in the problem. Now that we know there is a direct relationship between fatherless homes and prisoners behind bars, then we can proceed to change this reality. And, in fact, we already are.

Those of us who have been working to implement the California Mentor Initiative for the past six years are making giant strides in re-sodding the once parched soil of adolescent development in this state.

In California, there are upwards of two million kids who simply don't have a caring adult who holds aspirations for them, who is present for them in their lives.

The California Mentor Initiative introduces a significant adult role model to these kids, and what we are witnessing is a remarkable revolution of hope that is reconstructing the state one child a time.

Fatherlessness likely equals incarceration. Not the most profound of sociological equations, perhaps, but one that exists in all too vivid tones in our society today.

From not knowing how to study to being clueless about where to find employment; from being ignorant about the facts of life to becoming the teen mother of an unwanted infant; from being isolated from one's own dreams and goals to having every door in life slammed in one's face; from simply not knowing the difference between right and wrong to acting out one's rage in lawless acts of irresponsible crime and mayhem—all of these are clear and telling symptoms of children without solid adult direction.

We could spend anguished days of hand-wringing guilt bashing ourselves about why we abandon these young lives when they need us most. We could, in fact, go mad trying to figure out why, on God's great planet, there are so many of us who are good parents who have to strive against the negative tide of those who appear to thrive on indifference toward their young.

But these would be futile acts of self-indulgence at a time when the young don't need yet another form of abandonment. What they need is what we already have in place—the California Mentor Initiative, an inclusive movement of the human spirit that is making a profound and lasting statement in the war against isolation.

By identifying young, wayward teens at an age when adult direction is pivotal and critical, by introducing screened, stable, caring and responsible adult role models into their lives, we are actually allowing the kids to save themselves.

To truly understand the nature and the efficacy of the California Mentor Initiative, it is important to know this is not a rescue mission imposed from above. This is not a squadron of adult volunteers responding *en masse* to a 911 call.

This is, quite simply, a way for disenfranchised teens to empower themselves. They might not even understand the process, they don't even have to identify the powers that are unleashed, but what is happening is that they are profoundly and indelibly touched and changed by the mere presence of someone who—at last—cares enough to introduce the kid to himself.

We live in an era of tremendous awareness and talent among the young. There is an abundance of accessible information and a surplus of ways to cultivate raw ability into manifest creativity. The only thing holding back the aspirations of the young is the emotional impediment that springs like a weed from not having a loving presence in the person of a caring role model.

The California Mentor Initiative puts this apparatus of a working relationship firmly in place, and the young person is finally free to discover himself, place himself squarely onto the stage of the real world, and proceed with life with hopes, goals, and achievable dreams.

So then ... if 70% of the state's prisoners come from fatherless families, isn't it crystal-clear logic to see that the California Mentor Initiative is a grand idea whose time has come?

94

Story 94

Shortly after going to AA and emptying his heart of all the evil things that were keeping him emotionally oppressed, he got a new job, an AA sponsor, and, most importantly, a spiritual relationship with God that has kept him buoyant and on the right track.

Members of Alcoholics Anonymous frequently talk about the ways they have escaped their addiction, and one often-heard remedy is behavior modification, an extremely effective tactic that can be applied to the problems of youth in today's complex world.

Alcoholism, as we have come to know it, is a progressive illness, which means that the suffering victim can beat himself up for years and years before coming to any sound resolution of recovery.

Behavior modification is a coldly clinical term that, boiled to its simplest core, begins with making your bed in the morning. One member of AA laughs at himself when he recounts how this incredibly easy task became, for him, incredibly daunting.

At a meeting one day, he shared how, in the midst of his heaviest drinking bouts, he could never bring himself to making his bed in the morning. Perhaps it was the chaos in his life brought on by the disease or the depression that went along with binge drinking, but he found himself powerless to do this simplest of tasks most Americans can perform sleeping.

He doesn't know what triggered the change, but one day he grew sick and tired of feeling sad and blue that he astonished himself by making his bed. That, in turn, led to his beginning each day on his knees, because that was how he could reach all the sheets hanging down everywhere, which induced him to start saying his prayers every morning.

He was amazed. His days became brighter, he felt better about his very modest one-bedroom apartment in downtown San Francisco, and he began to buy things to decorate his simple pad. Ever so slowly, a new sense of freshness, redemption and resurrection began to take root in his heart, and he started attending AA meetings with a vengeance.

Shortly after going to AA and emptying his heart of all the evil things that were keeping him emotionally oppressed, he got a new job, an AA sponsor, and, most importantly, a spiritual relationship with God that has kept him buoyant and on the right track.

In his "shares" at AA meetings, he talks about this bed-making experience frequently. What he discovered was that, after years of berating himself for having a bad attitude and a negative slant on life, he finally realized that if you want to change your attitude, you must first change your behavior.

This was a blockbuster revelation to him. He had always assumed there were people in life blessed from birth with a rosy outlook. His lack of self-esteem reinforced the notion that there are those with a good attitude and those with a bad attitude. Once stuck, there was no hope.

However, as circumstances forced his hand and got him to literally fall on his knees to make his bed one morning, he began to see that each man is responsible for all the good that comes to him, and he must work to discover the key that unlocks the mystery.

Change your behavior first, then the attitude will follow. What a profound lesson for this man, who began to see that it is the tiny baby steps in life that lead to an accumulation of achievement, even if they seem totally insignificant or boring or menial at the time.

This is a vital lesson for children today, as well, too many of whom have no clue that you have to invest in life in order to reap something at harvest time.

Children need to be told that being born with a good attitude just doesn't happen—we are born with the tools to discover that good attitude, and those tools help us operate all those hundreds of daily tasks that we often find distasteful or overly tedious.

But all these tasks are character builders that lead to a positive, mature attitude where real happiness is finally possible.

In California today, two million children are absent from a significant adult role model, someone who can impart to them such simple and necessary lessons as this. This is how the California Mentor Initiative came into existence, to create an apparatus whereby stable mentors can enter the lives of needy young people to guide them through the treacherous pitfalls of adolescence and introduce them to life choices that will be sane, healthy and fulfilling.

For you to be a mentor is as simple as ... making your bed.

Story 95

But as wild and as dangerous as Selena may have wanted to be, the love she felt from her father was an unbreakable bond, and you knew she would always honor and respect the communion that existed between them.

A movie currently making the rounds of HBO TV gives a very vivid portrayal of true mentoring.

The movie is *Selena*, a biographical drama about the immensely popular young Mexican-American pop singer whose life was so tragically ended in gunfire from a disturbed and once-trusted employee.

The character of Selena is played by Jennifer Lopez, a fine actress who captures the tension that existed in the person of Selena—all the clashing emotions and turbulent life struggles that might've gone astray were it not for the imposing presence of her stern yet loving father played by the brilliant actor Edward James Olmos.

Anyone interested in becoming a mentor should watch the Olmos character carefully.

There is no question that he loved his daughter unconditionally. He knew early on that she possessed immense talent, and he took it upon himself to shepherd her life accordingly.

Selena positively bubbled with adolescent enthusiasm, exhibiting a limitless hunger for life that became documented in her music and the way she reached out to her adoring throngs. She was the Hispanic Madonna, maybe not as irreverent or brash, but certainly as vulnerable and mortal.

Olmos had the unenviable task of walking that precarious parental tightrope between discipline and letting go, and he played the part effortlessly.

Selena was a flirt and mild troublemaker, and you attained the feeling as the film unfolded that she would've been a gang member or an angry dropout or an unwed mother were it not for the watchful eye of her strong father who had to endure all the trappings that come to young rock stars—foolish groupies, groping hustlers, opportunistic hangers-on offering drugs and booze for friendship and love.

But as wild and as dangerous as Selena may have wanted to be, the love she felt from her father was an unbreakable bond, and you knew she would always honor and respect the communion that existed between them.

Her father was an honest, hard-working man, and he wasn't about to let his daughter drown in a world of sycophants and sideshow hucksters. He knew his fatherhood was never finished, that fame could not strip him of his responsibility to Selena, and vice versa.

As Selena sailed through the passages of her life—be it a new CD or an engagement to her future husband or a crisis about disciplining her craft—you watched with admiration as Olmos exhaled with a spirit of humble resignation at each step in her development. Selena was free to make her own choices because of, not in spite of, the honorable parenting offered by Olmos.

It is with effective mentoring—it's all about trust, respect, and tapping into the true potential of the mentee. It has nothing to do with control, loveless discipline, possessiveness and fear of letting go from the mentor.

Mentors don't rescue kids and they don't micro-manage their lives. Kids have been given incredible resources that need to be supported, affirmed and gently urged out of them by caring adult role models.

The potential for full personhood resides within the individual, and they need to spend quality time with an experienced adult who has the wisdom and the genuine loving interest to unlock this secret from the hearts of the young—namely, that each of us is directly responsible for the path that will eventually unroll in front of us. There is simply no other way.

If each one of us, like the Olmos character in the movie, does just a little bit to enhance the life of someone young and troubled, then together we can make an extraordinary difference on the landscape of our communities.

Our children need our time and personal input, not our money that merely shoos them away. Many things in life can wait, but our children cannot. Selena's father, like many mentors actively working with kids today around California, is a profound beacon, a clarion of hope, for the future of our young ones.

Story 96

"With Mentoring," says Jacks, "We are trying to artificially reconstruct the extended family. But family means different things to different cultures, and we are trying to come at it through that lens."

This imposing figure is the executive director of the Oakland Mentoring Center, where kids come to find positive, alternative lifestyles to the dead-end cycle of drugs, alcohol and gang involvement.

The 49-year-old community activist and longtime youth leader brightens when asked if he has a conviction that his chosen path in life is the right one.

Hear it from Michael Gibson, a 20-year-old reformed gang-banger, drug dealer and thief: "Martin has taught me that being a man is not about how much money you make. I learned to value my life, all life, over material things.

"I'm making about $20,000 a year now, and I used to make that in a day as a drug dealer. It's hard, but it's AC Transit now instead of a Lexus or a Ford Explorer."

Jacks sees mentoring as a healthy replacement for the parents and role models these kids never had.

"Part of my job," he says, "is to help adults understand the appropriate perspectives for addressing kids' issues. If our concerns are to help young people, then there must be a certain attitude conducive to helping young people.

"It's not just giving help, but also cultivating a healthy relationship, not one that's regimented or punitive. It must be one that's designed to take care of kids' needs, to help kids grapple with the things that I have grappled with as someone who has moved through life.

"An awful lot of young people are drawn to criminal activity because they simply don't have access to adults who can help them develop appropriate attitudes and behaviors to become productive citizens.

"We don't come out of Mom's womb with these understandings—we don't intuitively know what our values are and how we should behave. These things have to be taught. Now, if the society I have been born into hasn't given me that, I must look elsewhere. That's where mentoring programs designed for kids come into play.

"This is not a rigid, militaristic thing, mind you. We don't say, 'This is what you're gonna get, and if you get it this way, you pass, and if you don't, you fail.'

"Our attitude is if the kid doesn't get it, it's the school that fails, and the teachers that fail to teach. If we look at it this way, the onus is on the adults, the program operators. There is not one modality. The true teacher takes into account all sorts of diverse cultures and backgrounds, to serve all people.

"Basically, if I have a program designed to educate kids toward the acquisition of certain values, I as a teacher must have more than one learning style.

"Genuine teaching, you see, is about drawing from within the student. It's derived from the Latin word 'educare,' which means to draw out what's already in there. This opens up a whole new area of doing business. For the kid, it's now my choice, and this is the only kind of education, the only kind of mentoring, that sticks."

Jacks draws a huge breath, then gazes for a moment upon a teenaged kid tending to the flowers outside the stately Victorian that houses Jacks' office.

"Mentoring has already worked its way into the fabric of society," he says. "It is definitely one of the catalysts for how we work with kids in the future. Back in the old days, we used to have very stable family situations with not many surprises.

"Things aren't as fixed anymore. Families are transient. The average person will have three or four careers in a single lifetime. The basic family structure has changed radically. We have to find modalities and mechanisms that fit the changing times.

"Mentoring is a means of artificially structuring the extended families and inserting adults in young people's lives in a long-term, sustaining, mutually positive relationship. Families used to do it naturally, now we have to do it artificially.

"And it's so much more than preventing criminality—it's about nurturing and making yourself available to the needs of a kid who sometimes is just a kind word away from turning the corner into adulthood. It's an attraction to positive living. Remember that gangs are structured very close to how functional communities are structured—there's leaders, a code of discipline, uniforms and a sense of mission and community. Gangs are just a thin layer away from active, healthy engagement in positive community activism.

"And most of the kids we serve are not of the criminal mentality, anyhow. Some are 4.0 students who just happened to be born into a family where the parents never went to college, for instance, and they merely lacked a sense of direction.

"This is what apprenticeship programs are all about—talk to someone who's been out in the real world for awhile. The trades, for example, where you learn the nuts 'n bolts of living and working. It's about igniting the desire for a kid to stand on his own two feet, learning how to manage your money if you only work a certain amount of time per year.

"So, mentoring is about sustaining relationships, yes, but once a kid gets served by this program, then it's incumbent upon him to become a mentor to someone else—that's where the cycle gets complete and where you see the beauty and effectiveness of the whole reciprocal program."

On the other end of the state is Patrice Theard.

"From my heart," says Theard, who speaks with warmth and love about kids in trouble, "I've been doing this for six and a half years in Los Angeles, eight and a half years in my life. Mentoring works, and I have great compassion in my heart for kids. I love kids. There's so much work that needs to be done, but I have been fortunate enough to have a job where I can help facilitate people coming together all for the good of youth.

"I'm still doing it after all this time because it's so powerful.

"I'm very encouraged about what I see happening, in terms of the kinds of people, the large numbers of people from all sectors of the community, all ethnic backgrounds, religious, socio-economic, responsible, caring people who are coming to the table to address how we're helping our kids realize their potential.

"People understand the concept of mentoring. Yes, there's that whole educational piece that we still very much have to do, to help people understand just how powerful it is and how it really does work as a strategy when it's complemented with other resources for youth. But, at this time, it's very exciting when you can be part of the solution, where there are so many people coming together.

"It's very, very exciting, because we're going to reach that many more kids because of it.

"This is not like a job for me, this is life itself. This is what I choose to do, and I'm so fortunate to be in this position. I am doing this for kids, but the truth is I have gained so much from my involvement.

"We say to mentors all the time—there's so much power in helping other people, and seeing the results of young persons coming into their own and appreciating themselves, solidifying their strengths and positive characteristics.

"People often ask me, 'Why are you doing this? You've been doing this for so long. It's so sweet.' People just don't understand, but once you do this, nothing could possibly compare.

"What completes the cycle, of course, and what gives us ultimate satisfaction is when a mentee turns around and mentors another, and we're seeing more and more of that. Mentees are doing that as a priority for their own lives. That is so powerful.

"I think we are headed toward mentoring becoming a part of the fabric of society. We have broken major ground. The thread is there, the needle and thread are in motion, but we still have work to do. Our goal and vision is for mentoring to become a part of American life. It's why we're still working at this.

"The goal, you see, is to make mentoring natural the way it used to be, symbolic of the African proverb, 'It takes a whole village to raise a child.' The goal is not to craft and create relationships, but that they will happen naturally, because it's the right thing to do and because people will want to do it.

"We are seeing more and youth becoming comfortable enough to seek out mentoring relationships, due in part to work people are doing in the mentoring movement to advocate that youth think about people they admire and whom they would like to learn from, whose career they would like to emulate.

"We also advocate that youth do this in conjunction with a program, because there's still the need for the structure of a program. But instead of managing it where youth come into an agency to wait for an adult, they are instead seeking out a mentor, asking their teachers and parents for further guidance.

"We're seeing that happen more and more. And the attraction to good is so much more compelling than an attraction to criminality. We have to believe in our youth. They want the American dream like everyone else.

"We have to realize how very devastating it is to youth to have adults think negatively of them, to know that they are stereotyped in so many cruel ways. We have a newsletter coming out that was entirely produced and written by young mentees, and the cover story is about eliminating stereotypes, and it's a pitch to adults to become mentors.

"This young person who wrote the story makes an eloquent plea for adults to become mentors, because we have so many kids who are waiting to get a good mentor. Her theme is, 'We're not all bad people.' It's a very moving piece. She asks that we not be stereotyped just because of our neighborhoods, or how we dress, look and talk. We are good people who need mentors, and that's a cry for help and assistance. It's very real.

"There is such a ripple effect that happens with mentoring, also. The direct link, the reason we're all doing this, is to direct our youth, and that is our priority. We could talk for hours about the success stories, kids from all socio-economic levels and backgrounds.

"There used to be a profile of those kids who need mentoring, but the truth today is that all kids need mentors. That's where I see the positive steps toward making mentoring a part of the fabric of society—it's not just for a targeted group of people anymore.

"The challenges kids are facing today are so great, all kids need mentoring for one reason or another. Mentoring is not a panacea, but part of a successful strategy that works in complement with other resources for kids.

"In a successful mentoring relationship, you have two people who are giving love and guidance, giving unselfishly to each other, because it's mutual, so then you look at those two, then multiply it by the numbers of people who are doing the same thing, and we are rebuilding our communities. That is the ripple effect, and it is very, very real.

"And this is long-term. Mentors are going to be kinder to their employees and employers at work, and everyone becomes kinder to each other. This concept is reinforced and applied, and it sticks, changing your life forever.

"We are rebuilding communities, and therefore rebuilding society. We create love, friendship and understanding—people are beginning to understand how we got to where we are today. They become more tolerant and celebratory of commonalties, and from there we can really do anything."

97

Story 97

Mentors are vital to these young people because mentoring provides the texture, flavor and appeal to change young people's environment and future.

In his clumsy, yet heartfelt stabs at rhetoric, former President George Bush was fond of talking about "a thousand points of light" that illuminated America's path for struggling citizens.

The illusion was a poetic attempt to cast praise upon the nation's unsung heroes, toilers in the trenches who steadfastly maintain in their hearts and chosen vocations a determined vision for all that this nation promises.

In California, the most diverse and troublesome of the country's 50 states, there are thousands of points of light in each major urban sprawl.

One of those is Gregory Hodge, an eloquently upbeat African-American historian/activist/minister who helps shepherd California youth through the perils of adolescence.

To hear Hodge speak is to embrace hope—he is that dynamic.

When he speaks on his favorite subject, mentoring, the passion of his convictions is palpable, the power of his message profound.

"I like to talk about both the challenges and assets of the mentoring movement," Hodge told a recent gathering of mentors in California.

"There are immense challenges facing African-American kids today, but I always quickly follow this up by asserting that they are children, not an endangered species—not an owl or a whale that we need to save from extinction."

"In California, roughly 47 % of African-Americans live in poverty, yet nearly 84 % of school suspensions are handed out to black students, even though we comprise only about half the student population."

"Mentors are vital to these young people, because mentoring provides the texture and flavor and appeal to change young people's environment and future. It's going to take mentors to create the rich fabric. Social isolation among black kids is a huge challenge, and mentors will fill in the gap to show the opportunities."

As the California Mentor Initiative takes root in this vastly diverse state, Hodge emphasizes that it is absolutely vital to be consistent—there should be nothing casual or half-hearted about a mentor's approach to a child, who needs structure and continuity.

He also points out that programs and ideas must be culturally based. Culture is to people what water is to fish. There will be hope and an opportunity to do better, but it must be based on a cultural value system, one that accepts the young person for who he or she is today.

Culture is a way of looking at life—it's not just about music and books. First, you learn history, and then there is hope. And mentoring is all about a sense of history—the effective mentor shares, for example, that your African-American ancestors are a great people because they survived slavery.

What's particularly unique about the mentoring movement as it exists in California today is that, perhaps for the first time in the history of government, this is not a program that induces people to swivel their heads toward the establishment for help. It is, rather, an inspiring tidal wave of hope and promise that empowers citizens to cultivate themselves as talented and worthwhile human beings.

Most importantly, we have to be honest with children, because they're good, sharp thinkers, and they've shut down to most role models. Very simply, mentors provide the surrogate example of what should have been in place quite naturally from parents and the extended family members.

There's an ancient African-American adage that best sums up the whole concept of mentoring—"It takes a whole village to raise a single child."

That is the essence, the beauty and the simplicity of mentoring as it prospers today.

Story 98

For mentoring to work authentically, people have to step up responsibly. This isn't an exercise in mere altruism or an outgrowth of one's feeling good about himself on any particular day.

Directing the alcohol and drug programs for the State of California has given me a renewed sense of participatory democracy in its most radically effective form—restoring sanity and hope for upcoming generations of young Californians.

Participating in service oriented programs is what American democracy is all about. Bringing disenfranchised youth into the watershed of full engagement of their lives heals the wounds brought on by alcohol and drug abuse.

We should not underestimate the epidemic of social alienation currently surging like cancer through the veins of our younger citizens' lives. Our work on the grassroots level in cities and communities around the entire state has boiled this epidemic of estrangement down to four raging symptoms—teenage drug and alcohol abuse, educational failure, gang involvement, and teen pregnancy.

Kids gripped in the vise of emotionally wrenching primal screams are mortgaging their precious futures by acting out devastating and life-threatening behaviors that are nothing more than dramatic cries for help. They live in fear and isolation, bereft of any significant adult role models. Abandoned emotionally and physically, they are unleashed into the world without a map, without a clue. The pitfalls have pitfalls, and kids without direction are, quite literally, lost souls.

What terrible thing happens to adults making them forget what it's like to be young, restless, without roots? What horrible indifference to life's very pulse seeps into an adult's arteries to make him turn away and reject that very young life which is his responsibility? What makes people turn away so perversely from the bouncing bundle of joy they once so warmly embraced at life's onset?

We can't bemoan tired old adult behavior because that would be tired old adult behavior. We don't have time for that kind of sanctimonious whining. We are living in a crisis situation. We need to change urgently and fundamentally the way we think and act.

One of our successes in this regard is the California Mentor Initiative, which is in place throughout the state and flourishing as an essentially healing and guiding principle in the lives of our younger citizens. Isolation is the disease of the young and the disenfranchised, and mentoring is the tool whereby we reintroduce these people to themselves. We have come to realize that the best way to heal the scars of absentee and non-existent parenthood is the return of community. Mentoring is the beginning of community, and the ripple effects from its dynamism are re-sodding the once barren emotional and psychological fields of California's adolescents.

For mentoring to work authentically, people have to step up responsibly. This isn't an exercise in mere altruism or an outgrowth of one's feeling good about himself on any particular day. With its roots firmly planted in ancient time, the birthplace of an actively free citizenship yearning for democracy, mentoring is quite literally a function of society. It is a good citizen's duty, every bit as vital as jury summons, taxpaying or watchful neighborhood vigilance.

It doesn't take much thought to fully understand that mentoring crushes isolation, which is the disease eroding the underpinnings of a healthy society. Mentoring isn't designed as a full-service package equipped with all of life's answers, but it is offered as a creative way to trigger self-reflection and realization. It is a catalyst that helps inspire and motivate a scarred and scared youth toward adulthood. It is a spark that ignites the engine, which will propel youth from the perils of adolescence to the opportunities of maturity.

I would like to present the concept of mentoring in its most simple terms because it is a giant phenomenon built with tiny steps. It takes minimal effort for an adult role model to nudge himself toward activism, and the fruits of his labor yield maximum results. It is a joyful decision of citizenship that induces one good person to come to the assistance of another good, albeit troubled person.

And mentoring really is as simple, as straightforward, as refreshing, and as wise as saying to a young person: "The goodness in me salutes the goodness in you." That, my friends, is a power-packed salutation that will re-stitch the fabric of California currently at stress and strain under the oppressive weight of the four-headed epidemic hounding our kids. It's time to reclaim what is rightfully ours, and that is our future. It is far better to light a candle than to curse the darkness, and mentoring is the candle and the path to personal maturity and civic responsibility.

There is a chance, already proven, that life can be bright and fun again for once-beleaguered, overly tortured souls. There is a chance, already in action, that young people mired in negativity and unhealthy life choices, can still opt for positive, growth-enhancing, satisfying lifestyles that will free them forever.

Story 99

Everything in life seems to be enhanced by a mentoring relationship even the story behind publishing this book.

This past summer two energetic students came to work with the California Mentor Foundation. Being a streamlined operation, I enthusiastically embraced the young minds to contribute their ideas and vision. To my surprise my two mentees turned the table on me and I became the mentee.

From devising a media plan targeted at raising public awareness of mentoring to giving new depth to current projects these two women added a new current dimension to the foundation. They come from a different time. Raised with computers, the Internet and being twenty something Jenny and Mary bring special experiences to the table, which they used to modernize CMF.

If you can imagine the generation of the sixties with maturity and responsibility, then you can picture the unique spirit of my mentors. Through them I see the power of mixing of passion with accountability. Contrary to what most individuals view as an apathetic generation, they believe in a cause, mentoring. They hold a profound work ethic and spend many hours making their dreamt up visions reality. They infuse CMF with innovative ideas relating to their age group. In short time they have given a new sense of heart to the mentoring revolution.

I am grateful for their tireless energy, boundless ideas and sensitive hearts.

Story 100

100

Step up and share your expertise.

Mentoring programs are not exclusive to younger students they are present at many different levels of education. Young adults rely on mentors' advice whether it is for climbing the corporate ladder, or transitioning careers. Most of the time young professionals need aid even earlier while they are going through school.

In our society, after the long haul through undergraduate studies many students pursue graduate and professional schooling. Graduate programs have a competitive nature that mimics that field's working environment. Schools initiate mentoring programs to help ease students burden of finding their career path. These programs bridge the gap between the theoretical world behind the profession and the practical knowledge to find your way in that profession.

Historically law school reflects one of the most demanding educational structures. The training to become a legal advocate is harsh and laborious. A student can get lost in the daily routine of studies without a sense of purpose.

Like most other areas of graduate study, law schools are able to connect interested legal minds with students. The lawyers are able to relate to the rigorous program and show that there is a light at the end of the law school tunnel. They offer support, guidance and are a vast resource of professional information.

It was wonderful hearing Mary's perspective on the legal world. As a law student, she finds the most amazing thing to be that distinguished attorneys and judges will take time to share their experiences with a new student. Sharing one's experiences with a student enriches that student's academic life and shows them that they can succeed in a competitive profession. She has spoken with many attorneys all of whom have different views, motivation, and passion for areas of the legal profession. These conversations enable her to develop her own interests and see the infinite possible areas to apply her education.

"I know that I am eternally grateful for the advice of my elder mentors and look forward to one day being able to help other aspiring attorneys find their path to fulfill their own dreams and positively impact the world."

Anyone can be a mentor, won't you step up and share your life expertise.

101

Story 101

Just do it, Become a Mentor

There are far more than 101 reasons to be a mentor and no written publication could express each and every one. I sincerely hope that these stories I have collected will light that spark inside of you to further develop your mentoring relationships. I ask that you consider your ability to impact young peoples' lives, and take those relationships seriously.

Mentors build self-esteem, human engagement and many other areas of ones life. Mentoring stands as a universal opportunity for human development. There are no limits to the way that many people are able to affect the life of a child especially since mentors are able to touch many aspects of their lives.

While I was crisscrossing the state to grow strategic partnerships with the initiative, these stories and many others inspired me to write them down. Now I share them with you in hopes that you will understand the power of mentoring and its ability to change lives. I am already compiling the second edition of wondrous stories representative of millions of reasons to be a mentor.

There are two universal messages. Mentors testify that they get more out of the relationship and the mentees say that the most potent ingredient is that their mentor was often the first person that held aspirations for them.

I invite you to join this movement and grow America one child at a time by becoming a mentor.

Appendix A

Resources

California and National

California Resources

Governor's Mentoring Partnership
Mentor Resource Center
1700 K Street
Sacramento, CA 95814
www.adp.ca.gov/cf/GovernorsMentoring Partnership

California Mentor Foundation
100 Main Street
Tiburon, CA 94920
www.calmentor.com

Secretary Kerry Mazzoni
Office of the Secretary for Education
Governor's Academic Mentoring Program
1121 L Street, Suite 600
Sacramento, CA 95814
Phone: (916) 323-0611
www.ose.ca.gov

California Mentor Initiative
(800) 444-3066 in California
(916) 323-6589 outside California

California Commission on Improving Life Through Service
www.cilts.ca.gov
(916) 323-7646

Volunteer Centers of California
Contact: Ellen Reay
1110 K Street, Suite 210
Sacramento, CA 95814
Phone: (916) 341-3121

Foundation Center
www.fdncenter.org

The Higher Education Center
www.edc.org/hec

California Partnership for Responsible Parenting
www.dhs.ca.gov/prp/home.html

Schools to Career
www.stc-clearinghouse.com

National Resources

National Mentoring Partnership
www.mentoring.org

America's Promise
www.americaspromise.org

Big Brothers Big Sisters of America
National Office
230 N. 13th Street
Philadelphia, PA 19107
(215) 567-7000
(215) 467-0394 (FAX)

HOSTS Corporation
8000 NE Parkway DRive, Suite 201
Vancouver, WA 98662
Phone: (800) 833-4678
www.hosts.com

National Boys and Girls Club
1230 West Peachtree Street, NW
Atlanta, GA 30309
Phone: (404) 487-5700
www.bgca.org

Corporation for National Service
1201 New York Avenue, NW
Washington, DC 20525
(202) 606-5000
email: webmaster@cns.gov
www.nationalservice.org

Points of Light
The Points of Light Foundation
1400 I Street, NW Suite 800
Washington, DC 20005
(202) 729-8000
(202) 729-8100 (FAX)
email: volnet@pointsoflight.org
www.pointsoflight.org

National YWCA/YMCA
101 North Wacker Drive
Chicago, IL 60606
Phone: (312) 477-0031
www.ywca.org
www.ymca.net

Northwest Regional Educational Labs
101 South West Main Street, Suite 500
Portland, OR 97204
Phone: (800) 547-6339
www.nwrel.org

Children's Defense Fund
25 E Street NW
Washington, DC 20001
(202) 628-8787
email: cdfinfo@childrensdefense.org
www.childrensdefense.org

Children's Health Fund
The Children's Health Fund
317 East 64th Street
New York, NY 10021
www.childrenshealthfund.org

Department of Juvenile Justice
Delinquency Prevention
810 Seventh Street NW
Washington DC,
Phone: (202) 307-5911

Junior Achievement
One Education Way
Colorado Springs, CO 80906
www.ja.org

Bureau of the Census
www.census.gov

Congressional Quarterly's American Voter
www.cq.com

Department of Housing and Urban Development
www.hud.gov

Teach for America
315 W 36th Street, Floor 6
New York, New York 10018
Phone (800) 823-1230 x225
www.tfanetwork.org

DOJ Kids Page (Justice for Kids & Youth)
www.usdog.gov/kidspage

Department of Labor
www.dol.gov

Fedstats
www.fedstats.gov

Benton Foundation's Best Practices Toolkit
www.benton.org/Practice/Toolkit

CapWeb (the Internet Guide to Congress)
www.gsa.gov/fdac

Center for Science in the Public Interest
www.cspinet.org

Project Vote Smart's Congress Track
www.vote-smart.org/congress track

U.S. Nonprofit Gateway
www.nonprofit.gov

National Regional Education Labs
www.nwrel.org/national

Public/Private Ventures
www.ppv.org

US Department of Justice
www.ojp.usdoj.gov

Special Issue on Intergenerational Reading Programs
www.siu.edu/offices/iii/nl_fall93.html

Western Regional Center
www.wested.org

Join Together Online
www.jointogether.org

Fight Crime Invest in Kids
www.fightcrime.org

Monitoring the Future
www.monitoringthefuture.org

CityCares
www.citycares.org

The City Kids Foundation
www.citykids.com

Kiwanis International
www.kiwanis.org

Lions Club International
www.lionsclubs.org

Mentoring USA
www.mentoringusa.org

National Youth Leadership Council
www.nylc.org

Rotary International
www.rotary.org

Soroptimist International of the Americas
www.soroptimist.org

Youth Frontiers, Inc.
www.youthfrontiers.org

Youth Service America
www.ysa.org

Youth Volunteer Corps of America
www.yvca.org

YouthBuild USA
www.youthbuild.org

Appendix B

State Initiatives

(Outside California)

ALABAMA
The Attorney General's Mentoring Initiative
11 South Union Street, 3rd Floor
Montgomery, AL 36130
334-242-7300
334-242-7458 fax
Email: mentoralabama@ago.state.al.us
Volunteer Hotline: 1-888-356-2400

COLORADO
Governor's Commission on Community Service
1391 North Speer Boulevard
Suite 600
Denver, CO 80204
303-595-1541
720-904-9738 fax
Email: greg.geissler@cccs.cccoes.edu

CONNECTICUT
Connecticut Mentoring Partnership
30 Arbor Street
Hartford, CT 06106
PH: 860-523-8042
FAX: 860-236-9412
E-mail: susan.patrick@preventionworksct.org
alison.glaser@preventionworksct.org
Volunteer Hotline: 1-877-CT-MENTOR

DELAWARE
15 Willard Hall Building
University of Delaware
Newark, DE 19716
302-831-0520
302-831-0523 fax
E-mail: tclower@udel.edu
Volunteer Hotline: 1-800-815-LINK

FLORIDA
The Governor's Mentoring Initiative
State of Florida
Executive Office of the Governor
Room B-06, The Old Capitol
Tallahassee, FL 32399-0001
850-410-0697
850-487-1866 fax
Email: mcfaddl@eog.state.fl.us
Volunteer Hotline: 1-800-825-3786

MAINE
Maine Mentoring Partnership
c/o The Avalon Group
P.O. Box 821
Waterville, ME 04903
207-861-8131
207-873-4531 fax
E-mail: klh@mint.net

MASSACHUSETTS
The Mass Mentoring Partnership
105 Chauncy St, 3rd Floor
Boston, MA 02111
(617) 695-1200
(800) 397-1861
Email:info@massmentoring.org
Volunteer hotline: 1-800-367-1861

MINNESOTA
The Mentoring Partnership of Minnesota
81 South 9th Street, Suite 200
Minneapolis, MN 55402
612-370-9180
612-370-9195 fax
Email: joelleng@mentoringworks.org
karid@mentoringworks.org
Volunteer Hotline: 1-877-343-0300

NEW HAMPSHIRE

Granite State Youth Mentors
15 Constitution Drive, Suite 105
Bedford, NH 03110-6041
(603) 589-8003
(603) 589-8004 fax
E-mail: mbergere@nhmentors.org

NORTH CAROLINA

North Carolina's Promise
Governor's Mentoring Initiative
Office of the Governor
116 West Jones Street
Raleigh, NC 27601
919-715-3470
919-733-2120 fax
Email: lhcisnc@aol.com
Volunteer hotline: 1-800-820-4480

OREGON

Oregon Mentoring Initiative
920 SW Sixth Ave., Suite 1010
Portland, OR 97204
503-450-0890
503-450-0887 fax
E-mail: tom@ormentor.org
katie@ormentor.org

TEXAS

Texas Commission on Volunteerism & Community Service
Governor's Mentoring Initiative
P.O. Box 13385
Austin, TX 78711
PH: 512-936-9282
FAX: 512-463-1861
E-mail: celeste.padilla@twc.state.tx.us

UTAH

Utah Mentor Network
3450 South 900 West
Salt Lake City, UT 84119
801-538-9811
801-261-2753 fax
E-mail: awarner@hs.state.ut.us
bdrake@co.slc.ut.us

VIRGINIA

Virginia One to One: The Mentoring Partnership
327 W. Main Street
P.O. Box 843066
Richmond, VA 23284
PH: 804-828-1536
FAX: 804-828-1418
E-Mail: jjsmith@vcu.edu

WASHINGTON

Washington State Mentoring Partnership
Department of Social and Health Services
Division of Alcohol and Substance Abuse
612 Woodland Square Loop SE, Bldg "C"
Post Office Box 45330
Olympia, WA 98504-5330
PH: 360-438-8494
FAX: 360-438-8053
E-mail: pennetx@dshs.wa.gov
Volunteer Hotline: 1-877-301-4557

Appendix C

California Coalitions

(Listed by County)

ALAMEDA COUNTY

The Mentoring Coalition of Alameda County
C/O The Mentoring Center
Contact: Katie Robinson, Mentor Coordinator
1221 Preservation Parkway, Suite 200
Oakland, CA 94612
Phone: (510) 891-0427

AMADOR/TUOLUMNE COUNTIES

Amador Contact: Kelley Sargeant
935 South State Highway 49
Jackson, CA 95642
Phone: (209) 223-1485

TuolumneContact: Terry Skaff
427 North Highway 49, Suite 302
Sonora, CA 95370
Phone: (209) 533-1397 x221

BUTTE COUNTY

Butte County Mentor Coalition
Contacts: JoAnna Tauscher Birdsall
Butte College
3536 Butte Campus Drive
Oroville, CA 95965
Phone: (530) 89-2369

HUMBOLDT COUNTY

Northcoast Mentor Council
Contact: Lorey Keele
904 G Street
Eureka, Ca 9501
Phone: (707) 269-2052

KINGS COUNTY

Kings Mentoring Partnership
Contact: Jo Scott
905 N. Fulton
Fresno, CA 93733
(559) 592-9253

LOS ANGELES COUNTY

Contact: Keith Padgett

Big Brothers of Greater Los Angeles/Big Brothers Big Sisters of the Inland Empire
1486 Colorado
Los Angeles, CA 90041
Phone: (323) 258-3333 Ext 212

California Collaborative of Big Brothers Big Sisters Affiliates
Contact: Ken Martinet
Catholic Big Brothers
3300 W.Temple Street
Los Angeles, CA 90026
Phone: (213) 251-9800

ORANGE COUNTY

Community Mentor Partnership of Orange County
Contact: Carolyn Secrist
405 W. 5th Street, Suite 211
Santa Ana, Ca 92701
Phone: (714) 834-3076

RIVERSIDE COUNTY

Riverside County Mentor Collaborative
Contact: Maria Juarez
2038 Iowa Avenue, Suite B-102
Riverside, Ca 92507
Phone: (909) 955-4900

SACRAMENTO COUNTY

Communities in Schools of California
Contact: Karen Rothsein
400 Capitol Mall, Suite 900
Sacramento, CA 95814
Phone: (916) 447-2477
California Conservation Corps
AmeriCorps Ambassadors
Contact: Joan Bennett
1719 24th Street
Sacramento, CA 95816
Phone: (916) 341-3121

SAN DIEGO COUNTY

The Mentoring Coalition of San Diego County
Contact: Lisa Varela
204 North El Camino Real
Encinitas, CA 92024
Phone: (858) 581-5880

SAN BERNARDINO COUNTY

San Bernardino Mentoring Coalition
Contact: Rhonda Morken-Rose
One-2- One Mentors
16245 Desert Knoll Drive
Victorville, CA 92392
Phone: (760) 245-1997
San Francisco
San Francisco Mentoring Coalition
Contact: Eve Libertone
450 Mission Street, Suite 408
Phone: (415) 896-0909 x318

SAN LUIS OBISPO COUNTY

Mentor Alliance of San Louis Obispo
Contact: Lana Adams
POB1380
San Louis Obispo, CA 93406
Phone: (805) 544-4355 x485

SAN MATEO COUNTY

Mentoring Coalition of San Mateo County
Contact: Rebecca S. Cooper
C/o Friends for Youth, Inc.
1741 Broadway, Floor 1
Redwood City, CA 94063
Phone: (650) 368-4464

SANTA BARBARA COUNTY

South Coast Mentor Collaborative
Contact: Sonia Kroth
C/o BBBS of Santa Barbara County/Family Services Agency
123 West Gutierrez Street
Santa Barbara, CA 93101
Phone: (805) 965-1001x243

SANTA CLARA COUNTY

Mentoring Coalition of Santa Clara County
C/o Friends for Youth, Inc.
1741 Broadway, Floor 1
Redwood City, CA 94063
Phone: (650) 368-4464

SOLANO COUNTY

Solano Mentor Collaborative
Contact: Mel Orpilla
505 Santa Clara Street, Floor 3
Vallejo, CA 94590
Phone: (707) 648-5230

SONOMA COUNTY

Sonoma County Mentoring Partnership
Contact: Ben G Ray
Operation Getting It Together
500 North Main Street
Sebastopol, CA 95472
Phone: (707) 823-6967

STANISLAUS COUNTY

Stanislaus County Mentor Network
Center for Human Services
1700 McHenry Village Way, Suite 11
Modesto, CA 95350
Phone: (209) 550-4950

TULARE COUNTY

Mentors Matter Collaborative
Contact: Mary Alice Escarcega
POB 1350
Visalia, CA 93279
Phone: (559) 732-4194 x614

California Friday Night Live Partnership
Contact Carol Hodson
2367 W. Burrel
POB 5091
Visalia, CA 93278
Phone: (559) 733-6496

YOLO COUNTY

Yolo County Youth Connections Mentor Coalition
Contact: Tania Garcia Cardena
327 College Street, Suite 100
Woodland, CA 95695
Phone: (530) 669-3285

Appendix D

California Mentor Program Directory

A complete directory of California mentor programs can be downloaded at the California Department of Alcohol and Drug Programs' website <www.adp.ca.gov>. The Mentor Program Directory is located under the Resource Center option.

Appendix E

California Quality Assurance Standards

For Purposes of the California Mentor Initiative, Quality Mentoring Programs need to have the following:

A Statement of Purpose an a Long Range Plan including:

Who, what, where, when, why and how activities will be performed.

Input from originators, staff, funders, potential volunteers, and participants.

Assessment of community need.

Realistic, attainable, and easy-to-understand operational plan.

Goals, objectives, and timelines for all aspects of the plan.

Funding and resources development plan.

A Recruitment Plan for both Mentors and Mentees Including:

Strategies that portray accurate expectations and benefits. Year round marketing and public relations. Targeted outreach based on participant's needs.

Volunteer opportunities beyond mentoring (i.e. event organization, office support, etc)

A basis in your program's statement of purpose and long-range plan.

An Orientation for mentors and mentees including:

Program overview.

Description of eligibility, screening process, and suitability requirements.

Level of commitment expected (time, energy, and flexibility).

Expectations and restrictions (accountability)

Benefits and rewards they can expect.

A separate focus for potential mentors and participants.

A summary of program policies, including written reports, interviews evaluation, and reimbursement.

Eligibility Screening for Mentors and mentees including:

An application process and review.

Face-to-face interview.

Reference checks for mentors which must include criminal history record checks (finger printing), and may include character references, child abuse registry check, and driving record checks.

Suitability criteria that relate to the program statement of purpose and needs of the target population. Could include some or all of the following: personality profile; skills identification; gender; age; language and racial requirements; level of education; career interests; motivation for volunteering; and academic standing.

Successful completion of pre-match training and orientation.

If you have Youth Mentors, the following will apply:

An application process which must include a parental consent form.

Face-to-face interview.

Reference checks of at least two personal non-related adults.

Successful completion of a pre-match training and orientation.

A readiness and training curriculum for all mentors and mentees including:

Trained staff trainers.

Orientation to program and resource network, including information and referral, other supportive services, and schools.

Skills development as appropriate.

Cultural/heritage sensitivity and appreciation training.

Guidelines for participants on how to get the most out of the mentoring relationship.

Do's and don'ts of relationship management.

Job and role descriptions.

Confidentiality and liability information.

Crisis management/problem solving resources.

Communication skills development.

Ongoing sessions as necessary.

A Matching Strategy including:

A link with the program's statement of purpose.

A commitment to consistency.

A grounding in the program's eligibility criteria.

A rationale for the selection of this particular matching strategy from the wide range of available models.

Appropriate criteria for matches, including some or all of the following:

Gender; age; language; requirements; availability; needs; interests; preferences of volunteer and participant; life experience; temperament.

Signed statements of understanding that both parties agree to the conditions f the match and the mentoring relationship.

The program may have pre-match social activities between mentor and mentees.

Team building activities to reduce the anxiety of the first meeting.

A Monitoring process including:

Consistent scheduled meetings with staff, mentors, and mentees.

A tracking system for ongoing assessment.

Written records.

Input from family, community partners, and significant others.

A process for managing grievances, praise, rematching, interpersonal problem solving, and premature relationship closure.

A Support, Recognition and Retention Component that may include:

A formal kick-off event.

Ongoing peer support groups for volunteers, participants, and others.

Ongoing training and development.

Relevant issue discussion and information dissemination.

Networking with appropriate organizations.

Social gatherings of different groups as needed.

Annual recognition and appreciation event.

Newsletters of other mailings to mentors, mentees, supporters, and funders.

Closure Steps including:

Private and confidential exit interviews to debrief the mentoring relationship between:

Mentee and staff

Mentor and staff

Mentor and mentee without staff

Clearly stated policy for future contacts between mentor and mentee.

Assistance for participating in defining next steps for achieving personal goals (for the mentee).

An Evaluation Process based on:

Outcome analysis of program and relationship.

Program criteria and statement of purpose.

Information needs of board, funders, community partners, and other supporters of the program.

About the Author

Andy's sensitive heart and nurturing personality have touched and changed the lives of many people. Former Drug Czar for California, Dr. Andy Mecca brings over 35 years of professional experience to the California Mentor Foundation. Dr. Mecca served as Executive Director of the California Health Research Foundation and gained a national reputation for his role as Chairman of the California Task Force on Self-Esteem. He has written eight previous books on self-esteem and health promotion. Andy has run 50 marathons and completed the Ironman triathlon in Hawaii. He has also participated in two cross-country runs to raise funds for drug prevention programs. Andy lives with his wife Kate and golden retriever Daisy, in Marin County, California.